Superbrands®

Volume 21

uk.superbrands.com

CHIEF EXECUTIVE OFFICER
ACADEMY OF CHIEF MARKETERS
Damon Segal

DIRECTOR
ACADEMY OF CHIEF MARKETERS
Nathan Mathan

CHIEF OPERATING OFFICER
ACADEMY OF CHIEF MARKETERS
Felisa Kennard

BRAND LIAISON DIRECTOR
ACADEMY OF CHIEF MARKETERS
Tennessee Van Der Vyver

EDITORIAL DIRECTOR
SUPERBRANDS UK
Angela Cooper

DESIGN DIRECTOR
SUPERBRANDS UK
Verity Burgess

To order further books, email books@chiefmarketer.co.uk

Published by
Academy of Chief Marketers
William Old Centre
Duck's Hill Road
Northwood
HA6 2NP

© 2020 Superbrands Ltd

Printed in Italy

ISBN 978-1-8382519-0-1

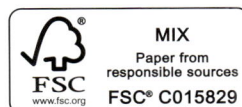

FSC
www.fsc.org
MIX
Paper from
responsible sources
FSC® C015829

Contents

CONTENTS

THOUGHT PIECES

About Superbrands

Superbrand status is awarded for quality, reliability and distinction by a combination of an independent expert council and business executives or consumers, voting on a comprehensive list of more than 3,200 consumer and business-to-business brands

---

The Superbrands Annual tells the story of many of these successful brands, exploring their history, development and achievements, showcasing why they are so well-regarded. These case studies provide valuable insights into the strategies and propositions of the brands that consumers and business professionals trust and admire.

The Superbrands organisation identifies and pays tribute to exceptional brands throughout the world.

The UK programme is run under license by The Academy of Chief Marketers.

The Academy of Chief Marketers

About The Academy of Chief Marketers

World-Class Learning and Personal Development for Chief Marketers Everywhere

Damon Segal, the joint co-founder of The Academy of Chief Marketers, has had involvement with Superbrands over several years, initially as a member of the business expert council and now as the custodian of the license. Using his three decades of experience working with brands and marketers, he has translated this experience into building the Superbrands proposition into one of even greater strength and value.

The Academy is a unique offering for Senior Marketing and Branding professionals to have access to a personal and professional development forum for expert learning and peer-to-peer insights; It's excellent for keeping marketing skills sharp to enhance your brand, business and career.

The Academy provides a confidential way to gain invaluable support from a group of highly qualified marketing and brand professionals from different industries. There is no better way to exchange knowledge than to sit around a table (or Zoom Room) of peers discussing ideas on how to overcome challenges and drive businesses forward.

Whether it is to learn what is new in the marketing arena, how to manage team members and suppliers, perhaps it's how to solve board-level challenges best. Having a group of experienced people to help you navigate these questions can help achieve both personal and business goals.

We believe it's time to bring world-class learning and personal development to Chief Marketers everywhere. For a long time CEO's have had access to this sort of development through various organisations, and now we bring the same opportunities to you with a marketing focus.

CMOs and marketing directors are all involved in leadership in some form, be it with their board, teams and / or suppliers. The Academy of Chief Marketers provides world-class speakers and events to enable marketers to realise their full potential.

Our purpose is to build a community of collaborative senior marketing and branding professionals where one great idea can change the world for the better.

The Academy of Chief Marketers was founded by veteran marketer and CEO, Damon Segal and tech guru and CEO, Nathan Mathan.

After spending over two decades in leadership and personal development and three in the digital, design and marketing arena, Damon wanted to facilitate a completely confidential environment for senior marketers and brand professionals to learn, inspire and grow. "Often a marketer's role is a lonely misunderstood one in an organisation, and The Academy can provide the learning and guidance that marketers often miss out on in their businesses, which is great for both the marketer and business growth."

Nathan Mathan has come from a blue-chip background in managing and consulting the full cycle of a technology solution for a business. Having worked in senior positions with companies like Capita, British Airways and Barclays Capital, Nathan has an excellent understanding of how to integrate the marketing function with a business's technology seamlessly. Nathan has spent over five years in leadership learning and coaching and brings a unique dynamic to The Academy meetings.

The Academy offers Superbrands members networking and learning events, such as bi-weekly, 'Inspiration Hour', private dining events, workshops and networking events.

Academy of *Chief Marketers*

Endorsements

SOPHIE DEVONSHIRE

CEO
The Marketing Society

Author of Superfast: Lead At Speed

THE MARKETING SOCIETY

The publication of the Superbrands Annual is a moment in time for the industry to mark each year; looking at what has changed and celebrating success for those brands who have built followers, fans and financial impact.

Its publication marks a good moment to 'pause' to reflect and to celebrate what's worked. In a world that's been challenging for many and changing rapidly for all, great brands matter more than ever – to consumers, the economy and to us as a marketing industry.

We love to hear about the stories of success, of creativity and innovation, of bravery and brilliance. Superbrands inspire the industry by driving economic growth and business survival. The tales of commercial and creative intelligence behind these stories help remind us of the importance and power of marketing excellence.

Great brand stories are a beacon of inspiration for the marketing leaders of tomorrow. Vive the Superbrands!

JOHN NOBLE

Director
British Brands Group

British Brands Group

Has there ever been a more testing time for brand management? I mean 'testing' in a good way. This edition of Superbrands comes in the midst of a pandemic the scale of which has never been seen before, when concern for the world is at its highest and awareness of social inequalities is acute. So much is shifting – what we value, how we live our lives, how we shop and much else.

For brand managers, this is a time for re-evaluation and potentially re-definition, hence the test. As ever, there will be winners and losers. One certainty though is that the force of 'brand' will remain as powerful as ever, with each of us using it instinctively in our daily lives, informing our choices on so many levels. While the influences on our choices may be shifting, it is a pleasure to mark and celebrate the constant of 'brand' and the part it continues to play in our changing lives.

JENNIFER SPROUL

Chief Executive
Institute of Internal Communication

Institute of Internal Communication

The power within

We are delighted to support this year's edition of Superbrands. Brands which achieve this accolade are clearly investing in their people, relationships as well as the purpose and values which they stand for and promise to their customers. Great brands not only focus on the customer, they are built from the inside out, where their words are supported by their actions and embedded within the culture of their organisation.

It is wonderful to see so many amazing brands that are creating meaningful relationships and experiences for all their stakeholders. At the IoIC we believe that truly great brands also make truly amazing experiences for their employees who become their own champions and ambassadors living and breathing the values they create. It is a privilege to support Superbrands and to see those amazing brands recognised which are essential to our lives, economy and society.

Superbrands Selection Process

About the Superbrands Selection Process

Superbrands UK Volume 21, 2020/21

The annual Consumer Superbrands and Business Superbrands surveys are long-running brand sentiment studies that identify the UK's strongest consumer and business-to-business brands respectively.

Brands do not apply or pay to be considered for Superbrands status. In order to provide a broad review of the market and ascertain the strongest brands in each category, all the key players in each sector are evaluated through the voting process. More than 3,200 brands across 142 categories were voted on in this year's surveys. These initial brand lists were compiled using a range of relevant data sources, such as market share, share of voice and industry league tables.

Since 2006 this has been independently managed by The Centre for Brand Analysis (TCBA), which undertakes brand research, evaluation and strategy projects.

Consumer Superbrands

A total of 2,500 British adults voted on a list of 1,623 brands across 78 different categories. The list is also ratified by the independent and voluntary Consumer Superbrands Council; 30 leading marketing experts, providing a secondary quality control mechanism. Brands not highly rated by the experts are vetoed from attaining Consumer Superbrand status.

Business Superbrands

This list is jointly chosen by 2,500 British business professionals with purchasing or managerial responsibility, and the independent, voluntary Business Superbrands Council; 20 leading business-to-business marketing experts. Both audiences voted on 1,610 brands in 64 categories.

Definition of a Superbrand

All those involved in the voting process bear in mind the following definition:

'A Superbrand has established the finest reputation in its field. It offers customers significant emotional and/or tangible advantages over its competitors, which customers want and recognise.'

In addition, the voters are asked to judge brands against the following three factors:

- **Quality**   Does the brand provide quality products and services?

- **Reliability**   Can the brand be trusted to deliver consistently?

- **Distinction**   Is it well known in its sector and suitably different from its rivals?

Naturally, as a brand perception and sentiment survey, individual opinions will be impacted by a number of additional factors.

Only the most highly-regarded brands from these surveys are awarded Superbrands status. These brands do not pay for this status and can proclaim their success to stakeholders. Member brands are also able to use the Superbrands seal (shown to the right) to showcase their award.

To access the consumer and business professionals that vote in our surveys, TCBA has partnered with the global leader in digital research data, Dynata.

Dynata is the world's largest first-party data and insights platform. With a reach that encompasses over 62 million consumers and business professionals globally, and an extensive library of individual profile attributes collected through surveys, Dynata is the cornerstone for precise, trustworthy quality data. Dynata serves nearly 6,000 market research, media and advertising agencies, publishers, consulting and investment firms and corporate customers in North America, South America, Europe, and Asia-Pacific.

dynata.com

Introducing the Experts

Superbrands Councils 2020/21

The Business Superbrands (B) and Consumer Superbrands (C) Expert Councils
are chaired by Council Member Stephen Cheliotis, Chief Executive
at The Centre for Brand Analysis (TCBA)

Business Superbrands Council

Steve Aldridge
Chief Creative Officer
Wunderman Thompson UK

Rob Alexander
Partner, Headland

Chris Ashley-Manns
Chief Marketing Officer
Webeo

Alex Bigg
CEO, Engine | MHP + Mischief

Fran Brosan
Co-Founder & Chairman
Omobono

Kate Cox
CEO, Bray Leino

Kirsty Dawe
CEO, Webeo

Steve Dyer
Managing Director
Oil The Wheels

James Farmer
Co-Founder
B2B Marketing

Jason Fletcher
Executive Creative Director
Gyro UK

Steve Kemish
Managing Partner
Junction

Mark Lethbridge
Group Chief Executive
Gravity Global

Claire Mason
Founder & CEO, Man Bites Dog

Stephen Meade
Chief Executive, McCann Enterprise

Rob Morrice
CEO, Stein IAS

Sandy Purewal
Founder, Superfied

Susanna Simpson
Co-Founder
Definition

David Willan
Co-Founder
& Former Chairman
Circle Research (now Savanta)

Prof. Alan Wilson PhD
Professor of Marketing
University of Strathclyde

Consumer Superbrands Council

Andrew Bloch
Founder, FRANK.

Ed Bolton
Principal (Creative), Yonder

Catherine Borowski
Founder & Artistic Director
PRODUCE UK

Vicky Bullen
CEO, Coley Porter Bell

Simon Dixon
Co-Founder, DixonBaxi

Katie Edwards
Managing Partner, Publicis.Poke

Rachel Forde
CEO, UM UK

Phil Hakim
Managing Director, Flipside

Jed Hallam
Chief Strategy Officer, Initiative

Vanella Jackson
Global CEO, Hall & Partners

Rob Kavanagh
Executive Creative Director,
OLIVER UK

Nick Liddell
Director of Consulting
The Clearing

Avra Lorrimer
Managing Director
Hill + Knowlton Strategies

Peter Martin
Group Managing Director
SMP & Melody

Amy McCulloch
Founder & Managing Director
eight&four

Richard Moss
Chief Executive, Good Relations

Ita Murphy
CEO, SYZYGY UK

James Murphy
Co-Founder & CEO
New Commercial Arts

Andrew O'Connell
Managing Director, UK
Dynata

Giles Palmer
Founder & CEO, Brandwatch

Caroline Paris
Creative Director, Brave

Tim Perkins
Deputy Group Chairman
Design Bridge

Julian Pullan
Vice Chairman &
President International
Jack Morton Worldwide

Lisa Riordan
Creative Director, Imagination Ltd

Graham Sykes
Creative Director, FITCH

Jade Tomlin
Creative Director
Tribal Worldwide London

Adrian Walcott
Managing Director,
Brands with Values &
Co-Founder, BAME2020

Guy Wieynk
Global CEO, AnalogFolk

Dylan Williams
Chief Strategic Officer, Droga5
London & Managing Director,
Accenture Interactive

Foreword

Welcome

Superbrands UK Volume 21

Firstly, welcome to Superbrands UK Volume 21. I believe this is an extraordinary volume based on what we've been through while putting the annual together during lockdown in 2020. It's fantastic to see how many brands have rallied to support the nation in such an impactful and generous way.

Becoming a Superbrand is a fantastic achievement. To award this status we go through a rigorous independent process to identify brands that have excelled when it comes to Quality, Reliability and Distinction. We are very excited to bring you some of the extraordinary stories of what these Superbrands are accomplishing and how they got where they have today.

We have seen an enormous amount of change over the past months with a need for brands to pivot to meet the new purchasing and engagement behaviours brought on by the coronavirus pandemic. I think now more than ever it is vital to recognise the role that marketing and brand play in communicating to customers. What it is that a brand stands for, its message and how it meets its customer expectations. These areas have a direct impact on consumers' relationships with brands, and I think for those businesses who have recognised this, the faster they have been able to understand and positively engage their customer base.

Being a brand today, it is critical to understanding your position in the world and tell that story effectively to your audience. It's about understanding the power of trends, like personalisation and experiential offerings, and then being adaptable enough to apply these to your business while remaining authentic and trustworthy.

The Academy of Chief Marketers is the custodian of the Superbrands UK programme. It is our mission to build a collaborative community of senior marketing and branding professionals. The ability to connect so many Superbrands in one place means that just one great idea generated by our community has the potential to affect good in the world at scale.

I would like to thank those brands who have joined us on our journey for the 2020/21 programme, and you for taking the time to read my foreword, all the way through! I hope you all enjoy the fantastic stories in this volume and find them as inspiring as I did.

Until next time, keep fighting the good fight and stay strong.

Damon Segal
Co-Founder, Academy of Chief Marketers

ACCA Think Ahead

ACCA is the **world's most forward-thinking professional accountancy body**. It has a **thriving global community of 227,000 members and 544,000 future members based in 176 countries**. It upholds the **highest professional and ethical values** and supports both the private and public sectors

Market

ACCA's global community are among the world's best-qualified and most highly sought-after accountants, working across a multitude of sectors. ACCA supports them, and the organisations in which they work, through its qualifications, research and insights delivered through a global network of 110 offices and centres in 49 countries.

Connecting the market is a strategic objective for ACCA and one way it does this is through its International Assembly (pictured below and on the right hand page), a global representational group of members, which meets at its London headquarters every year. Due to Covid-19 travel restrictions, in 2020 ACCA held its International Assembly online for the first time.

Product

Award-winning research and insights that answer today's questions are at the heart of ACCA. In turn, this knowledge prepares its members as well as the accounting and finance profession, as a whole, for tomorrow. From global economics and emerging technologies to risk management, understanding the impact of a range of factors helps ACCA shape and lead the profession into the future. Its vast membership, spanning 176 countries, puts a highly skilled network of professionals

and forward-thinkers in place. They are able to feed into ACCA's research and insights, giving further depth and diversity. This is of immense value to the organisation's members as well as employers, standard setters, policy makers, regulators and academic institutions. ACCA's expertise, opinions and input are regularly sought to help the development of national and international policy and standards.

ACCA's qualifications are considered to be the gold standard in accountancy, opening doors to highly respected, interesting work in any sector. Furthermore, the ACCA professional qualification has been officially benchmarked to Master's level. Public trust has been built over the years by ACCA through the creation and development of an inclusive profession, with people from all backgrounds. The organisation is committed to providing open access at multiple

DID YOU KNOW?

ACCA has been an **advocate for inclusivity** for more than **100 years**

entry points, welcoming graduates, school leavers as well as those with no formal academic awards. Once qualified, members remain at the forefront of emerging trends with access to ACCA's professional insights and by having the opportunity to continually update their skills through its extensive programme of online CPD and events.

ACCA Careers is an employability portal, which supports the career success of members and future members. It includes the world's largest specialist accountancy job board and also provides practical careers advice and services such as CV writing.

During the turbulence of Covid-19, in early March 2020 ACCA also introduced more support including a dedicated Covid-19 Hub for members and future members. This included extra CPD resources and news items to keep ACCA's community connected and informed on key developments.

ACCA's Accounting and Business (AB) magazine, for members, covers topical issues and supports and inspires their careers and work. It is published in app and web formats.

Achievements

ACCA is proud to have an 81.3% satisfaction rating by its members and future members, the highest in five years. In addition, 82.8% of members and future members and 87%

of employers agree that ACCA is an innovative and forward-thinking organisation.

ACCA has also been recognised as the Professional Body of the Year, 2020 and 2019 by The Accountant/International Accounting Bulletin digital accountancy awards. Also in 2020, it was recognised by the PQ Magazine Awards as Accountancy Body of the Year as well as receiving the Innovation in Accountancy award for its Student Wellbeing Hub. In 2019, ACCA

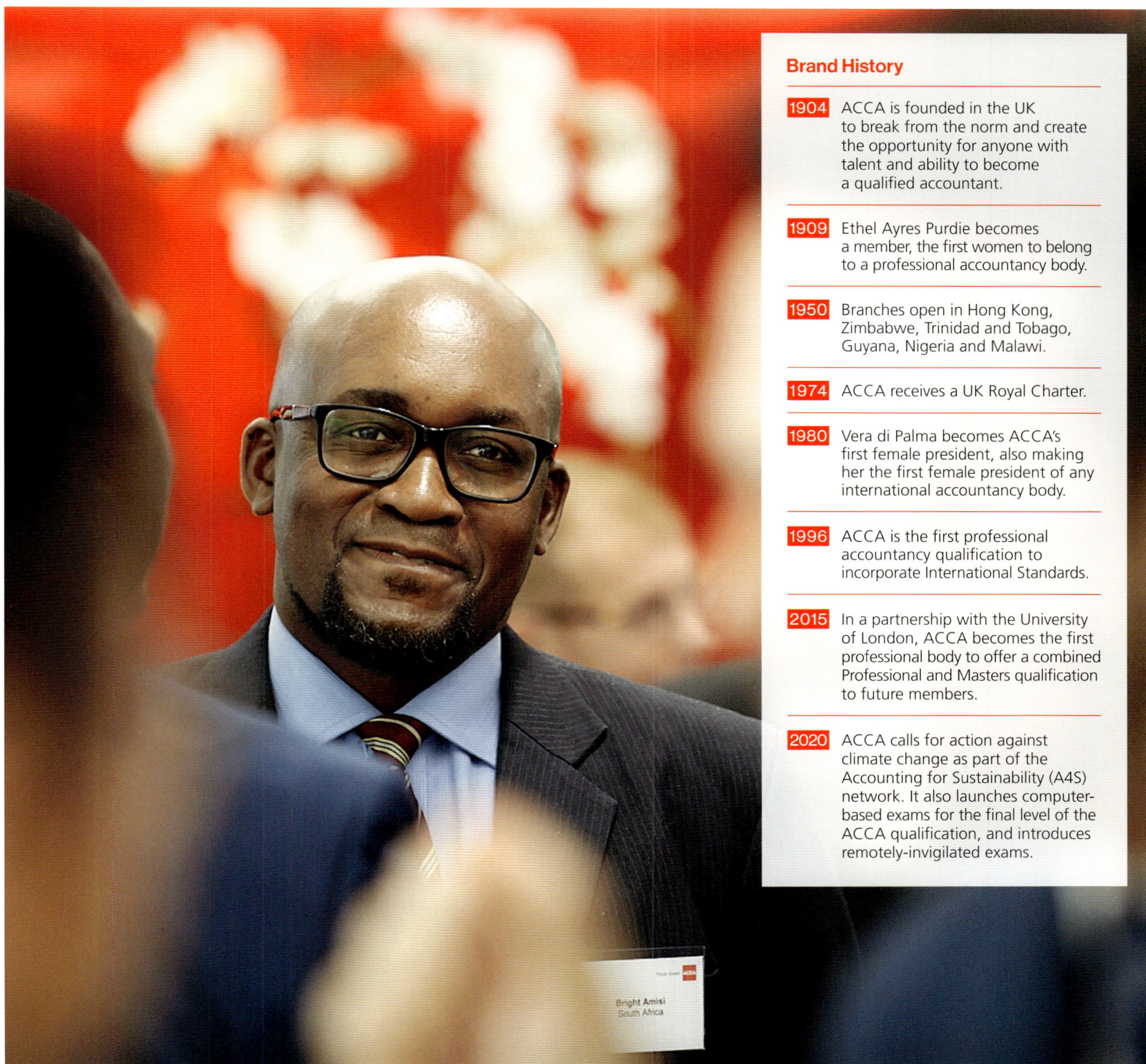

Bright Amisi
South Africa

Brand History

1904 ACCA is founded in the UK to break from the norm and create the opportunity for anyone with talent and ability to become a qualified accountant.

1909 Ethel Ayres Purdie becomes a member, the first women to belong to a professional accountancy body.

1950 Branches open in Hong Kong, Zimbabwe, Trinidad and Tobago, Guyana, Nigeria and Malawi.

1974 ACCA receives a UK Royal Charter.

1980 Vera di Palma becomes ACCA's first female president, also making her the first female president of any international accountancy body.

1996 ACCA is the first professional accountancy qualification to incorporate International Standards.

2015 In a partnership with the University of London, ACCA becomes the first professional body to offer a combined Professional and Masters qualification to future members.

2020 ACCA calls for action against climate change as part of the Accounting for Sustainability (A4S) network. It also launches computer-based exams for the final level of the ACCA qualification, and introduces remotely-invigilated exams.

was recognised as the Professional Body of the Year at the MemCom membership excellence awards and was also honoured with Thought Leadership Initiative of the Year, 2019.

Recent Developments
In 2019, ACCA launched its award-winning Student Wellbeing Hub, providing invaluable support to its entire student community, which proved vital in light of the coronavirus pandemic.

ACCA also accelerated its future exam vision by introducing remotely invigilated exams allowing students to take exams at home and continue their qualification journey where exam centres are closed because of Covid-19.

2020 also saw ACCA launch its first ever Virtual Careers Fair. This provided a much-needed forum

for employers and ACCA talent to connect during the Covid-19 pandemic. Run globally across ACCA's market network, the fairs attracted 40,736 registrations from ACCA members, future members and prospective future members, with 342 employers participating making 3,065 jobs available on the days of the fairs.

Promotion
Over the past two years, ACCA has amplified the power of its brand by focusing on a key external theme each quarter that demonstrates its relevance and leadership. These include 'The power of connections', 'The power of digital' and 'The power of future-ready talent'. Using one shared global voice across all its markets and communications channels, it has delivered clear and consistent messages and outputs on key issues of importance to the business and finance

world. ACCA's award-winning professional insights have been a core part of these campaigns.

Brand Values
For 116 years, serving the public good has been embedded in ACCA's purpose which was relaunched in 2020 as: 'We're a force for public good. We lead the global accountancy profession by creating opportunity'. This marries with ACCA's three core values; Inclusion, creating opportunity for all, removing artificial barriers, creating connections and embracing diversity; Integrity, being ethical, honest and accountable as well as encouraging the same from others. Acting in the public interest and focusing on long-term value; Innovation, thinking ahead and exploring new ideas, creating solutions that ensure that the ACCA community, as well as the wider profession, is ready for today and tomorrow.

AUTOGLASS®

Autoglass® is a **leading consumer and business automotive brand**, providing **vehicle glass repair**, replacement and recalibration to more than **one million motorists** every year

Market

Autoglass® is the UK's favourite vehicle glass repair, replacement and recalibration specialist. Autoglass® is part of Belron® Group, which operates in 35 countries on six continents and served 18.2 million customers in 2019. Autoglass® has the widest-reaching network in its field in the UK, with more than 1,000 technicians providing a world-class service to motorists.

Windscreens play an integral role in modern automotive design and the average car in the UK car parc uses 15% more glass than 10 years ago. The windscreen is important for vehicle safety – its correct fitting and bonding can save lives. Windscreens now incorporate complex technologies such as cameras and sensors to enable Advanced Driver Assistance Systems (ADAS) that form part of the journey to autonomous driving, such as Autonomous Emergency Braking and Lane Departure Warnings.

Autoglass® is exceptional in the vehicle glass repair, replacement and recalibration market, as it has its own dedicated research and development team: Belron® Technical – a network of innovators and thinkers, all focused on driving technical standards and developing innovations that break new ground to improve the service provided to its customers.

DID YOU KNOW?

A **windscreen repair** can be up to **six times cheaper** than a replacement

Autoglass® works with insurance, fleet and lease companies – large and small – across the full spectrum of industries. Autoglass® handles the vehicle glass claims for eight of the top 10 motor insurance companies in the UK, providing a world-class service to policyholders demonstrated by its NPS score of 73 in 2019. The company has a dedicated specialist glazing division which repairs and replaces glass on everything from trains to combine harvesters, and a sister company, Autoglass® BodyRepair, which offers a mobile bodyshop repair service.

Product

Autoglass® exists to make a difference with real care. By providing exceptional customer service at every touchpoint and being an ambassador for road safety, Autoglass® has become one of the UK's most trusted service brands.

The company operates a 'Repair First' philosophy, ensuring that, wherever possible, it will repair a chipped windscreen rather than replace it, a safe solution that saves time and money, as well as being better for the environment. If the damage is beyond repair, Autoglass® will replace the glass. It only uses Original Equipment Manufacturer (OEM) standard glass, ensuring that each replacement windscreen is as good as the original.

Autoglass® is an industry leader in safety and champions the role that ADAS technology plays in improving driver safety. The recalibration service provided by Autoglass® delivers a seamless customer journey with the glass replacement and recalibration happening at the same appointment. As well as being a far better customer journey, this eliminates any risk that may exist between the time of glass replacement and subsequent recalibration – including on-board diagnostic checks prior to the windscreen removal to understand if there are any existing faults to the vehicle.

Achievements

Autoglass® has more than 80,000 customer reviews online with an average score of 4.4 out of five, the highest number of reviews from any UK-based vehicle glass repair and replacement specialist.

Autoglass® is proud of being a trusted and respected company in the eyes of its people, customers and partners. Its work for charity is extensive and in 2019, through the annual Spirit of Belron® Challenge, Autoglass®, Belron® and associated brands raised €1.5m for Afrika Tikkun.

Autoglass® is committed to achieving continual improvement in environmental as well as Health and Safety management. It is certified to ISO 14001, ISO 9001 and OHSAS 18001 standards and constantly strives to reduce its relative use of non-renewable fuel and CO_2.

Autoglass® is also committed to embracing new technologies to provide a smoother customer journey and has utilised Artificial Intelligence (AI) technology to allow customers to take a photo of their car's damage, upload it to the website and receive a quote instantaneously – choosing this option means a quote is calculated 70% quicker than through the previous method.

Recent Developments

Autoglass® prides itself in being at the forefront of innovation in the automotive after-market and has invested heavily in understanding the implications of ADAS technologies. In 2016, it became the first to offer a nationwide ADAS recalibration service.

Autoglass® has over 550 trained ADAS technicians and more than 80 centres offering recalibration across the UK and continues to invest as the adoption of this technology grows.

Autoglass® has also spearheaded the creation of an industry standard ADAS training accreditation in collaboration with the Institute of the Motor Industry (IMI). The new accreditation will ensure technicians can identify and interpret information relating to a specific vehicle and its ADAS features, in order to determine which method of recalibration is required and then calibrate correctly – significantly reducing the completion time. In 2020, around 20% of vehicles that have a replacement windscreen fitted require an ADAS recalibration, in 2015 it was only just over 2%.

Autoglass® has continued to expand its partnership with a range of prestigious fleet companies, signing new contracts with WS Transportation and Eddie Stobart.

In 2019, Autoglass® launched a new Over The Air recalibration service which added to its existing market-leading ADAS proposition. This addition now gives a Total Calibration solution to the accident damage market for Advanced Driver Assistance Systems (ADAS) diagnostics, coding and recalibration.

Promotion

Autoglass® became a household name in the 1990s after becoming the main sponsor of Chelsea Football Club. Since then, it has invested in several high-profile brand campaigns to ensure it remains at the forefront of motorists' minds, cementing its position as a great British brand.

In 2005, its 'Heroes' advertising campaign was launched, featuring real technicians. Autoglass® firmly believes its people are 'everyday heroes' that deliver its brand promise consistently to customers.

This format has been extended throughout the company's brand communications, with employees appearing on vans and online. Sonic branding, in the form of the famous 'Autoglass® Repair, Autoglass® Replace' jingle, is one of the most recognisable assets of the brand.

Brand Values

Autoglass® has the philosophy that it makes a difference with real care.

Brand History

1972 Autoglass Supplies Ltd is launched, providing mobile vehicle glass replacement.

1982 Autoglass Ltd becomes part of Belron®, the world's largest vehicle glass repair and replacement company.

1983 Autoglass Ltd merges with Windshields Ltd to become Autoglass Windshields, rebranding to Autoglass® in 1987.

1990 The windscreen repair service is launched and Autoglass® becomes a registered trademark.

1997 Autoglass® becomes the main sponsor of Chelsea Football Club.

2005 Autoglass® launches its 'Heroes' advertising campaign.

2009 The Autoglass® Specials brand is launched.

2015 Autoglass® leads the industry with its Advanced Driver Assistance Systems (ADAS) recalibration investment, and it is rolled out nationally in 2016.

2017 AutoRestore® rebrands to become Autoglass® BodyRepair.

2018 Autoglass® launches Rain Repel – the Advanced Windscreen Kit as well as the industry's first skill for the Amazon Echo, enabling customers to book an appointment using voice. Autoglass® also expands its ADAS expertise to 70 centres offering recalibration.

2019 Autoglass® launches Over The Air, a Total Calibration solution for the accident damage and repair market and becomes a member of the National Body Repair Association (NBRA).

2020 Autoglass® expands its ADAS expertise to more than 80 centres offering recalibration.

Avast believes in an open and connected world, where people everywhere have the right to access the same information, ideas and experiences. Today, **Avast safeguards more than 435 million people worldwide**, protecting their digital data, identity, and privacy

Market

From the start, our digital world was designed to be free and open; made by people for people. Today, 4.5 billion people – more than 50% of the planet – are connected, in 200 languages, spending a third of every day online.

While the digital world offers entirely new ways to connect, learn, work and innovate, there are many modern-day challenges that need to be addressed. Fake news, hate speech, cybercrime, disinformation, internet censorship, machine learning and AI biases are all undermining the original freedom and openness for which the internet was designed.

Avast's mission is to create a world that provides safety and privacy for all. Its aim is to help shape the digital world to be a freer, fairer place through the application of science, technology and human ingenuity.

Product

As the world's largest global consumer security company, Avast blocks 1.5 billion attacks and analyses 200 million new files each month, detecting more than 6,500 new threat samples per day.

Avast's comprehensive range of online security, privacy and performance products give consumers protection and peace of mind for all their online needs. Its security products for PC, Mac and mobile devices, such as Avast Free Antivirus, protect against all malware including ransomware, viruses, spyware and phishing.

Homes are increasingly filled with smart devices that connect to the internet – doorbells, thermostats, cameras and many other electronic devices – with two in five households containing at least one vulnerable device. Avast provides products for families, connected households and telecommunications providers which make securing and managing Internet of Things devices in the smart home simple.

Avast's privacy products let users design their online privacy levels. Some of its most popular products include Avast SecureLine VPN, which keeps users anonymous online; Avast Secure Browser, which provides security and privacy without compromising on performance; and Avast AntiTrack, which keeps users' digital footprint hidden.

The Avast Family Space app helps parents and children agree upon important boundaries through parental control settings that allow children to safely enjoy educational, fun and interesting content online, while protecting them from the darker corners of the web.

Avast Business products support small to mid-size businesses, helping them to get online and

DID YOU KNOW?

Avast **blocked 1.3m phishing attacks misusing the Covid-19 crisis** between Jan-May 2020

manage digital transformation. It also works with channel partners to deliver cloud-based solutions, offering endpoint and network protection as well as management, update and patching services.

Achievements

Avast recently received a number of industry leading accolades and awards for its product portfolio. Avast Free Antivirus was named a Best Buy by Which? Magazine in 2020 and was also awarded the Top-Rated Products accolade in 2019 by the respected test lab, AV-Comparatives, surpassing many paid-for alternatives.

Avast's flagship Internet of Things security product, Avast Omni, was named Best of Innovation Honoree in the CES 2020 Innovation Awards. The product won the Best of Cybersecurity and Personal Privacy category for outstanding engineering and design.

Avast's mobile apps rank amongst the most downloaded. Avast Antivirus has a rating of 4.7 stars from more than six million reviews in the Google Play store. In addition, its iOS version, Avast Privacy & Security, is ranked as one of the most popular utilities products, scoring 4.7 stars from more than 21,000 user ratings.

In June 2020, Avast reached a major milestone when the brand was admitted to the FTSE 100, just two years after originally listing on the London Stock Exchange on the FTSE 250.

Recent Developments

In a year when cybercriminals exploited the fear and confusion around Covid-19, Avast made a number of contributions to help fight the pandemic.

Through its charitable body, the Avast Foundation, it donated US $25m to a number of programmes using technology to support advances in medical science. This encompassed fields of testing and prevention including CEPI, the Bill & Melinda Gates Foundation's Therapeutics Accelerator and Folding@home. Worldwide, Avast colleagues

Brand History

1988	Avast is founded in the Czech Republic.
1997	Avast antivirus software is licenced to McAfee.
2001	Avast makes the defining decision to change the traditional antivirus business model and offer a fully featured free antivirus product to all.
2003	Within 30 months of going free, Avast is used by more than one million people around the world.
2006	The number of people using Avast reaches 20 million.
2011	Avast expands into business security, focusing on the SMB market.
2012	Avast Free Mobile Security becomes the best rated security app on Google Play.
2014	Avast mobile products reach the 100 million download milestone, faster than any other mobile security tools in Google Play history.
2016	Avast acquires cybersecurity giant AVG, doubling its number of users and bringing in new talent and technologies.
2017	Piriform is acquired, bringing the total number of active users to more than 435 million.
2018	Avast is listed on the London Stock Exchange in the FTSE 250 index.
2020	Avast joins the FTSE 100 index.

volunteered their time and technical skills to support local community relief efforts.

Avast also made its new parental assistance app, Avast Family Space, available for free in the UK to help families safely manage the increasing reliance on internet and device usage during the pandemic lockdown uncertainty.

Another side effect of the pandemic was the significant increase in spyware and stalkerware apps against the backdrop of escalating domestic abuse. In 2020, Avast protected more than 43,000 users worldwide from such malware.

Promotion
In 2019/20, Avast collaborated with London's Science Museum to sponsor the 'Top Secret: from Ciphers to Cyber Security' exhibition, which lifted the lid on GCHQ as it reached its centenary. In addition, Avast's partnership shed light on the exciting and rapidly evolving world of cybersecurity.

Avast also partnered with Neighbourhood Watch to establish the Cyberhood Watch initiative, a partnership programme aiming to raise awareness and educate people about online threats and risks. Neighbourhood Watch has been expanding its focus to include online safety issues in addition to physical safety, and Avast provides insights, advice and helpful content for members, including an online training course. Avast is also working with a group of active Neighbourhood Watch ambassadors to train them on today's major security threats so that information can be shared within local communities.

In 2020, Avast also became a member of the UK's Internet Watch Foundation to support its vital mission to remove online child sexual abuse content. Its technology filters out websites which host such content in video and non-photographic formats and blocks it. Avast believes in championing the online rights of those who are vulnerable and will not compromise in its mission to stop online harm.

Brand Values
Avast believes in an open and connected world, where everyone everywhere has the right to access the same information, ideas and experiences; and where communities can explore, participate and thrive. Avast uses its science-driven technology to prevent the cyber harms that threaten digital freedom, to enable access, privacy and safety online, for all.

BARCLAYS

With more than 330 years of history and expertise in banking, Barclays is a British universal bank. It operates in business to business and consumer sectors, united by a **common set of values** and a single guiding purpose, **'Creating opportunities to rise'**

Market

Barclays is a player on the global banking stage. It provides diversification by business line, geography and customer, enhancing financial resilience and contributing to the delivery of consistent returns through the business cycle. Its strong core business is well positioned to deliver long-term value for Barclays' shareholders.

Product

Barclays operates in more than 40 countries and employs approximately 80,000 people. It moves, lends, invests and protects money for customers and clients worldwide, utilising the latest technology in unison with its wealth of banking expertise. Its service company supports these operations by providing technology, operations and functional services across the Group.

Achievements

Barclays aims to be a company of opportunity makers, working together to 'help people rise' – customers, clients, colleagues and society. It is an industry leader in championing diversity and inclusion within the workplace and in delivering services. It also consistently appears in The Times Top 50 Employers for Women as well as ranking highly on the Bloomberg Gender Equality Index.

DID YOU KNOW?

In **1958 Barclays** appointed the **UK's first ever female branch manager**, Hilda Harding

Barclays was the first bank to roll out 'talking' ATMs and high visibility debit cards in the UK, assisting those with visual impairments. It is also recognised as a Disability Confident Leader by the UK Government and works to promote the scheme to other employers.

Having launched the Dynamic Working campaign, its approach to flexible working, in 2015, Barclays has been recognised with the accolades of Best for Embedded Flexibility and Top 10 Employer for Working Families. In 2018, the bank was one of the first signatories to the UK Government's Race at Work Charter and is one of 12 Stonewall Top Global Employers for LGBT+ colleagues.

Barclays is increasingly recognised as a pioneer in green finance. It has successfully launched an inaugural green bond, green mortgage and asset finance facilities to name a few, as well as corporate deposits. In 2020, Barclays won UK's Best Bank in the annual Euromoney magazine Awards for Excellence and UK's Best Investment Bank, the eighth win over the last nine years as well as Excellence in Leadership in Western Europe, for its response to the Covid-19 pandemic.

Recent Developments

Since 2013, LifeSkills has been supporting youth employment by raising the confidence, motivation and aspirations of more than 10 million young people, making the move from education into work. The programme helps develop core, transferable skills that businesses increasingly need. In 2019, the programme was extended to encompass the whole of the UK workforce, across all ages, aligning with current employment trends, such as under-employment and an ageing workforce. In addition, Barclays Connect with Work is a global programme providing people that face barriers to work with job-ready skills and connecting them to businesses that are recruiting. In 2019, the programme helped to place 66,000 people into work globally.

Barclays also has a range of specific services for the armed forces. Products include tailored loan policies and the ability to pause or cancel insurance policies if deployed at the last minute. Specialist branches near major military installations deliver the Community FLEX proposition – including a revised employment policy to support Barclays colleagues wishing to deploy as military reservists.

Barclays' Unreasonable Impact programme is an international network of accelerators. It's dedicated to scaling growth-stage entrepreneurs whose ventures have the potential to employ thousands worldwide, while solving some of the most pressing societal and environmental challenges. Since 2016, 124 ventures have been part of Unreasonable Impact; collectively they have reduced greenhouse gas emissions by 55 million tonnes, supported 30,000 net new jobs and are positively impacting the lives of more than 200 million people globally.

Since the outbreak of Covid-19, Barclays has been helping its personal, SME and corporate customers to access both financial and wider support, including loan schemes, repayment holidays, training sessions and resources. In April 2020, Barclays announced a £100m Community Aid Package to support charities that are helping people and communities most impacted by the pandemic.

Promotion

In 2020, Barclays partnered with Nextdoor to help local businesses advertise to their neighbourhood for free. Through the partnership, businesses can add themselves to the 'Open for Business' directory and reach thousands of households with two free 'business posts' every month.

Barclays launched the 'Make money work for you' campaign across the UK in 2019, to help customers take control of their money. The aim was to show Barclays standing beside business and consumer customers, helping them to have a more positive relationship with their money. Also in 2019, Barclays sponsored Pride in London, Northern Pride, Pride in Liverpool, Pride Glasgow and Bury Pride. For the second consecutive year, Barclays unified all UK Pride activity under the creative identity, 'Love Goes The Distance'. This celebrates how far the march towards equality has come, as well as highlighting where progress is still needed.

Barclays became the title sponsor of the Barclays FA Women's Super League in 2019 and lead partner of the FA Girls' Football School Partnerships. It has made a commitment to ensure girls in England have equal access to football in schools by 2024. A total of 100 Girls' Football School Partnerships have now been created, each with an education expert overseeing the introduction and delivery of the programmes to primary and secondary schools across the country.

Designed to help businesses and communities create, innovate and grow, Barclays Eagle Labs, are in 25 locations nationwide. Advice and digital skills have been provided to more than 100,000 individuals and Eagle Labs is currently home to 546 resident businesses. Reflecting its commitment to Backing the UK, Barclays is supporting innovative, high-growth UK businesses to create new employment opportunities and growth within the UK. In 2019, in partnership with Airlabs, Barclays created a fleet of London electric black cabs filled with air as clean as in the Peak District, thanks to Airlabs' innovative air filtration technology.

Barclays' Investment Bank engages its C-suite and institutional investor audiences in strategic dialogue, through ideas and video-based storytelling. With the aim of delivering its understanding across sectors, asset classes and economies, thought-leading insights provide a window into the way in which Barclays works with clients and the impact its services can have on their businesses. In 2017, the first solution for corporate clients to combine biometric technology with advanced digital signing was launched to help customers feel more confident online and to prevent malware and remote access trojan fraud.

In 2016, Barclays Corporate Banking facilitated the first global trade transaction executed using blockchain technology, alongside Wave. This business was a graduate of Barclays Accelerator, a 13-week programme designed to accelerate Fintech start-up businesses.

Brand History

1690 John Freame and Thomas Gould start trading as goldsmith bankers in London.

1728 Freame and Gould move to 54 Lombard Street, beneath the sign of the Black Spread Eagle.

1920 Barclays finances William Morris, helping him become the biggest car manufacturer in the UK.

1966 Barclaycard, the UK's first credit card, is launched.

1967 The world's first ATM is unveiled by Barclays.

2007 Barclays launches the UK's first contactless payment card.

2012 Barclays Pingit launches, the first payment service allowing money to be transferred with a mobile phone.

2015 Barclays launches Rise, a community for Fintech start-ups to connect, co-create and scale innovative ideas.

2017 The first solution for corporate clients combining biometric technology with advanced digital signing, biometrically tying a transaction to an individual, is launched.

2018 Barclays launches its Purpose – 'Creating opportunities to rise'.

2019 Barclays becomes the first lead sponsor of the Barclays FA Women's Super League, the biggest ever investment in UK women's sport by a brand.

2020 Barclays launches a £100m Community Aid Package to support charities that are helping people and communities most impacted by the Covid-19 pandemic.

Brand Values

Barclays' strategy is underpinned by the energy, commitment and passion of its people who deliver its Purpose – 'Creating opportunities to rise', spanning customers, clients, colleagues and society as a whole. Everything that the bank does is underpinned by five values; Respect, Integrity, Service, Excellence and Stewardship.

bp

bp's purpose is to **reimagine energy** for people and our planet. Its ambition is to be a **net zero** company by 2050 or sooner and to help the world get to net zero

a very *different* kind of *energy company*

Market

bp is an integrated energy business focused on delivering solutions for customers. bp provides customers with fuel for transport, energy for heat and light and lubricants to keep engines moving. It has operations in Europe, North and South America, Australasia, Asia and Africa.

Product

bp has a 111-year history (since 1909) operating in energy markets. Some of its well known brands include Castrol, Wild Bean Cafe and Aral.

A global producer of oil and gas, in 2019 it produced 3.8 million barrels of oil equivalent per day. As part of its new strategy, to be a very different company by 2030, it aims to reduce oil and gas production by over 40% over the next decade.

bp holds a rapidly growing low carbon electricity and energy portfolio, with a focus on building scale in renewables and bioenergy. Biofuels are an essential part of advancing towards a low carbon future by reducing emissions from transport and electricity. BP Bunge Bioenergia is a world-scale, highly-efficient producer of sugarcane ethanol in Brazil.

In 2017 bp joined forces with Lightsource, one of Europe's largest solar developers, to accelerate worldwide growth of solar. bp is a key wind energy producer; in the US, its nine onshore windfarms produce enough electricity to power more than 450,000 homes.

Air bp is one of the world's largest aviation fuel suppliers and has been innovating and shaping the industry for more than 90 years. Air bp has been providing fuel for flights and supporting customers in beginning their low carbon journey since 2010 when it undertook the supply of sustainable aviation fuel. It is the first aviation fuel provider to turn its global fuelling operations carbon neutral.

In the UK, bp has more than 1,200 service stations, which provide trusted quality fuels and everyday convenience items, while Wild

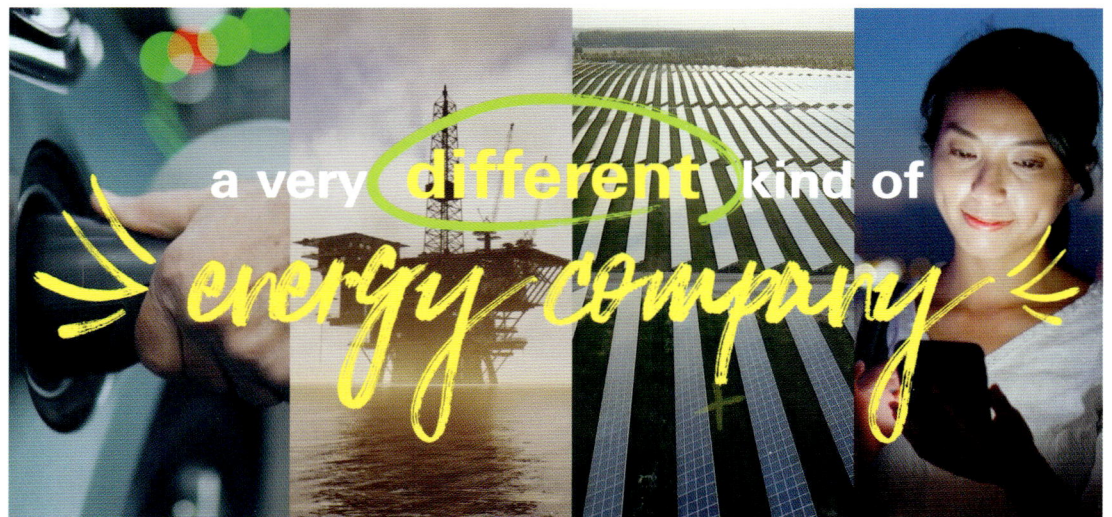

DID YOU KNOW?

bp's Helios logo, named after **the Greek god of the sun**, celebrated its **20th anniversary in 2020**

Bean Cafes (in selected sites) provide food and drink for on-the-go motorists. In addition to its own offering, bp has partnered with Marks & Spencer Simply Food at selected locations across the UK to provide customers with an even greater choice.

bp also has the UK's largest public electric vehicle charging network which continued its growth by introducing more ultra-fast charging points throughout 2020.

Achievements

In 2020, bp started taking steps to deliver on its new strategy – it began with bp's first venture into offshore wind by partnering with Equinor, a recognised leader in its sector. bp also announced a partnership with Uber to help their UK drivers

transition to electric with discounted access to the bp charging network. bp also revealed plans to help the city of Aberdeen decarbonise to meet its target to be net zero by 2045.

bp's contribution to the UK extends to helping societies connect with world-class art and inspiring more young people into STEM subjects. For more than five decades it has been one of the country's most prominent investors in the arts, culture and education.

Recent Developments

In 2020, bp set a bold new ambition to become a net zero company by 2050 or sooner and to help the world get to net zero. bp announced a new strategy to deliver on that ambition and to transform the company in the next decade. By 2030 bp aims to be a different kind of energy company – increasing annual investment in low carbon to US $5bn – a 10-fold increase on the US $500m it currently invests. As part of its pivot from an international oil company to an integrated energy company, it aims to reduce oil and gas production by more than 40%. bp also revealed it would be aiming to provide 70,000 electric vehicle (EV) charging points globally – up from 7,500 on its public network in 2020.

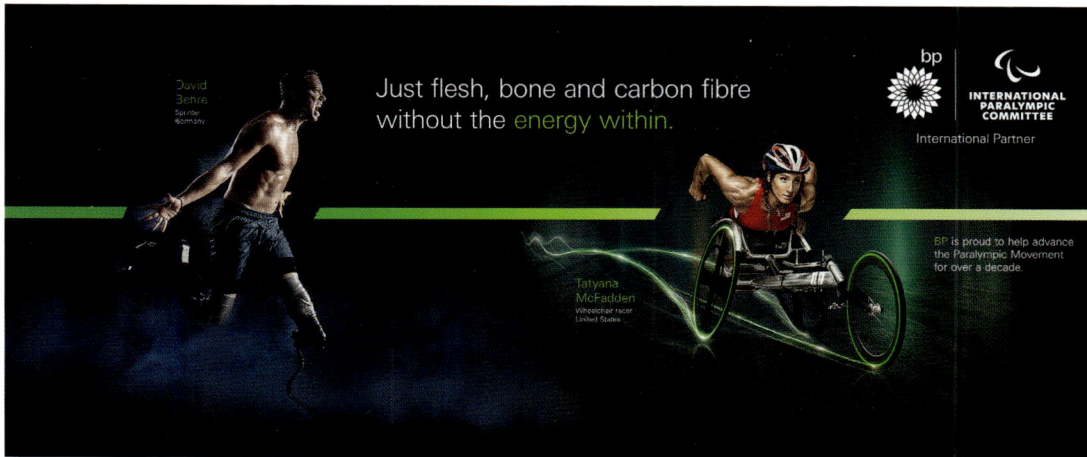

Just flesh, bone and carbon fibre without the energy within.

bp
INTERNATIONAL PARALYMPIC COMMITTEE
International Partner

BP is proud to help advance the Paralympic Movement for over a decade.

David Behre
Sprinter
Germany

Tatyana McFadden
Wheelchair racer
United States

Brand History

1909 The Anglo-Persian Oil Company, as bp was first known, is formed.

1940s bp's sales, profits, capital expenditure and employment all surge upwards as post-war Europe restructures.

1975 bp pumps the first oil from the North Sea's UK sector ashore after purchasing the Forties field – financed by a bank loan of £370m.

1990s bp merges with US giant Amoco, and the acquisitions of ARCO, Burmah Castrol and Veba Oil turn the British oil company into one of the world's largest energy companies.

2000 The brand relaunches, unveiling the new 'Helios' brand mark.

2005 bp Alternative Energy is launched, a new business dedicated to the development, wholesale marketing and trading of low carbon power.

2012 bp supports Britain in staging the world's biggest sporting event – the London 2012 Olympic and Paralympic Games – as an Official Partner.

2017 bp and Lightsource agree to form a strategic partnership, bringing Lightsource's solar development and management expertise together with bp's global scale. The company is renamed Lightsource bp.

2018 bp announces it is to buy the UK's largest public electric vehicle charging network, which operates more than 6,500 charging points across the country.

2020 bp pivots from being an international oil company focused on producing resources to an integrated energy company focused on delivering solutions for customers. Concurrently, the Helios logo celebrates 20 years.

Promotion

In response to the Covid-19 crisis, bp offered free fuel and electric vehicle charging to emergency services vehicles. It also provided support to the NHS Heroes Initiative, enabling drivers of electric taxis to offer reduced fares to NHS workers.

Recognising the anxiety and uncertainty brought about by the pandemic, bp made a substantial donation to mental health charity Mind to help more people across the country access mental health support.

bp continues its focus on digital solutions for customers. In 2018, bp launched a national rollout of its smartphone app-based payment platform, BPme. The technology revolutionised customer's fuel buying experience by allowing contact-free payment entirely through the app, from the comfort of the driver's vehicle. Today, the platform also supports the bp retail loyalty programme in the UK; BPme Rewards. BPme has been adopted in more than 1,100 UK bp filling stations with 1.5 million downloads.

New Instagram and Linkedin accounts for the company's CEO, Bernard Looney, were set up in 2020. This provided a platform to speak more directly to society on the energy transition and other key issues such as business leadership, diversity and mental health.

Brand Values

bp upholds values of safety, respect, excellence, courage and one team. In a fast-changing world, these five values provide a fixed point of reference for the way the company operates and behaves.

bp has been supporting the Paralympic Movement since 2008 when it became an official partner for the London 2012 Paralympic Games. It recognises the power of the movement and supports its vision to create a more inclusive world through Para sport.

BRITISH AIRWAYS

Throughout its history, **spanning over 100 years**, British Airways has been at the **forefront of innovation** in aviation. **Its pioneering spirit has led to numerous industry and world firsts**. Although 2020 has been a difficult year for air travel, **British Airways is committed to safely getting customers back in the air** and continuing to connect Britain with the world and the world with Britain

Market

British Airways, part of International Airlines Group, is one of the world's leading global premium airlines and the largest international carrier in the UK. With its home base at London Heathrow, last year British Airways flew to more than 200 destinations in more than 80 different countries. In 2019, the airline carried more than 46 million customers.

Product

British Airways operates a range of flights to UK domestic, short-haul and long-haul destinations. It offers a choice of travel classes, with something for every taste and budget, from First, Club World, World Traveller Plus and World Traveller on long-haul routes, to Club Europe and Euro Traveller, on short-haul routes.

Achievements

During the global pandemic the airline did all it could to support the fight against Covid-19, operating more than 100 repatriation flights to bring more than 40,000 UK customers back home. In addition, a taskforce of volunteer British Airways staff helped out in communities across the country. The airline is continuing to fly vital PPE and medical supplies to the UK and temporarily converted two Boeing 777 passenger jets into dedicated cargo aircraft to enable the airline to carry as many supplies as possible.

DID YOU KNOW?

British Airways donated more than **200,000 essential items** to **charities and communities** across the UK in the **fight against Covid-19**

Throughout 2020 the airline expects to take delivery of several new aircraft, including the Airbus A321neo, Airbus A320neo, Airbus A350-1000, Boeing 787-10 and Boeing 777-300ER. British Airways is also fitting out some of its long-haul aircraft with new interiors and most will include its new business class seat the Club Suite. The Boeing 777-300ERs will be delivered fitted with the airline's improved First seat with a sliding door.

All short-haul aircraft are to be fitted with wifi and more than 60 of British Airways' long-haul aircraft are now fitted with full streaming capability, high-speed wifi. The system will be installed in 90% of long-haul aircraft by the end of 2021.

In 2020 British Airways expanded its route network with the launch of new routes to Dalaman, Bodrum, Lahore, Pristina and Newquay.

Recent Developments

British Airways always puts the safety and security of its customers and staff first and, during the Covid-19 pandemic, the airline has been making changes to increase contactless interactions, while still delivering a great customer experience.

The airline has introduced a new premium contactless lounge experience at London Heathrow. Customers can choose to use self-scan machines to gain entry to some lounges. It has also launched 'Your Menu'. Customers simply scan a QR code to order food and drink from the comfort of their seat and have it delivered directly to their table.

The airline has also moved its award-winning on-board magazine, High Life, online. The monthly content packed magazine will now be available digitally before, during and after a flight. High Life will continue to include travel inspiration articles and is downloadable, free of charge, in-flight using the on-board wifi.

As British Airways continues to update its fleet with more modern, fuel-efficient and quieter aircraft, 2020 saw the emotional retirement

Brand History

1919 AT&T operates the first commercial scheduled flight.

1924 Imperial Airways is formed as the UK's first nationalised airline to operate UK air services.

1936 British Airways Ltd is formed from United Airways, Hillman Airways and Spartan Airlines.

1974 BOAC and BEA merge to form British Airways.

1987 British Airways is privatised.

1988 Club World and Club Europe cabins are launched. British Caledonian joins British Airways.

1999 The oneworld® alliance launches with British Airways, American Airlines, Canadian Airlines, Iberia and Qantas as the founding members.

2010 A redesigned first class cabin is unveiled and a joint business with American Airlines and Iberia launches.

2011 British Airways and Iberia complete their merger to form the International Airline Group (IAG).

2012 IAG finalises the purchase of bmi in April. The brand sponsors the London 2012 Olympic and Paralympic Games.

2019 British Airways celebrates its 100-year anniversary on 25th August.

2020 British Airways retires the last of its iconic 747 fleet and continues to take delivery of new quieter and more fuel-efficient aircraft.

Main image: Photo taken before Covid-19 restrictions were put in place

of British Airways' last Boeing 747-400 aircraft. At one point the airline held the world's largest fleet of jumbo jets, affectionately nicknamed 'The Queen of the Skies'. In October, British Airways' final two 747s received a special send-off from London Heathrow, as hundreds braved the British weather to say farewell to the iconic aircraft.

Promotion

When travel restrictions were eased, British Airways worked hard to ensure its customers felt safe and secure returning to air travel. Its communications focused on reassuring customers around the changes made to each step of the customer journey. Alongside taking a leadership position to get Britain and the world flying again, its summer campaign inspired customers to take off to the people, places and experiences they love and had missed.

The British Airways Executive Club loyalty programme has more than 10 million members worldwide. Executive Club members can collect Avios, the reward currency of the Executive Club, in various ways; including booking flights, hotels, car hire and shopping at their favourite online retailers through the Avios eStore or Rewards App. Once collected, members can then spend their Avios on reward flights, on-board food and drink, upgrades and more.

During the height of the Covid-19 lockdown, a time when travel was not an option for most, British Airways inspired customers to collect Avios in ways other than flying and celebrated how members had collected Avios via online purchases. Nearly 20,000 UK members used the Rewards App during lockdown to purchase Home, DIY and Garden products, collecting almost

14 million Avios. British Airways encouraged members to build up their Avios balance, ready to redeem when they could fly again.

Brand Values

The British Airways brand is built upon the belief that it is the flow of people and ideas around the world that make Britain great. The brand looks to embody four modern British values – openminded, pioneering, creative and welcoming.

It is a modern, forward-facing outlook, and one that evokes a feeling of pride, while confidently showcasing the best of modern Britain to the rest of the world. British Airways' service ethos is built around delivering personalised, intuitive and friendly service that makes its customers feel cared for and excited about their next British Airways journey.

With donations from the public, the British Heart Foundation (BHF)
invests in ground-breaking research that strives to get closer than ever
to a **world free from the fear of heart and circulatory diseases**

Market

There are 168,000 charities registered in the UK. In 2019, charities that fund medical research invested £1.9bn in UK research (Source: Association Medical Research Charities). This may sound like a lot of money, but robust medical research is a long, expensive process. On average, it takes 12-15 years and £1.15bn to produce a new drug (Source: Association of British Pharmaceutical Industry). Even before the Covid-19 pandemic decimated charities' incomes, the proportion of people giving money either by donating or via sponsorship had been declining steadily (Source: Charity Aid Foundation). This is partly due to the tough economic climate and the new GDPR legislation which significantly impacted charities' ability to connect with people. In 2018/19 fundraising income at the top 100 charities fell by £92m.

DID YOU KNOW?

There are **7.4 million people in the UK living with heart and circulatory diseases** – that's around **twice the number** of people **living with cancer and Alzheimer's disease** combined

Despite a challenging market, over the last four years the BHF has grown its fundraising income by 12% and its brand has gone from strength to strength.

Product

Since the BHF was founded in 1961, it has funded transformative research which has contributed to reducing UK deaths from heart and circulatory diseases by half. The BHF also offers support for the millions of people living with these conditions to live better, healthier lives.

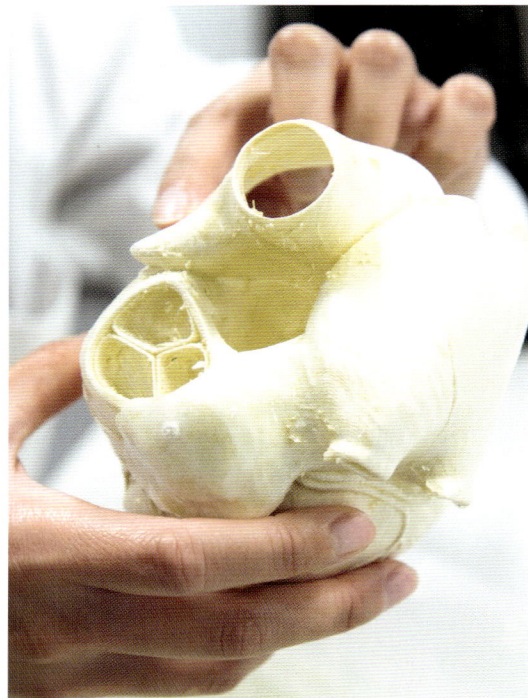

Every six hours, a BHF-funded research paper is published. The BHF funds more than half of non-commercial research into heart and circulatory diseases in the UK. It currently funds around 900 projects, at 47 universities and institutions across the country investigating heart and circulatory diseases and the risk factors that cause them.

Achievements

To help change the way people think and feel about the BHF, the team embarked on a strategic brand review. A new proposition to Beat Heartbreak Forever saw them completely overhaul the brand with a new marcomms strategy and a fresh, contemporary brand identity. The 2018 launch campaign had a crystal-clear message that while BHF research starts with your heart, it doesn't stop there. Its efforts have seen BHF's brand metrics reach their highest recorded levels. In 2019, YouGov's BrandIndex ranked the BHF as the third most improved charity brand of 2019 and in April 2020 the BHF's brand campaign 'starts with your heart' won the Charity Film of the Year Award in the £100 Million Plus Turnover category.

Recent Developments

While it is primarily a medical research charity, the BHF also offers patient services such as a nurse helpline. At the height of the UK's lockdown, its helpline saw a tenfold increase in calls, and its website's Covid-19 information and support pages were viewed millions of times. The BHF's initial reaction to the pandemic was to ensure its services reached as many people as possible. It ramped up its nurse helpline – extending its hours and bringing in more nurses from across the organisation – and transformed its customer service centre into a triage system so it could manage the volume of calls. The BHF also launched its 'Coronavirus on their minds' campaign in May 2020 to let the public know that the BHF was there for them. Looking forward, the BHF's new marketing campaigns will focus on the impact of Covid-19 on its research to save and improve lives, and the urgent need for regular donations to support its longer-term research ambitions.

Brand History

1961 The British Heart Foundation is born.

1968 Mr Donald Ross performs the first UK heart transplant following five years of BHF-funded research into transplant surgery techniques.

1975 BHF Professor, Sir Magdi Yacoub, develops the 'arterial switch', a procedure that is now used all over the world to treat heart defects that occur in babies in the womb.

1976 BHF Professor Michael Davies shows that heart attacks are caused by a blood clot in a coronary artery.

1980 BHF Professor, Sir Magdi Yacoub, establishes the first UK heart transplantation service at Harefield Hospital.

1986 The BHF funds clinical trials of new medicines to treat heart attacks.

1995 Two BHF-funded trials show the life saving benefit of statins.

2019 BHF research shows that high levels of air pollution can increase the risk of a heart attack or stroke.

Promotion

Over the last two years, the BHF's marketing campaigns have aimed to communicate the scope of its research, which extends beyond heart diseases to include other heart and circulatory conditions such as stroke and vascular dementia. During this time, awareness of its research into vascular dementia and diabetes has doubled.

In March 2019 the BHF launched its 'Boy' campaign which saw a young boy, Billy, waxing lyrical about how important the heart is. The campaign also featured a free glow-in-the-dark poster of the heart and circulatory system. The poster was a huge success – with demand exceeding targets by 675%.

In February 2020 the story continued with the BHF's 'swear jar campaign' which followed Billy's rampage against his family as he attempted to get them to swear. After some saint-like self-control from his parents, the family visits a care home where Billy's grandad is suffering from vascular dementia and memory loss. The story ends as it becomes clear that Billy is acting up to raise money for his grandad in a bid to find a cure for the disease.

Brand Values

Even with the challenges that the pandemic has caused, the BHF has a clear strategy to realise its vision of a world free from the fear of heart and circulatory diseases, and will continue to focus on what is important for the charity: funding life saving research and providing support and information to those affected by heart and circulatory diseases.

During this time of inevitable change, the BHF is guided by its values. Taking decisions in the face of uncertainty requires bravery. Making the best possible decisions relies on being informed and working with partners. In addition, compassion for people affected by heart and circulatory conditions, alongside supporters, volunteers and colleagues, is key. Above all, the charity is driven to bring about positive change for its beneficiaries.

CANCER RESEARCH UK

Cancer Research UK (CRUK) is the **world's leading independent cancer charity**. The **only charity fighting more than 200 types of cancer**, its pioneering work into the prevention, diagnosis and treatment of cancer has **helped save millions of lives**

Market

There are more than 195,000 charities registered in the UK and 1,400 cancer charities. With a lower proportion of people supporting charities and consumer confidence at a low, building trust is more important than ever. Charities need to fight even harder for their share of a decreasing market, and to maintain relevance they must move with the times, be innovative, bold and brave.

CRUK is the world's leading independent cancer charity dedicated to saving lives through research, influence and information. CRUK funds nearly 50% of all publicly funded cancer research here in the UK and is the only charity fighting more than 200 types of cancer, from the most common types to those that affect just a few people.

Product

The number of people around the world who receive a cancer diagnosis each year is expected to rise dramatically, from 18.1 million in 2018 to 29.5 million in 2040. In the 1970s, less than a quarter of people in the UK with cancer survived their disease. But over the last 40 years, survival has doubled – today half will survive their cancer. CRUK's ambition is to accelerate

progress and, by 2034, see three-quarters of people surviving the disease for 10 years or more.

CRUK is pioneering new ways to prevent, diagnose and treat cancer, as well as finding ways to optimise existing treatments. The infrastructure it has created for scientists enables world-class research. It engages and empowers patients, policymakers and the public

to make sure advances in research have a positive impact. It also provides information to approximately 38 million people each year – from prevention and diagnosis, to treatment and beyond.

CRUK's work is funded by the generosity of its supporters and partners, raising money through donations, legacies, community fundraising, events, retail and corporate partnerships. All of this is supported by an incredible network of around 40,000 dedicated volunteers.

Achievements

CRUK is number one in Third Sector's 2019 annual Charity Brand Index and also ranked second most famous in YouGov's 2020 CharityIndex.

In 2019 the charity was awarded 'Brave brand of the year, 2019' by The Marketing Society for its national obesity awareness campaign. An award that recognises brands that take risks and stand out from the competition.

In July 2020, the UK Government launched a significant new strategy to help tackle obesity. This included a ban on TV and online adverts for junk food before 9pm – something CRUK has been campaigning for over several years.

Brand History

1930s CRUK lays the foundations for modern radiotherapy.

1940s CRUK develops the first chemotherapies.

1980s CRUK discovers how cancer-causing genes form and develops the brain tumour drug, temozolomide.

1990s CRUK develops abiraterone for treating prostate cancer and uncovers the role diet plays in cancer.

2000s CRUK scientists win a Nobel prize for medicine, help bring in the smoking ban, and launch the first trial of the HPV vaccine (something that will prevent millions of cases of cervical cancer).

2010s CRUK launches AddAspirin, the world's largest clinical trial and discovers how cancer evolves, paving the way towards personalised cancer treatments.

In 2019/20 CRUK spent £455m on research covering almost every aspect of cancer, including £66m on research into some of the hardest to treat cancers. It supported over 150 clinical trials that tested the latest treatment advances on more than 8,000 patients.

In 2019/20 around £108m was raised through goods sold in over 600 shops and other online trading platforms. More than 6,000 people left a gift to CRUK in their Will, and over 425,000 people took part in one of its fundraising events.

Recent Developments
Research is at the heart of progress. CRUK works across the prevention, early diagnosis and treatment of cancer, and despite the setbacks from the pandemic, it has still made great progress to beat cancer.

For example, in the area of early diagnosis, research funding has helped develop the Cytosponge, a simple and cheap tool that can detect Barret's oesophagus – a condition that can lead to oesophageal cancer. The tool has already been shown in clinical trials to be 10 times better than the current method for detecting the condition and could help save thousands of lives worldwide each year.

DID YOU KNOW?

One in two people in the UK, **born after 1960 will get cancer** in their lifetime

The Cytosponge is just one of many methods in development right now for the early detection of cancer. CRUK's scientists are currently developing blood and breath tests that can spot early signs of some cancers. Validation studies are showing that these may be more effective than current standard practices.

Promotion
CRUK's award winning Right Now campaign brings to life real and inspiring stories which demonstrate the positive human impact of cancer research and creates hope that cancer can be beaten.

As a result of Covid-19, CRUK predicts a drop of 25% in fundraising income over 2020/21 and in response the brand has reacted quickly to adapt the campaign, launching an integrated Brand Response Appeal to the UK public to drive

income. The new campaign demonstrates why CRUK's work is so important and now more than ever it needs everyone's help to fund life-saving research. The creative continues to show the reality of day-to-day life for those affected by cancer, but this time under the effects of the Covid-19 restrictions by using authentic user generated content. The campaign also features a CRUK researcher who highlights the charity's continued role in carrying out life-saving research in the face of the pandemic. So far, the campaign has been utilised across a range of channels including TV, VOD, digital, social, partnerships, PR and supporter communications such as email, SMS as well as direct mail and continues to drive donations.

Brand Values
Working together with its supporters and partners, CRUK's vision is to bring forward the day when all cancers are cured – to prevent, control and cure cancer, with three in four patients surviving their cancer by 2034. Its pioneering work is changing lives on a global scale.

Cancer Research UK is a registered charity in England and Wales (1089464), Scotland (SC041666), the Isle of Man (1103) and Jersey (247)

Continental

Continental develops pioneering technologies and services for sustainable and connected mobility of people and their goods. Founded in 1871, the technology **company offers safe, efficient, intelligent and affordable solutions for vehicles, machines, traffic and transportation**

Market

Continental is renowned as a leading premium tyre manufacturer, offering best in braking across all weather conditions. The German manufacturer is in fact much more than a tyre brand; also being one of the world's leading automotive suppliers, shaping the automotive landscape for a safer future with the aim of zero fatalities, zero injuries and zero crashes. Generating sales of €44.5bn in 2019, it currently employs more than 230,000 people in 59 countries and markets. Continental continues to succeed in independent tyre tests across Europe.

Product

Over the last 149 years, Continental has built a rich heritage of developing ground-breaking technologies and mobility solutions, offering a range of tyre fitments for all applications. Continental works with manufacturers to develop ground-breaking solutions, whilst looking to the future with tyre concepts such as Conti C.A.R.E. This revolutionary concept facilitates efficient mobility management for fleet operators. Sensors built into the structure of the tyre enable data on tread depth, possible damage, tyre temperatures and pressure to be provided to the ContiConnect Live application. Additionally, the Conti C.A.R.E concept features technology concepts that allow tyre pressures to be adjusted.

Sustainability is at the heart of everything Continental does, which is why it has continued with the development of Taraxagum dandelion rubber. Since the opening of the Taraxagum Lab in 2018, Continental has released the popular Urban Taraxagum bicycle tyre, the first mass production product to use this material. Although still in its development stage, in the future Taraxagum will be used in car and truck tyres.

Achievements

The market-leading approach of Continental has been frequently recognised with a range of UK tyre test wins and international awards. In 2019, Continental was awarded the Auto Express Product of the Year following a hat trick of wins in the Auto Express summer, winter and all-season tyre tests, the first tyre manufacturer to win all three tyre test awards in a single year. Continuing its tyre test success, Continental also won the Tyre Reviews Ultimate Summer Tyre Test with the PremiumContact™ 6.

DID YOU KNOW?

Continental soles feature on **137 different** models of **adidas trainers**

Continental's commitment to technical excellence and innovation ensures its tyres deliver superb braking, handling and performance. It is the only tyre manufacturer to have an automated braking test centre, enabling 24/7 year-round testing. Continental completes more than 700 million test miles annually and more than 200 rubber compounds daily. Continental is the leading tyre choice for the world's top car manufacturers, with more than 800 current model approvals. If car manufacturers trust the tyre brand's products, drivers can too.

Over the past year, Continental Tyre Group Ltd was named as the inaugural winners of the Tyre Industry Environmental & Sustainable Solution

Award. Sustainable management and social responsibility are among the fundamental values of Continental. This was recognised by the judges who praised Continental's approach to reducing carbon emissions and its use of alternative sustainable materials.

Continental's forward-thinking approach can also be seen in its partnership with Kordsa to produce sustainable Cokoon dip technology. This revolutionary process introduces an eco-friendly dip technology during the textile reinforcement process. To assist with making this an industry standard, the innovative technology is available as an open source, with the first 250,000 passenger car tyres now in series production.

Recent Developments

Over recent years, Continental has developed a range of partnerships to maximise its brand awareness across audiences. Working closely with adidas, Continental continues to bring advanced tyre technology to the soles of trainers, creating rubber compounds with exceptional grip in both wet and dry conditions. Marking 10 years since the beginning of the partnership, 2020 has seen more than 137 different models featuring Continental soles.

The brand's commitment to safety and performance extends to its partnerships with leading cycling events such as Prudential RideLondon, Tour de France, Giro d'Italia and

Brand History

1871 Continental-Caoutchouc-und Gutta-Percha Compagnie is founded in Hanover.

1904 Continental presents the world's first automobile tyre with a patterned tread.

1914 There is a triple victory for Daimlers fitted with Continental tyres at the French Grand Prix.

1979 The takeover of the European tyre operations of Uniroyal, Inc., USA, gives Continental a wider base in Europe.

2003 The world's first road tyre approved for speeds up to 360km/h, the ContiSportContact 2 Vmax, is unveiled.

2006 The automotive electronics business of Motorola, Inc. is acquired by Continental.

2010 Continental partner with adidas to produce trainers with Continental compound technology built into the soles.

2017 Continental launches the new AllSeasonContact.

2018 Recognition in UK tyre tests continues with Continental winning the Auto Express summer, winter and all-season tests – the first time a manufacturer has won all tests in a single year.

2019 Continental is announced as the Founding Partner and exclusive tyre supplier of the new racing series, Extreme E.

La Vuelta, which provide the perfect platforms to engage with keen cyclists and strengthen Continental's position as safety experts, 'whatever the wheel'.

In addition, Continental has entered its seventh year as a Partner in Excellence at Mercedes-Benz World, the pioneering brand experience centre located at Brooklands motor racing circuit in Surrey. Throughout 2019 and 2020 Continental has continued to offer free driving experiences, demonstrating the benefits of premium tyres through a range of driving demonstrations.

Continental will be Founding Partner and exclusive tyre supplier for the new race series, Extreme E, which will see electric SUVs race in extreme and remote areas of the world to highlight the challenges within the location's ecosystems. As the exclusive tyre supplier, Continental has worked closely with Extreme E to develop tyres capable of tackling a range of difficult terrains.

Promotion

For more than 140 years, Continental has continued to invest and improve its tyres to bring consumers premium products. Choosing a Continental tyre means there is no need to worry about anything other than driving safely. This concept lead to the new brand campaign story – 'We care about tyres, so you don't have to'. The campaign shows everyday situations where Continental is the one that consumers can count on.

In past years, Continental has hosted events to support its Vision Zero initiative. A series of Vision Zero Live driving events enabled consumers and retailers to experience advanced vehicle and tyre technologies through a series of live demonstrations. Continental also continues to be a proud corporate supporter of TyreSafe, educating motorists about the simple tyre safety checks all drivers should undertake.

Brand Values

With its tyre technologies, and automotive knowhow, Continental works towards its Vision Zero mission of zero fatalities, zero injuries and zero crashes. Its contributions not only make for an exciting driving experience, but a safe one. Continental's pioneering safety technologies, paired with educating road users globally, reflects the company's commitment to road safety.

drax

Drax is **enabling a zero carbon, lower cost energy future**. Drax Power Station is the **UK's largest single site renewable power generator** and has **ambitions to be carbon negative by 2030** – helping the UK meet its zero carbon target

Market

Drax's portfolio of power generating assets make it the fourth largest power generator in the UK.

Drax Power Station in North Yorkshire is the country's largest, producing enough power for six million homes and has been the backbone of electricity generation in the UK since 1974.

Since converting two thirds of the power station from coal to use sustainable biomass, it has reduced emissions by more than 80% making it the biggest decarbonisation project in Europe.

Drax Power Station will stop using coal in 2021 – a key milestone in achieving its world-leading ambition to be a carbon negative company

DID YOU KNOW?

Drax uses rail to transport its pellets, **saving 32,622.50 tonnes of CO$_2$ per year**

by 2030, using bioenergy with carbon capture and storage (BECCS) – a ground-breaking negative emissions technology needed globally to address the climate crisis.

In 2018 Drax acquired a portfolio of flexible, low-carbon and renewable electricity generation assets in strategic locations across Britain. These include the iconic Cruachan pumped storage power station and two hydro schemes in Scotland, which have enhanced Drax's role supporting the UK grid as more intermittent renewables such as wind and solar come on line.

Drax is the world's fourth largest producer of sustainable biomass pellets. In the US, Drax manufactures compressed wood pellets produced from sustainably managed working forests. It supplies around 20% of the biomass used by Drax Power Station to produce 11% of the UK's renewable power.

Drax's customer facing businesses – Haven Power and Opus Energy – supply renewable electricity and energy solutions to UK businesses, and provide a route to market for more than 2,300 renewable energy installations – mainly wind and solar.

Product

Drax uses its expertise and experience to help UK businesses on their own sustainability journey via its energy supply brands, Haven Power and Opus Energy. Drax offers a variety of sustainable solutions to help businesses reduce their carbon footprint and energy costs. These include 100% renewable electricity, smart meters, energy and market insight, power purchasing agreements, electric fleets and asset optimisation.

Its latest suite of products support electrification. Drax Electric Assets helps customers optimise power-intensive equipment, delivering cost savings and opportunities to create new income streams. Drax Electric Vehicles supports and guides organisations through the process of electrifying their fleets to achieve further costs savings.

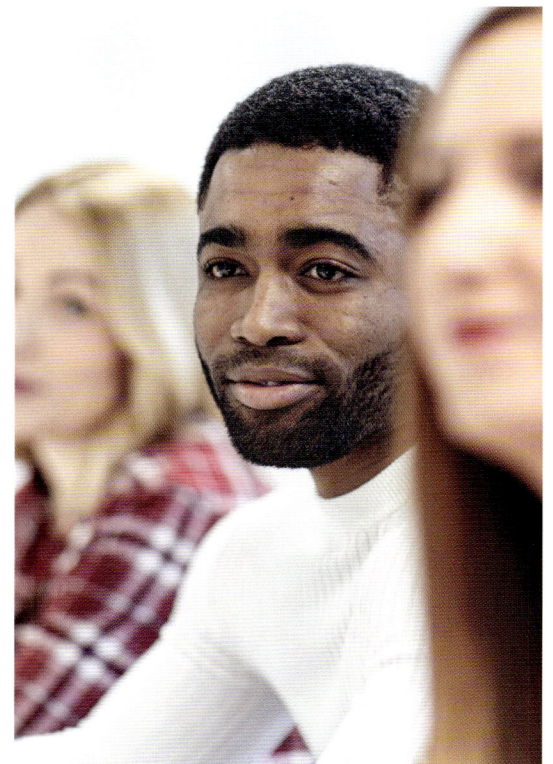

DID YOU KNOW?

Drax has a **hollowed-out mountain**, **two visitor centres** and a **nature reserve**

Drax also provides a route to market for more than 2,300 independent wind and solar power generators, and is trialling polyphase smart meters, giving large corporate customers more control of their energy.

Achievements

Carbon emissions from Drax's power generation were 85% lower at the end of 2019 than in 2012 and the company is on track to stop using coal in March 2021.

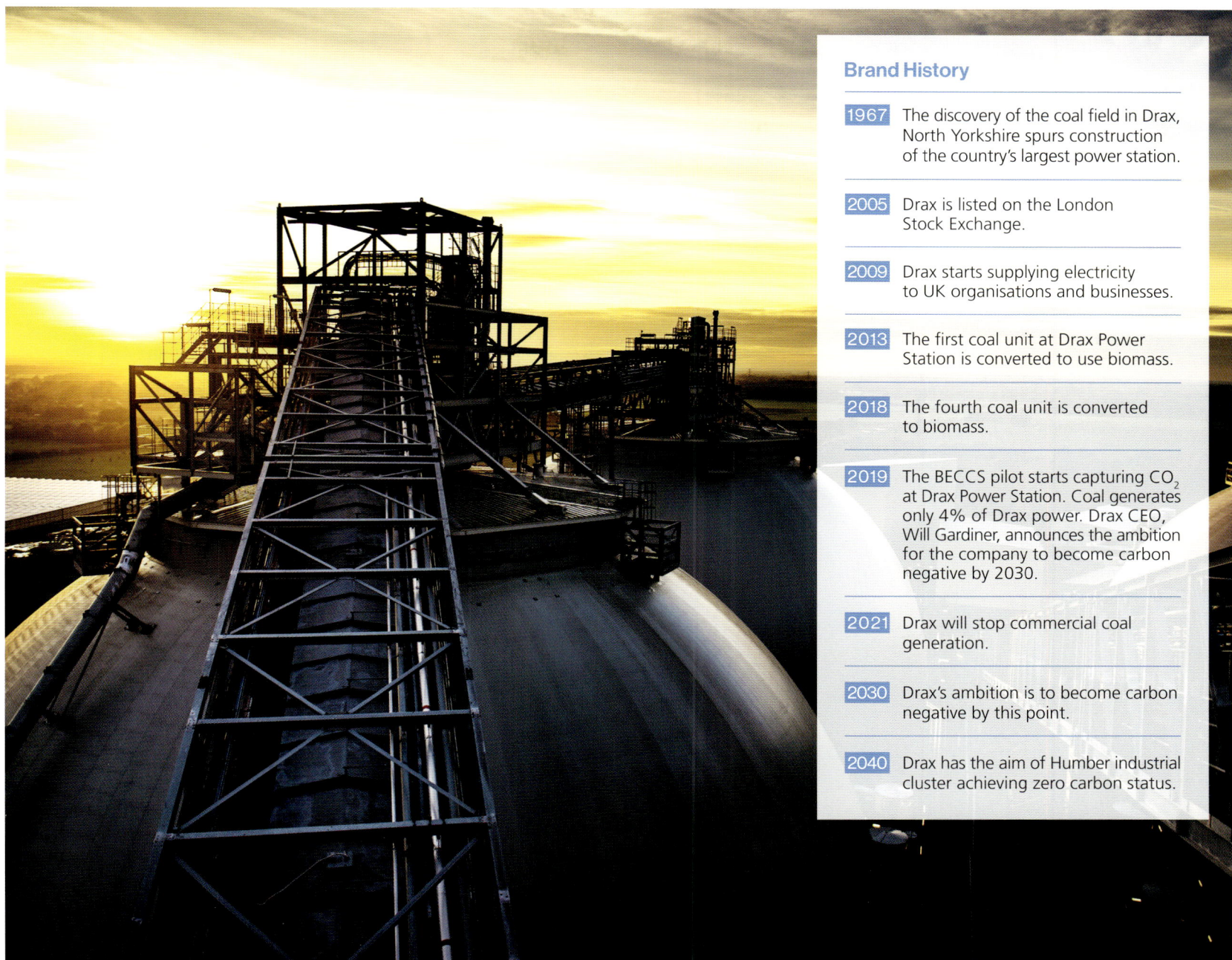

Brand History

1967 The discovery of the coal field in Drax, North Yorkshire spurs construction of the country's largest power station.

2005 Drax is listed on the London Stock Exchange.

2009 Drax starts supplying electricity to UK organisations and businesses.

2013 The first coal unit at Drax Power Station is converted to use biomass.

2018 The fourth coal unit is converted to biomass.

2019 The BECCS pilot starts capturing CO_2 at Drax Power Station. Coal generates only 4% of Drax power. Drax CEO, Will Gardiner, announces the ambition for the company to become carbon negative by 2030.

2021 Drax will stop commercial coal generation.

2030 Drax's ambition is to become carbon negative by this point.

2040 Drax has the aim of Humber industrial cluster achieving zero carbon status.

The transformation from coal to biomass at Drax Power Station was a world first, completed on time and on budget, preserving and creating jobs across the supply chain.

Drax's supply chain for sustainable biomass supports 5,700 jobs in The North and generates around £600m a year for the region's economy.

Drax was also the winner of Utility Week 2019 Innovation Award for its BECCS project.

Recent Developments
Drax was the first company in the world to announce an ambition to be carbon negative by 2030 by using BECCS – a negative emissions technology that the UN's Intergovernmental Panel on Climate Change (IPCC) says will be needed globally to address the climate crisis.

Drax was the first power generator in the world to capture carbon dioxide (CO_2) from a 100% biomass feedstock using BECCS in 2019 and has plans to use BECCS at scale as soon as 2027.

BECCS at Drax could anchor a zero carbon industrial cluster in the Humber – the UK's most carbon-intensive industrial region – creating opportunities for The North to lead in clean technologies, skills and jobs.

BECCS at Drax is an opportunity for the UK to lead globally in the development – and export – of a crucial negative emissions technology.

Promotion
Drax promotes education and employability through its support of science, technology, engineering and maths programmes as well as its apprenticeship programme.

Brand Values
As a brand, Drax is all about perpetual progress, continually moving forward, striving to improve on what has gone before. It recognises that today's solutions can always be bettered tomorrow. Drax's history is one of evolution and change, underpinned by inventiveness and a determination to do what it has said it will do. It is driven by finding practical, responsible and scalable answers to achieve its purpose, a zero carbon, low cost energy future.

To this end, achieving a positive economic, social and environmental impact is embedded in Drax's strategy. It has participated in the UN Global Compact since 2018 and is committed to universal principles on human rights, labour, environment and anti-corruption.

Drax has also identified six of the UN's 17 sustainable development goals where it can have the greatest positive impact: affordable and clean energy, climate action, sustainable forestry, innovation, sustainable cities and communities as well as collaboration and engagement with all stakeholders.

Drax's sustainable biomass sourcing policy exceeds the stringent regulatory requirements set out by the energy industry regulator, Ofgem and the EU. It only uses sustainable biomass from areas with managed forests which are growing at a greater rate than what is harvested. Drax does not use biomass that causes deforestation, forest decline or carbon debt.

EDWARDIAN HOTELS

LONDON

Offering a collection of **individual hotels, inspired by London** and rooted in the neighbourhoods the hotels inhabit, from **stylish boutiques through to luxury on the grandest scale**, each hotel boasts **stunning interiors and exceptional comfort**. With complimentary wifi throughout, chic bars and concept restaurants, **Edwardian Hotels London's service ethos delivers unforgettable experiences**

Market

Founded by Jasminder Singh OBE in 1977, Edwardian Hotels London is intrinsically linked to the landscape, with 11 of its 12 properties being in London and one in the heart of Manchester.

The group has been committed to establishing upscale hotels in the city for decades and is inimitably embedded within the London landscape. The luxury London hotel market is a highly competitive environment and Edwardian Hotels London is able to stand out from the crowd with stunning four and five-star properties in key London locations. What helps to distinguish the brand from other key players is its individuality. As a family business, the company offers top quality and unique design, combined with a style of service that is genuine.

DID YOU KNOW?

Set across **16 storeys**, **The Londoner** will premiere as the world's first **'super boutique'** hotel

Product

Known for its presence in London's most sought after locations, Edwardian Hotels London has eight hotels in Zone One alone. With strong and sustained investment across the portfolio and a contemporary environment in each hotel, the properties are designed for comfort and convenience. Adorned with tactile furnishings and original art throughout, each hotel is distinct in its look and feel.

Staying in an Edwardian Hotels London property is an experience. From Kensington to Covent Garden or Bloomsbury to Mercer Street, each has a unique personality. The group's 'Yes I Can!' service philosophy means nothing is ever too much trouble.

Achievements

Edwardian Hotels London has been ranked as one of the best hotel groups in the UK in Which? Travel consumer magazine.

Focused on creating bespoke experiences, each hotel is a one-off and strives to achieve the best in hospitality by creating exceptional memories. This ethos is further evident at its Manchester property, winner of The Beautiful South Gold award, as well as Manchester Tourism's Hotel of the Year over consecutive years. Sustainability is also high on the agenda, with numerous awards cementing the brand's reputation as one of the UK's greenest hotel groups, including a Green Tourism Business Scheme Gold Award, Best Carbon Reduction in a Hotel Chain, and a Sustainable Restaurant Association Two Star badge.

Edwardian Hotels London is the official corporate fundraising partner to Cancer Research UK, with funds raised by the wider company going to the Francis Crick Institute in London, a world-leading centre of biomedical research and innovation.

Digital innovation is at the forefront of the group's progression, with a number of new initiatives ensuring a seamless guest experience. Its multi-award-winning virtual host 'EDWARD' has been a huge success, with recent accolades

including 'Best Use of AI & Associated Technologies' at the 2019 ECCCSA ceremony. An automated, intelligent text-based interaction service, EDWARD responds to and executes guests' requests, enquiries and bookings via mobile phone. Online check-in and check-out has also become a popular feature, with guests given the freedom to choose their room prior to arrival, and check-out quickly and easily.

Recent Developments

Edwardian Hotels London remains part of one of the world's fastest growing upscale hotel groups, while retaining its individuality as a privately owned hotel collection. In 2019 the company developed its offering with, among others, the refurbishment of its Bloomsbury Street hotel and the August launch of Bloomsbury Street Kitchen.

DID YOU KNOW?

The **AI chatbot, EDWARD, responds to questions in 59 languages,** and counting

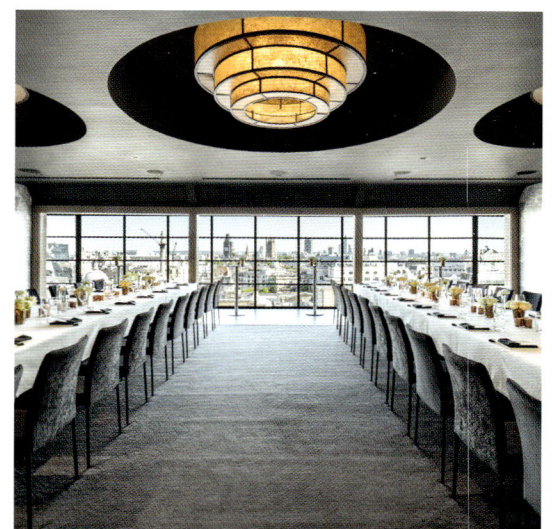

Brand History

1977   Edwardian Hotels is established by Jasminder Singh OBE.

1992   A marketing agreement with Carlson is signed to increase global reach and the brand becomes Radisson Edwardian Hotels.

2004   The first hotel outside London opens in Manchester, a five-star hotel in the city's iconic Free Trade Hall.

2007   The company opens a brand new hotel opposite The O2 at New Providence Wharf in London.

2012   An agreement is signed with Radisson Hotel Group (originally Carlson) to become part of the global Radisson Blu brand portfolio and the brand becomes Radisson Blu Edwardian, London.

2013   Radisson Blu Edwardian, London launches Steak & Lobster as well as Scoff & Banter.

2016   May Fair Kitchen opens at The May Fair Hotel, followed by Monmouth and Leicester Square Kitchens at the Mercer Street and Hampshire hotels, respectively.

2017   Plans get under way for The Londoner in Leicester Square, opening in 2021.

2018   At The Hampshire Penthouse opens and Manchester welcomes a multi-million-pound refurbishment, new restaurant and bar.

2019   Bloomsbury Street Kitchen opens, offering an exquisite selection of contemporary Mediterranean and Japanese small plates, alongside reserve wines, sake and signature cocktails.

Serving an exquisite selection of contemporary Mediterranean and Japanese small plates, Bloomsbury Street Kitchen is a distinguished sunrise to sunset destination with a diverse variety of wines, sake and signature cocktails.

The popular EDWARD service was also rolled out as an Apple and Android app, adding extra convenience for guests. The latest exciting development in Leicester Square comes in the form of a new hotel, The Londoner, which will open its doors to the public in early 2021. Sixteen storeys will feature 350 bedrooms, six concept eateries and bars, a private guest residence, an urban wellness retreat, seven inspiring meeting spaces and a stunning ballroom for up to 850 guests.

Promotion

The group's brand communications remain distinctive. Through cherry-picked partnerships and a cross-channel brand activation calendar, every hotel continues to weave itself into the fabric of the community in which it resides.

In the capital, Radisson Blu Edwardian, London properties demonstrate their affinity with the arts through longstanding partnerships with the National Theatre, Royal Shakespeare Company, and The Donmar Warehouse, to name three of its extensive partnership portfolio. The May Fair Hotel continues its status as the Official Hotel Partner to London Fashion Week and the London Film Festival. Meanwhile in the north, Radisson Blu Edwardian, Manchester continues to cement its place in the heart of Manchester through its title as the Official Hotel of Manchester Pride.

Brand Values

The essence of the Edwardian Hotels London brand is its core 'Yes I Can!' philosophy – an approach not only to service but also to the way it does business. This positive attitude enables the delivery of a customer promise that makes people feel special with individual service aiming to build mutually beneficial relationships with a commitment to creating business. Authenticity is at its core, the environment and experience guests enjoy at Edwardian Hotels London is uniquely cosmopolitan.

FitchGroup

Fitch Group is a **global leader in financial information services** with operations in **more than 30 countries**. Dual headquartered in **London and New York**, and wholly owned by Hearst Corporation, it is comprised of **Fitch Ratings, Fitch Solutions, Fitch Learning and Fitch Ventures**

Market

Credit ratings provide a forward-looking and relative assessment of credit risk – namely, how likely is it that investors will be repaid in-full and on-time. Credit risk is one of the most important considerations when investing in a bond, although it is only one of many factors that should inform an investment decision. Understanding credit risk is not easy, and it's a challenge exacerbated by the enormity and complexity of the bond market. Fitch Ratings helps make sense of this complexity with ratings based on a simple letter scale. AAA is the highest rating, indicating the least credit risk, and D is the lowest rating. Its rigorous analysis and deep expertise have resulted in a variety of market leading tools, methodologies, indices, research and analytical products, which have helped investors manage risk and funds over a century of growth.

Product

Fitch Group has a globally prominent team of analysts who are experts in credit and risk. The group comprises four businesses: Fitch Ratings is a global leader in credit ratings and research. Its analysts cover 5,000 financial institutions, 2,850 corporates and 160 sovereigns and supranationals. Fitch Solutions helps clients excel at managing their credit risk, offer deep insight into the debt investment market, and provide comprehensive intelligence about the macroeconomic environment. Fitch Learning is a preeminent training and professional development firm which educates 26,000

finance professionals in banking, credit, risk, wealth management and apprenticeships every year. Finally, Fitch Ventures is a strategic venture investment vehicle.

Achievements

Fitch is recognised as a market leader, with recent accolades including Fitch Ratings being named, for a second consecutive year, as the most transparent Credit Rating Agency for ESG. In 2020, Fitch Group received an impressive 94 FocusEconomics Awards and Fitch Solutions was named best Counterparty Data Provider by Waters Technology. Fitch also won the China Ratings Agency Award for a third consecutive year and Fitch Learning achieved the top Ofsted grade for its UK Apprenticeship Programmes.

Recent Developments

For 20 years, Fitch Group has been growing internationally, hand in hand with the growth of the financial markets around the world. The latest chapter in this story is in China, where in May 2020, Fitch Ratings announced that Fitch Bohua had received approval from the People's Bank of China (PBOC) and the National Association of Financial Market Institutional Investors (NAFMII) to rate financial institutions (including banks, non-bank financial institutions and insurers) and their securities as well as structured finance bonds in China's interbank market. Fitch Bohua is a wholly-owned subsidiary of Fitch Ratings and provides forward-looking ratings, in-depth research, valuable data tools and

insightful commentary for investors and other participants in the local Chinese bond market.

Fitch is committed to its corporate social responsibility goals. It has launched many employee-led networks including Fitch Pride Network, Fitch Women's Network, Fitch BALANCE, Fitch BAME Network and Fitch Green Wave, all aimed at increasing representation and affecting change. In 2019, Fitch launched the 'us.u.all' training programme which is designed for managers to explore diversity and inclusion.

In 2018, Fitch Group became a signatory to the United Nations Principles for Responsible Investment and the UNPRIs initiative on credit ratings and risk. Fitch launched an integrated scoring system that shows how ESG factors impact individual credit rating decisions. Fitch is the only CRA that currently offers this level of granularity or transparency about the impact of ESG on fundamental credit, maintaining more than 140,000 ESG scores on more than 10,000 entities, transactions and debt programmes.

As a result of Fitch's growth and acquisitions, it now has more than 4,000 employees, including in excess of 1,600 analysts, in more than 40 offices and affiliates worldwide.

Promotion

Fitch's brand is inextricably linked with its people and its thought leadership. It maintains an active presence in a wide variety of global media,

Brand History

1913 Fitch Publishing Company Inc. launches in New York and the Fitch Bond Book is published.

1924 Fitch develops the letter-grade scoring system for the credit-worthiness for corporations.

1975 Fitch gains NRSRO status, allowing it to supply financial information for regulatory purposes.

1997 Fitch merges with IBCA Ltd, owned by Fimalac S.A.

2000 Fitch IBCA and Duff & Phelps Credit Rating Co merge and acquire Thomson BankWatch.

2006 Hearst Communications, Inc. invest in Fitch.

2008 Fitch launches Fitch Solutions.

2013 Fitch acquires 7city Learning to become part of Fitch Learning.

2014 Fitch acquires BMI Research incorporating it into Fitch Solutions Country Risk & Industry Research (2018).

2015 Fitch Solutions launches Fitch Connect.

2016 Fitch Group and Hearst launch Fitch Ventures.

2018 Fitch Group becomes wholly-owned by Hearst and Fitch acquires Fulcrum Financial Data products.

2020 Fitch Bohua is approved by People's Bank of China and the National Association of Financial Market Institutional Investors to rate financial institutions, their securities, and structured finance bonds in China's interbank market.

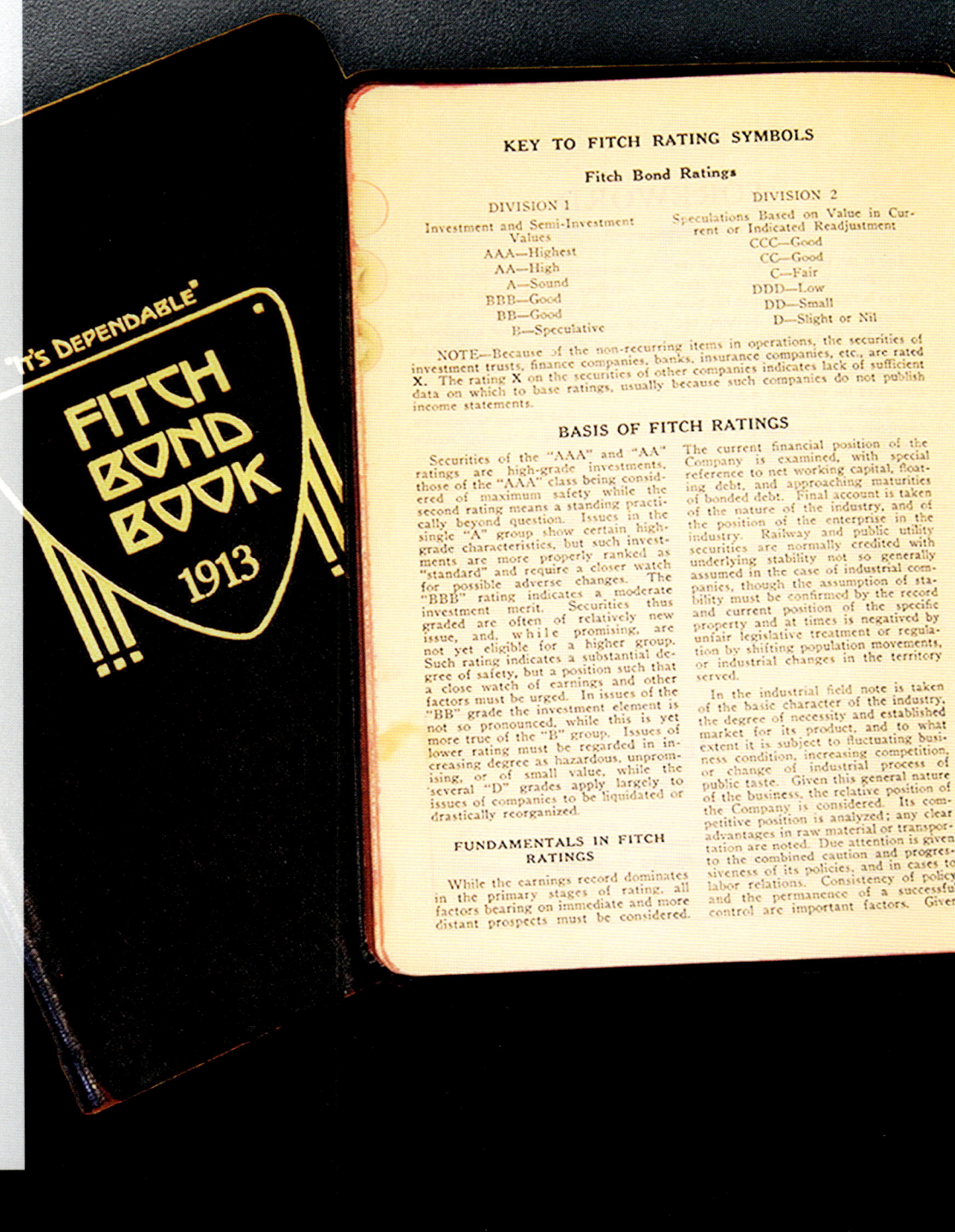

including top tier global print and broadcast outlets, business and trade media, and national and local newspapers. This helps to promote Fitch's research and ratings. In addition, its analysts are regularly quoted in print and interviewed on television and radio. In 2020, in particular, Fitch Ratings' views on the credit market impact of Covid-19 have generated extensive media interest.

Events are an integral part of Fitch's brand promotion. This vital communications channel conveys the Fitch message and demonstrate the quality of its thinking and research in an interactive environment. Recently, the increase in virtual events has allowed Fitch to experiment with the format, while also reaching a far wider audience.

Brand Values
Fitch aims to be the partner of choice for the global capital markets. Putting clients and partners at the centre of its business, it provides unparalleled service based on its best-in-class reputation for analytics, research, service, transparency and integrity. People are Fitch's most valuable asset and are at the heart of what makes Fitch Group different. Its values help shape its three-pronged philosophy: To foster a strong and inclusive culture; to be completely transparent and fiercely independent; and to be exceptional partners to stakeholders.

Fitch is committed to conducting its business in a responsible and sustainable way that is beneficial to its stakeholders and critical to its ongoing success. Its corporate social responsibility goals include fostering an inclusive culture, leadership development and being a diverse recruiter. Fitch also believes in giving back to its community and has a number of programmes aimed at increasing access to education and reducing the environmental impact of its business operations.

Flymo®

Since inventing the hover mower more than 50 years ago, **Flymo has become a market leader in effective and affordable garden care products**. Its range now encompasses everything from **grass trimmers to robotic lawnmowers**. With constant design and technological innovations being at the heart of Flymo, **the brand is continually revolutionising its range**

Market

Flymo is part of the Husqvarna Group, a leading global producer of outdoor power products which encompasses lawnmowers, robotic mowers, garden tractors, chainsaws and trimmers. In the UK, Flymo is a leading lawnmower brand as well as being at the forefront of design and innovation across a wealth of other gardening equipment segments.

Over the years, Flymo has built a very close relationship with UK gardeners, learning about what they need and what problems they have in the garden, then using its 'Easier by Design' philosophy to create and develop new products to make gardening easier. Customer satisfaction and support is a key priority. Flymo research has found that more than 70% of people who have bought from the brand would purchase a Flymo lawnmower again. The company therefore works hard to retain these high levels of brand loyalty.

Product

Flymo's consistent drive to make products 'Easier by Design' stems from its invention of the hover mower, back in 1963. The traditional heavy petrol lawnmower was transformed into a significantly lighter and easy to use product, literally floating on a cushion of air and easy to manoeuvre in any direction. Since then, Flymo has set the pace by producing high performance hover mowers alongside other gardening power tools.

Since launching the 1200R robotic lawnmower in 2013, when robotic lawnmowers were almost unknown in the UK, Flymo has helped grow the market segment by making robotic lawnmowers more available and affordable, now taking a significant share of the UK market. These lawnmowers leave no visible grass on the lawn because they cut such a small amount at a time. By cutting little and often, the lawn always looks healthy. The robotic lawnmower works within a set boundary in the garden, it will mow in the rain and will automatically return to its charging station.

DID YOU KNOW?

83% of DIY consumers **recognise that Flymo** is the **UK's leading lawnmower brand** *

*Source: Survey Sampling International (SSI)

In addition to its comprehensive lawnmower range, Flymo's garden power tool range has seen the launch of the Contour Cordless 20V Li, EasiCut Cordless 20V Li and SabreCut XT Cordless 20V Li, which tackle a variety of trimming jobs. All use a powerful 20V Lithium-ion rechargeable battery, eliminating the need for a power cord.

Achievements

For more than 55 years, Flymo has been an established and iconic sight in UK gardens. It has consistently held high market shares in the UK, at its peak taking more than a 50% share of the UK lawnmower market.

2021 will see the launch of the EasiLife GO robotic lawnmower. This is Flymo's smallest and simplest robotic lawnmower yet, with its intuitive Push & Go interface and enhanced app control, it is ideal for smaller lawns.

In addition, two new Flymo Hover Lawnmower ranges, SimpliGlide and EasiGlide, have also been introduced. Both of these ranges are lightweight and easy to manoeuvre. They are available in a 30cm, 33cm and 36cm deck size, with long life metal blades, powerful motors and ambidextrous handles, along with a host of other useful features.

The EasiGlide range is available across three models – the affordable EasiGlide, the advanced EasiGlide V and the feature-packed EasiGlide Plus model.

2021 also sees the introduction of the Flymo EasiClean Li and Li Plus pressure washers. These compact lithium-ion battery powered portable pressure washers are ideal for quick and easy cleaning around the home and garden.

In the 1980s, Flymo gained the Queen's Award for Technological Achievement as well as receiving royal recognition for its ability to export – taking its lawnmower to more than 60 countries worldwide. Heavy investment and research has seen Flymo introduce an automation programme, making it the first company in Britain to fully assemble and test its products using robots.

Recent Developments

In recent years, Flymo has been developing its range of battery-powered products. This technology can be used to solve some of the problems consumers face when using electric products that require power cables. Battery technology has rapidly advanced, becoming a more powerful and reliable power source.

Flymo launched the Mighti-Mo 300 Li, its first Lithium-ion battery lawnmower, ideal for typically small UK lawns, in 2017. Powered by a 40V battery, it is lightweight and compact, whilst being a surprisingly powerful small lawnmower.

Following on from this success, Flymo launched a new cordless, interchangeable battery system,

Brand History

1963 The Air Cushion mower is invented by Karl Dahlman, taking inspiration from the newly launched Hovercraft.

1964 Flymo Ltd is formed and manufacturing begins at Aycliffe, in the north of England.

1970 Flymo's first electric model launches.

1981 The first grass collecting air cushion mower is introduced. The following year, Flymo receives a Queen's Award for export achievement.

1988 The launch of the Multi Trim electric trimmer is the most successful in Flymo's history.

1993 Flymo GardenVac is successfully launched, going on to create a new market segment all over Europe.

1999 Flymo launches its first cordless, battery powered mower for small gardens.

2013 The 1200R Robotic Lawnmower is launched.

2014 Flymo launches a new hover collect lawnmower with unique twin chamber hovering deck for a cleaner neater cut and closer cutting up to edges.

2017 The first Flymo Lithium-ion battery lawnmower, Mighti-Mo 300 Li, launches.

2019 Flymo celebrates its 55th birthday and the first Flymo Lithium-ion interchangeable battery range, C-LiNK, is launched together with a complimentary range of C-LiNK compatible products.

2020 Flymo extends it Robotic lawnmower range with the launch of the EasiLife 200 sq m, 250 sq m and 500 sq m.

C-LiNK. This lightweight power head connects to three interchangeable gardening tools – a hedge trimmer, grass trimmer and blower. All three products within the range use a powerful 20V Lithium-ion battery, the first of its kind for handheld Flymo tools. The C-LiNK range is complimented by three C-LiNK compatible products, which use the same battery and charger system. These are a lightweight trimmer with an innovative, specially designed, in line edging wheel to make lawn edging easy, the Contour Cordless 20V Li; a lightweight hedge trimmer, the EasiCut Cordless 20V Li; and the SabreCut XT 20V Li, which is a versatile, long reach hedge trimmer, to tackle taller awkward hedges.

Promotion

Flymo supports its products and innovations with multi-channel promotions. Over the years it has run many national TV advertising campaigns alongside national media press campaigns. Going forward, a leading focus for 2020 and beyond will be to strengthen its digital and online presence to support the consumer shift from in-store to online shopping behaviour. Indeed, Flymo estimates that more than 40% of all its sales are now online via one form or another. Enhancing the customer experience online is now a major priority for Flymo at every stage of the customer journey.

2019 saw the launch of the Flymo e-commerce website where consumers can now buy direct. In addition, all the latest information about the brand is available and consumers can register products as well as keep up to date with the Flymo newsletter and enter special member competitions.

Brand Values

Flymo was founded on innovation and its thirst for design and technological development continues. Its aim is to create products that are 'Easier by Design', suited to today's modern lifestyle in order to help consumers maintain impeccable gardens.

GREEN FLAG
COMMON SENSE TO THE RESCUE

With over **45 years' experience**, Green Flag provides **breakdown cover 24 hours a day, 365 days a year**. Its ambition has been to **revolutionise the breakdown market by utilising a network of service providers throughout the country.** This innovative and efficient model provides a **high-quality service for customers**

Market

Green Flag is the UK's third largest breakdown brand (Source: Based on independent research by Consumer Intelligence, September 2020, survey of 1,015 policy holders). The market has grown in recent years but is increasingly under pressure from new players. Green Flag works with a flexible, nationwide network of local garages, providing a high-quality service for customers.

Product

Green Flag is a challenger brand that aims to keep people moving with smart solutions and meeting their motoring needs. Rather than relying on a fleet of owned vans, Green Flag partners with a smart network of specialist local mechanics up and down the country and in Europe, allowing them to provide a more agile service.

Green Flag believes that by not operating a fleet of owned vans also creates an efficient business model, eliminating costs, and allowing savings to be passed on to customers.

By not deploying a one size fits all model, Green Flag's network is flexible and adaptable. It also means that rescue vehicles are not kept on the

DID YOU KNOW?

Green Flag began as an **idea between two friends** above a fish and chips shop

road when they aren't needed and Green Flag can partner with the closest and best equipped mechanic to the customer to get them moving again. This can include the provision of hire cars and taxi services.

Achievements

Customer satisfaction is key to Green Flag's success. Its Recovery Plus product has received a five-star Defaqto rating in 2020. Furthermore, Green Flag ranks highly in a range of UK Customer Satisfaction surveys, results that are supported by its strong Trustpilot scores with an 'excellent' rating. Green Flag has also won Best Direct Breakdown Cover Provider at the Your Money Awards in 2018 and 2019 as well as having a Net Promoter Score (NPS) of +76 from customer satisfaction surveys on claims.

Recent Developments

Since launching in 2015, the Green Flag 'Rescue Me' app has been integral to the innovation of the rescue experience as consumer behaviour changes. Through the app, customers can register a call for help and track their technician. This helps Green Flag keep connected to broken down drivers and

DID YOU KNOW?

Nationwide, 1,700 rescues a day are attended to (based on Green Flag rescue data, for the last 12 months)

ensures that customers are kept informed and in control. The app itself has an NPS of +78 and registered 10% of all breakdown claims in 2019, a figure that is expected to increase year-on-year.

As the world of motoring changes with the rapid development of vehicle technology and ownership preference, Green Flag continues to innovate its products and challenge the industry norm through its challenger brand approach and in 2019 launched the Green Flag online shop selling products that meet motorists' needs.

Due to the Covid-19 pandemic, Green Flag has also recognised that NHS workers across the UK are heavily relied upon and offered free rescue for all NHS staff during lockdown and now offer discounts on breakdown cover as a way of saying thanks for all their incredible work.

Promotion

Thinking differently has always been Green Flag's approach since its beginning in 1971, built on the ambition to revolutionise the breakdown market. In 1994, it became the first ever brand to sponsor the England football team, which ran until the 1998 FIFA World Cup.

Brand History

1971 Green Flag is established under the name National Breakdown Recovery Club (NBRC).

1984 NBRC is acquired by National Car Parks (NCP).

1994 The company is renamed as Green Flag and begins sponsoring the England football team.

1999 Green Flag becomes part of RBS Group, which is then acquired by Direct Line.

2008 Green Flag branded vans launch across the network.

2014 Green Flag sponsors Premiership Rugby.

2015 Green Flag begins sponsoring ITV National Weather.

2017 Green Flag is named as Your Money, Best Online Breakdown Insurance Provider.

2017 Green Flag reboots its brand and marketing strategy.

2018 The company launches a new smart network of service providers and wins Best Automotive campaign at the PRCA Awards.

2019 The brand celebrates its 25th anniversary as 'Green Flag'.

2020 Green Flag launches its NHS offer to give all NHS staff access to free breakdown cover during the Covid-19 crisis.

Green Flag's brand review in 2017 strengthened its position in the market with its 'Common Sense to the Rescue' concept which boldly challenged the AA and RAC offerings. A fresh TV campaign connected with drivers across the UK, demonstrating that Green Flag is a smart, credible alternative and 50% cheaper at renewal. 'Common Sense' being shorthand for a smarter approach to breakdown, a service that is more agile and adaptable now and in the future. 'To the Rescue' has two meanings. It represents the quality of service as well as the customers' position, namely 'rescuing' them from the competition. The reinvigoration of the brand was brought to life through TV, radio, OOH and digital channels. The 'Common Sense to the Rescue' tagline continues to live through all communications today.

Brand Values

Built on 'Common Sense to the Rescue', everything Green Flag does is aimed at providing an efficient service to meet its customers' needs. Its innovative model enables customers to take ownership of their mobility and get them back on the road as soon as possible, in a smart and connected way.

HARIBO

Founded in 1920 by HAns RIegel in BOnn, HARIBO is a **market leader**
in creating great tasting, **fun sweets that delight consumers around the world**
and help friends and families **enjoy moments of childlike happiness**

Market

The HARIBO family has been producing great value, quality treats for three generations. Today, its range of confectionery is available in more than 100 countries and 16 factories operate worldwide, including two in the UK.

HARIBO's journey to becoming the UK's number one sweets manufacturer (Source: IRI Marketplace, 52 wks ending 19th April 2020) and producer of Britain's favourite treats (Source: Britain's Favourite Sweets, Channel 5, January 2019 & May 2020), began in 1972 when the company acquired majority stakes in British confectioner, Dunhills. Taking full ownership in 1994, the brand set about revolutionising the UK sweet market; this started with today's number one sweet brand HARIBO Starmix and the launch of Tangfastics, with its unique tangy recipe.

Product

HARIBO's universal appeal spans generations. As its famous slogan suggests, it is loved by both kids and adults; many remember growing up with their HARIBO favourites and have since, in turn, enjoyed sharing those moments of nostalgia with their children.

Through its popular gums and jellies, liquorice favourites and MAOAM fruity chews, HARIBO

DID YOU KNOW?

The UK has **more than 100 different varieties** of HARIBO

prides itself on its reputation for quality, great taste and for delivering fun, excitement and innovation into the confectionery aisle.

Offering something for everyone, HARIBO has created its own unique mixes that have become iconic, with Starmix, Tangfastics, Supermix and Giant Strawbs, to name just a few. This variety is complemented by the popularity of sister brand MAOAM, which delivers the category's leading fruity chews, including Stripes and Pinballs.

Achievements

From its operations and products, through to the way it markets its treats, HARIBO

strives for excellence throughout its business. This commitment has resulted in significant investment, achievements and growth.

Bolstering its success in the UK, HARIBO strengthened its infrastructure in 2016 with the official launch of a new Yorkshire based production facility; this marked a significant, multi-million-pound investment.

The brand's dedication to maintaining a safe workplace is also continuously endorsed. In 2020, HARIBO received the prestigious 'Order of Distinction' from the Royal Society for the Prevention of Accidents (RoSPA). This acknowledged its ability to demonstrate the highest standards

Brand History

1920 HARIBO is founded by Hans Riegel in Bonn.

1994 HARIBO takes full ownership of Dunhills which launched the world-famous Pontefract Cakes more than 250 years ago.

1995 Starmix is unveiled, introducing the brand's first mix bag of iconic pieces – the Egg, Heart, Ring, Cola Bottle and Bear.

2014 TV advert 'Boardroom', HARIBO's most iconic TV advert, is launched under the Kids' Voices campaign.

2016 The doors officially open to a new HARIBO factory in Yorkshire.

2017 HARIBO reacts to demand and launches its first HARIBO-owned retail store.

2018 HARIBO launch Fruitilicious, offering 30% less sugar, same great taste.

2020 HARIBO marks a global milestone – '100 years of happiness'.

year-on-year, achieving 15 consecutive gold awards to become recognised as world-leaders in health and safety practice.

Further endorsement was received in 2019 when Starmix was named Britain's Favourite Sweet. This coveted title was bestowed on this popular treat again in 2020, marking a year of celebration as Starmix enjoys its 25th birthday (Source: Britain's Favourite Sweets, Channel 5, January 2019 & May 2020).

Recent Developments
HARIBO focuses on delivering choice and variety, from much-loved sweets, reduced sugar offerings and portion-controlled formats suitable for many occasions.

Leading the way, HARIBO launched its first reduced sugar product, Fruitilicious, in 2018. Offering 30% less sugar* alongside the same great taste that consumers have come to love and expect from HARIBO, Fruitilicious is now the best-selling reduced sugar medium bag in the UK (Source: IRI Marketplace, Total Market, MAT to 22nd March 2020, £ Sales). It is sold nationwide and through HARIBO's own stores.

Following in the footsteps of its European colleagues, HARIBO opened its first outlet store in 2017 and has expanded its retail footprint across the UK. Those visiting HARIBO's stores

are treated to a fantastic showcase of HARIBO favourites from around the world, alongside highly sought-after merchandise.

Promotion
Best in class marketing is at the heart of HARIBO. Here, the brand outperforms competition across key marketing metrics with the highest levels of awareness and brand love – HARIBO is the first brand shoppers think about when asked to name a sweets brand.

DID YOU KNOW?

HARIBO is an acronym of HAns RIegel, BOnn

This is undoubtably supported by HARIBO's award-winning 'Kids' Voices' adverts; just like its treats, they have mass-market appeal and have become synonymous with the brand.

The 'Kids' Voices' creative, which initially launched in 2014 through the advert titled 'Boardroom', uses adults talking with kids' voices to capture moments of childlike happiness by bringing to life the fun and childlike enthusiasm that people have for the brand.

'Boardroom' was ranked number one in Nielsen's most impactful ads of 2015 (Source: The Grocer Top Products Survey 2015 Top Campaign – Sugar Confectionery 19th December 2015). This inspired a series of TV adverts using the same creative concept. The latest, titled 'Police', marks the fifth instalment. Here our nation's heroes make up a story about cops and robbers using the iconic sweets from Starmix.

Brand Values
HARIBO's ambition is to help friends and families enjoy moments of childlike happiness together for generations to come; this means continuing to make the right choices for its people, customers and the environment.

Whether this is giving back to the community in as many ways as possible, enhancing workforce skills and nurturing team members to become best in class, driving manufacturing excellence, or protecting and propelling the Yorkshire region's rich heritage in confectionery production.

All these factors support growth, which is ultimately driven by trust, popularity and delivering quality treats that people know and love. Combine this with the desire to provide moments of childlike happiness in everything that the brand does, and you can see why 'Kids and grown-ups love it so… the happy world of Haribo'.

*Fruitilicious contains 30% less sugar than regular fruit gum sweets

Heathrow

Heathrow is the UK's gateway to the world. During the **coronavirus pandemic**, Heathrow colleagues have **worked continuously to provide a safe and world-class experience** for passengers choosing it **for business and leisure travel**

Market

Although Covid-19 has disrupted travel immensely in 2020, Heathrow remained open during the pandemic, consolidating its operations into Terminals 2 and 5, to facilitate repatriation flights and cargo deliveries. Through the development of increased cleaning measures, Heathrow has been diligent in following Government guidelines to help reduce the spread of the virus. Whether assisting in the transportation of PPE for NHS staff or its generous donations to the local community, Heathrow has made conscious efforts to help those most in need during the pandemic.

Product

Heathrow aims to ensure its passengers have an enjoyable, but also safe, airport experience. Its colleagues and partners have worked tirelessly to re-open stores and restaurants in Terminals 2 and 5, all of which accept contactless payment, for a contact-free experience. Furthermore, the Heathrow app can be used to order food and drink remotely, as well as reserve items from Heathrow Boutique, in advance of heading to the airport.

Covid-19 has brought into focus the need for action in times of global crisis. In the face of climate change, and before the pandemic hit, Heathrow participated in industry plans to decarbonise aviation and reach net zero

DID YOU KNOW?

Terminal 5 has **30 miles** of **baggage conveyors** and **2.8 miles of tunnels**

emissions by 2050. Through the production of Sustainable Aviation Fuels (SAF), second-generation biofuels, the industry aims to establish the basis for synthetic fuels, made directly from renewably produced hydrogen and captured carbon. UK SAF production could also generate up to £2.7bn and support 18,800 jobs, providing a stimulus in areas across the UK such as Humberside, Teesside, Wales and Scotland.

Achievement

In 2019 the Heathrow Employment and Skills Academy Awards celebrated 15 years. To date it has supported 5,800 people into employment, contributing £13.5m to training and career development.

During 2020, an enhanced focus has been placed on ensuring the safety of staff and passengers, both through stringent cleaning measures and the participation in multiple testing trials.

Recent Developments

Heathrow has put many precautions in place to help prevent the spread of Covid-19. In August 2020, Heathrow began using technology to monitor and detect temperatures. Thermal screening technology was introduced, as a trial, to monitor the temperatures of multiple people moving through the airport in an effort to detect those experiencing Covid-19 symptoms.

Heathrow terminal staff wear full protective equipment, relevant to their role, whilst ensuring social distancing is observed and cleaning procedures are maintained. This is in addition to the provision of more than 600 hand sanitiser stations, enhanced cleaning regimes, prominent signage featuring government health advice, Perspex barriers for frontline contact points and social distancing reminders.

The airport implemented a number of pioneering technologies to thoroughly clean passenger touchpoints, including UV cleaning robots, which use UV rays to quickly and efficiently kill viruses and bacteria at night; UV handrail technology fitted to escalators to ensure continuous disinfection of the moving handrails; and anti-viral cleaning methods to security trays, lift buttons, trolley and door handles, aiming to provide long-lasting protection from Covid-19. Heathrow retrained 100 colleagues to serve as hygiene-technicians,

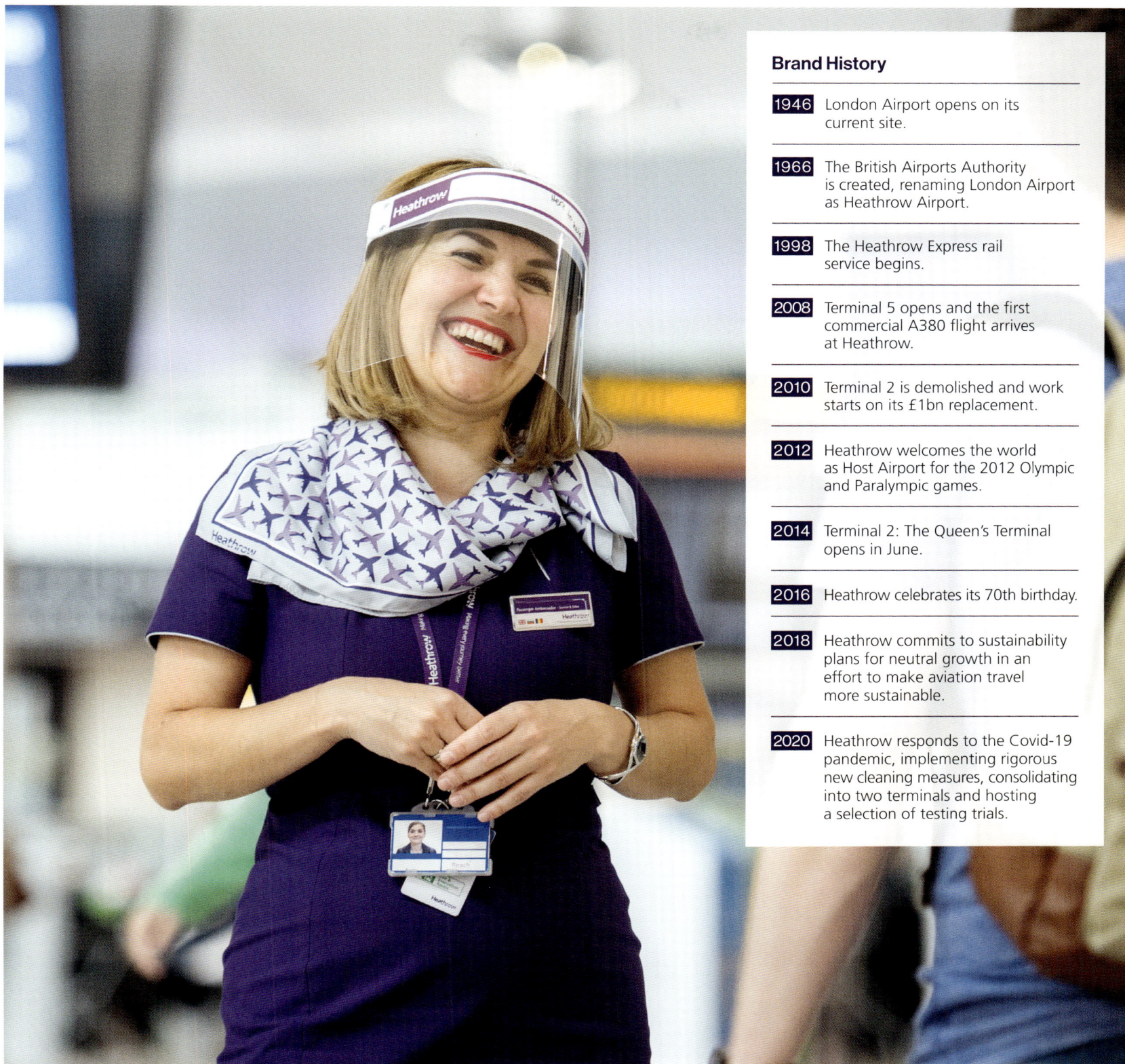

Brand History

1946 London Airport opens on its current site.

1966 The British Airports Authority is created, renaming London Airport as Heathrow Airport.

1998 The Heathrow Express rail service begins.

2008 Terminal 5 opens and the first commercial A380 flight arrives at Heathrow.

2010 Terminal 2 is demolished and work starts on its £1bn replacement.

2012 Heathrow welcomes the world as Host Airport for the 2012 Olympic and Paralympic games.

2014 Terminal 2: The Queen's Terminal opens in June.

2016 Heathrow celebrates its 70th birthday.

2018 Heathrow commits to sustainability plans for neutral growth in an effort to make aviation travel more sustainable.

2020 Heathrow responds to the Covid-19 pandemic, implementing rigorous new cleaning measures, consolidating into two terminals and hosting a selection of testing trials.

who thoroughly disinfect the airport and answer passenger queries on the methods being used.

Promotion

Heathrow launched its 'Fly Safe' message following the re-opening of borders, with the aim of reassuring passengers to travel again. This encompasses measures that have been put in place across the airport, including within the retail offering, as well as the safest ways to travel to and from the airport.

August 2020 saw the launch of the sixth series of ITV's prime-time documentary, Heathrow: Britain's Busiest Airport. Filmed before the pandemic, it gives an insight into normal daily life at the airport which brings an array of challenges, emotional moments and everything in between.

During the coronavirus pandemic, Heathrow made remarkable efforts to support the local community. For the younger generation, Heathrow compiled online educational resources to assist with homeschooling. It also donated 70 laptops to students who didn't have devices at home in order to aid their home learning. In addition, Heathrow also donated £95,000 in rapid emergency funding to support local community groups. One project in particular equipped elderly people with technology, allowing them to stay in touch with family and friends, in an effort to minimise the effects of loneliness.

Heathrow has also supported the wider community by donating vital PPE to the NHS. This has included 16,000 FFF3 face masks and 60,000 liquid bags.

As a business at the heart of the travel industry, Heathrow has been in a key position to comment in the media in response to the unfolding crisis and the repercussions of the Government's recommendations for the industry as a whole. This is a reflection of the importance of Heathrow's position as Britain's biggest international airport.

Brand Values

Heathrow's aim has always been to give passengers the best airport service in the world. It remains committed to delivering on this, making passengers feel secure and confident to fly again.

A trusted brand with optimum performance and consumer wellbeing at its core, Hoover continues to **integrate the latest practical advancements and style** into its **expansive portfolio** of freestanding, built-in and floorcare appliances

Market

Hoover Candy Group is part of Haier Europe; the number one worldwide group in home appliances.

The fastest growing company within the categories of Major Domestic Appliances (MDA) and Small Domestic Appliances (SDA), Haier Europe commands almost 16% of the global market for household appliances.

Smart appliances are becoming more prevalent, with a handful of manufacturers leading the way by tapping into demand for connectivity, functionality and bespoke solutions.

Waste and energy-efficiency are both subjects high on the customer agenda, meaning brands have had to adapt their technology to enable consumers to reduce food waste (refrigeration models) and water/energy usage (laundry appliances).

Product

Hoover UK offers an extensive range of small and major domestic appliances, from handheld vacuum cleaners to multi-door fridge freezers.

Its product portfolio spans vacuuming (cordless and corded), cleaning (steam cleaners and dishwashers), laundry (washing machines, tumble dryers and washer dryers), cooking (ovens, sous vide systems, microwaves, hobs and hoods) and cooling (fridges, freezers and fridge freezers).

A market leader in smart technology, Hoover was the first manufacturer to launch a range of fully-connected wifi appliances in the UK in 2015. Since then, and with support from Haier Europe, Hoover has gone from strength-to-strength with its impressive connected model offering.

Achievements

With a global reputation for performance and trust, Hoover's products have received recognition from a number of high-profile UK institutions, including the Good Housekeeping Institute (GHI), Which?, Quiet Mark, Shortlist.com, Real Homes, Tech Radar, Trusted Reviews and Expert Reviews.

Recipient of two world-famous Red Dot Awards in 2020, one for the H-FREE 500 cordless vacuum and another for the Haier Europe hOn Smart Home app, Hoover also received endorsement for its whole washing machine portfolio from the GHI in August 2020*. The well-respected organisation praised the brand for the performance, quality, reliability and design of its products.

Recent Developments

Hoover implemented a number of major product launches in 2020, most notably the H-WASH 500 laundry range, Collection 3 cooking models and the H-HANDY 700 EXPRESS next-gen handheld vacuum.

DID YOU KNOW?

Hoover **invented the first portable vacuum cleaner** more than **100 years ago**

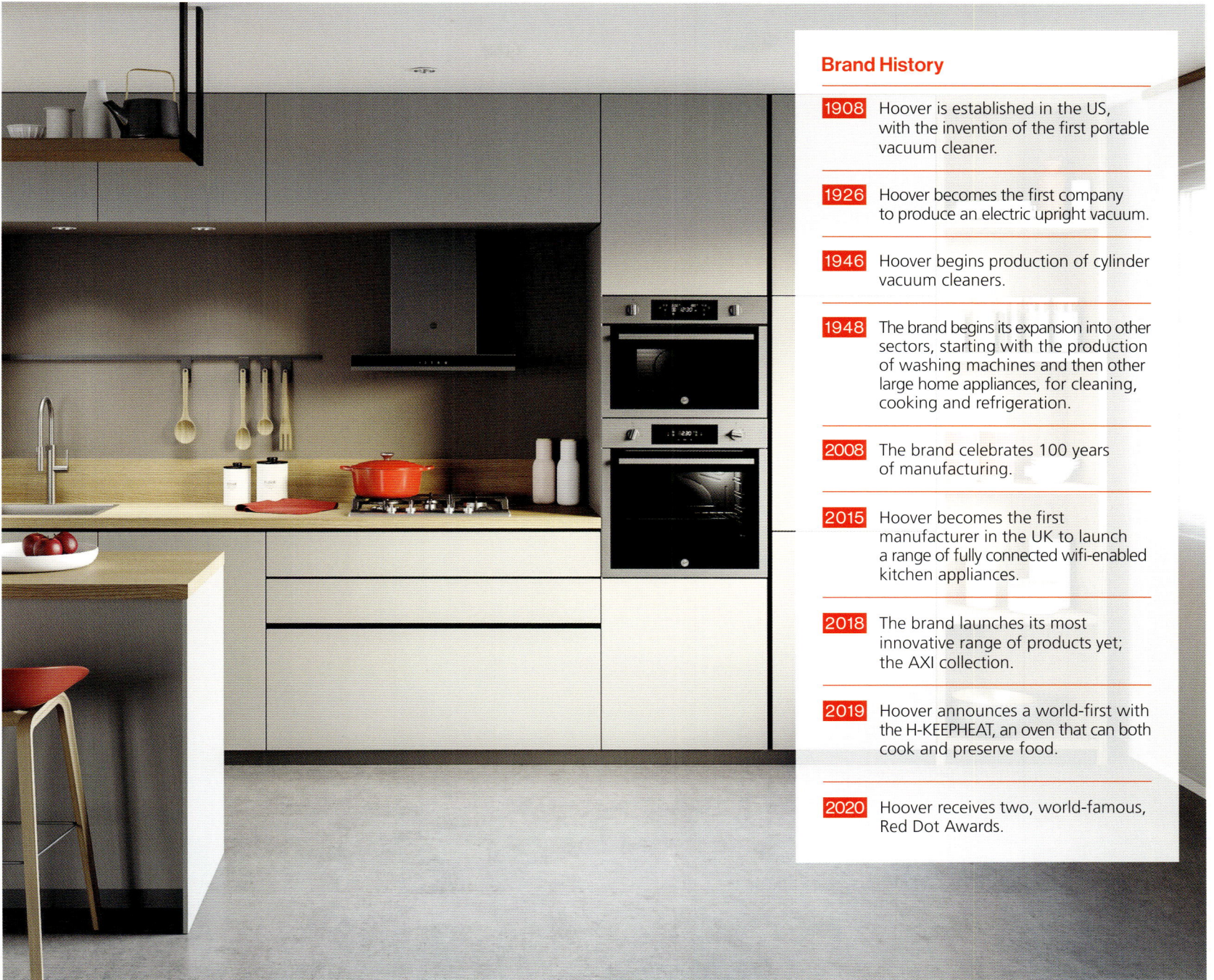

Brand History

1908 Hoover is established in the US, with the invention of the first portable vacuum cleaner.

1926 Hoover becomes the first company to produce an electric upright vacuum.

1946 Hoover begins production of cylinder vacuum cleaners.

1948 The brand begins its expansion into other sectors, starting with the production of washing machines and then other large home appliances, for cleaning, cooking and refrigeration.

2008 The brand celebrates 100 years of manufacturing.

2015 Hoover becomes the first manufacturer in the UK to launch a range of fully connected wifi-enabled kitchen appliances.

2018 The brand launches its most innovative range of products yet; the AXI collection.

2019 Hoover announces a world-first with the H-KEEPHEAT, an oven that can both cook and preserve food.

2020 Hoover receives two, world-famous, Red Dot Awards.

The H-WASH/H-DRY collection is Hoover's smartest ever range. Comprising 54 washing machines, washer dryers and tumble dryers, the products offer the very latest in appliance technology. Connected via the hOn app, models offer unique features such as 'click to wash' and 'scan to care' which use photos taken of laundry items to recommend the best washing programmes.

Collection 3 is Hoover's largest-scale cooking launch since 2018. Including smart, pyrolytic and steam ovens, as well as gas and induction hobs, Collection 3 features a brand-new look for Hoover ovens with clean lines and black glass or stainless steel finishes. Boasting the very latest technology, a number of models are wifi-connected, offering remote control, voice activation and access to more than 200 recipes.

H-HANDY 700 EXPRESS is a next-gen handheld model perfect for 'grab and go' spot cleaning at home or in the car. Compact, stylish and lightweight, the cordless vacuum offers ultra-powerful cleaning and is lighter than a loaf of bread. Designed to be left out on display,

DID YOU KNOW?

In 2020, Hoover was **awarded two**, world-famous, **Red Dot Awards**

the vacuum nestles neatly in a sleek charging base, complete with a 3-in-1 crevice, dusting and upholstery tool. It also delivers up-to 12 minutes runtime, an impressive 50% more than its closest competition (12 minutes versus eight minutes from the Shark WV200UK).

Promotion
Hoover has invested substantially to support its key 2020 launches with major, multi-channel marketing campaigns to both trade and consumer audiences.

All built on the foundations of Hoover's 'The Way You Live…' messaging, activity has

been disseminated via several online video on-demand (VOD) platforms, social media, PR, advertising and email marketing.

Hoover has also continued to amplify its sponsorship of both British chef and restaurateur, Simon Rimmer and Rugby League giants, Warrington Wolves, with the launch of 'Wellbeing Wednesday'. Complete with meal, fitness and mindfulness advice, the digital initiative saw Hoover reach millions with helpful tips and tricks to help people through the pandemic.

Brand Values
Hoover strives to meet the needs of all customers, both retail and consumer, with core values built on performance, wellbeing and trust.

Offering the latest technology for perfect results, Hoover believes in a healthy lifestyle and a better environment for all, building on a century of continuous research and development and offering reliability and build quality that people can trust.

*Survey on appliance brand recommendation (Washing Machines) from Good Housekeeping Reader Panel, 2020

HSBC UK

HSBC is one of the **world's largest banking and financial services organisations** serving more than **40 million customers** through its global businesses. HSBC UK offers a range of **retail, commercial and private banking services** in the UK including current accounts, mortgages, credit cards and savings accounts

Market

Often described as the UK's biggest bank in terms of assets, the HSBC UK brand often finds itself squeezed in the middle of the UK banking market. In terms of share of voice, HSBC UK is consistently outspent by other major retail banks such as Lloyds, Barclays and Halifax who dominate the market. On the other end of the scale, disruptors to the category such as Monzo and Starling are seeing a popular groundswell, utilising word of mouth tactics. This means HSBC UK's challenge is twofold; a need to punch above its weight in terms of awareness and finding ways to differentiate itself amongst a crowded competitor set.

Product

HSBC aims to be where the growth is, connecting customers to opportunities, enabling businesses to thrive and economies to prosper, and ultimately helping people to fulfil their hopes and realise their ambitions.

HSBC UK serves personal and business banking customers in the UK and has an extensive branch network across the country to support the needs of its customers.

HSBC UK was created on 1st July 2018 in response to the Financial Services (Banking Reform) Act 2013 which requires all banks to 'ring-fence' their core banking services in the UK.

Achievements

Over the past two years, HSBC UK has won 36 industry awards across its 'We Are Not An Island' campaigns, as well as achieving its highest ever levels of advertising awareness.

HSBC UK has introduced a scheme within its branches to help raise awareness of hidden disabilities, something that has come to the fore in light of the coronavirus pandemic. The globally recognised Hidden Disabilities Sunflower Lanyard scheme is being introduced across all HSBC UK branches. Wearing a sunflower lanyard indicates discreetly to others that the wearer, or somebody who is with them, may be living with a hidden disability – such as dementia, mental health conditions, autism, or sensory impairments – and may require additional support, extra help or a little more time.

Customers and colleagues can opt to wear a lanyard as a discreet signal that they may need additional support. For some, their condition may mean they cannot wear

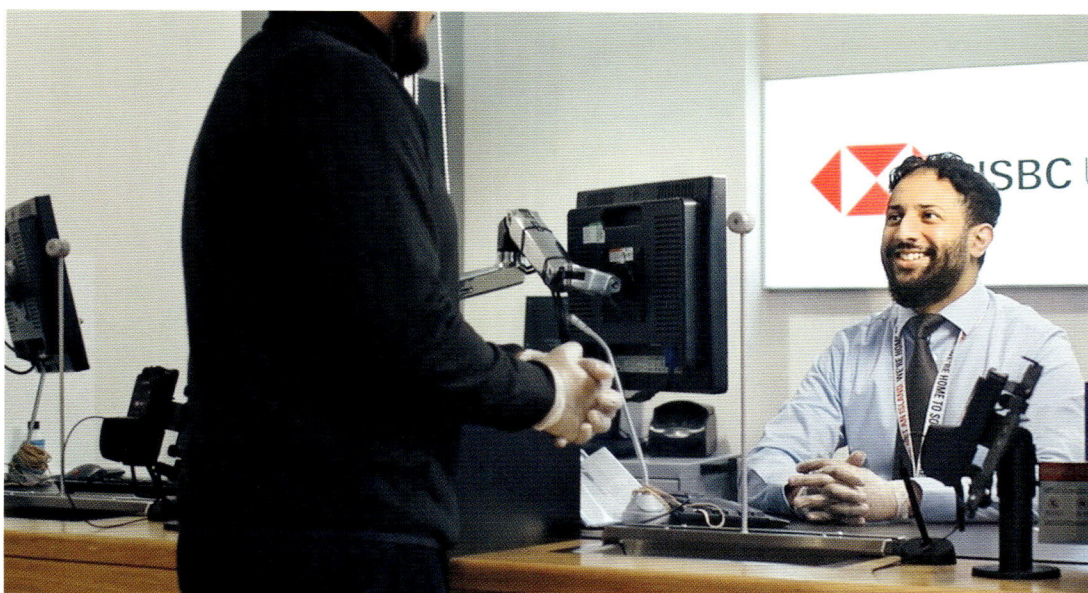

WE ARE NOT AN ISLAND.
WE ARE PART OF SOMETHING FAR, FAR BIGGER.

Together we thrive

HSBC UK

Brand History

1836 — The Birmingham and Midland Bank opens for business.

1851 — The first branch opens.

1958 — Midland Bank becomes the first bank to offer unsecured personal loans.

1992 — Midland Bank officially becomes a part of HSBC.

1999 — The Midland Bank name is replaced, creating a clear and consistent identity.

2002 — The Canary Wharf building is opened as the new head office in the UK.

2018 — HSBC UK moves to Birmingham.

2019 — The award-winning 'We Are Not An Island' campaign is launched.

---

a face covering, while others may require seating or have the need to be in a calm environment.

Recent Developments

In recent months, HSBC UK has responded to its customers' changing circumstances due to the Covid-19 pandemic by introducing a number of support packages for both businesses and personal banking customers ranging from loans for businesses to providing holidays on mortgages, loans and credit card repayments.

HSBC UK has recently launched VoiceID, voice-driven technology to its telephone banking. It enables callers to state their intent verbally and be directed to the correct team automatically, saving time for both customers and customer service colleagues.

The new service uses smart technology to recognise the reason for the call and navigates customers to the correct team for help, replacing the touch-tone menu and reducing the need for internal transfers. With the launch of the new Interactive Voice Response (IVR) system, customers will get the correct help, more quickly.

DID YOU KNOW?

HSBC UK recently **doubled the availability** of its service that enables **homeless people** to open a **bank account**

Since its introduction at the beginning of 2020, this technology has prevented £208m of attempted fraud.

Promotion

From 'The World's Local Bank' through to 'We Are Not An Island', HSBC has long been viewed as a global bank. The continuous challenge however is to show the bank's customers why its international and open mindset is relevant to them and their needs. With this in mind, in 2019, at a time when the UK was questioning its relationship with the rest of the world, HSBC UK captured the nation's attention with one clear message – We Are Not An Island. The aim was to celebrate how the things that make us quintessentially British, also make us inescapably international. Since the launch of the We Are Not An Island work, HSBC UK's creative output has sparked national and international conversation as well as driving significant increases in ad awareness levels. Brand communications have daringly tapped into important cultural conversations and provided an observational view on the social climate of the UK.

Most recently, in response to the Covid-19 pandemic, HSBC has started a conversation about what long-term, positive change can look like, and encouraged audiences to stop waiting for normal to return and use this opportunity to build a better world instead and realise the power of the new different.

Brand Values

HSBC UK's brand promise is to advance prosperity for the people, communities and businesses rooted in the UK. From sponsoring Birmingham Pride to supporting the most vulnerable with ongoing partnerships with Shelter and Children in Need, HSBC UK exists to help people thrive, whatever their circumstances.

INVESTORS IN PE○PLE

Investors in People's purpose is simple. **Make work better.** Three words. Easy to understand, but not always easy to get right. **Since 1991, it has been a force for making work better for more than 11 million people**, with ambitions for further growth

Market

For three decades Investors in People has strengthened positive bonds between businesses and their people, to enhance recruitment and retention, and increase value and output. Its purpose is 'Make Work Better', which it does for millions of people.

As consumers attune to worker/workplace relationships, the demand for Investors in People's help is growing – especially as the lines of home and office blur more in the Covid-19 era.

With ethical consumption soaring, consumers increasingly demand more of organisations, just as they expect workplaces where societal, individual and business objectives align. Investors in People helps to make that achievable.

Investors in People knows that it is people that create better outcomes and is unique in focusing on the entire organisation – not just leadership – because better organisations make better

DID YOU KNOW?

Since 1991, more than **11 million people** have **worked in an Investors in People accredited organisation**

outcomes. Over the years, it has helped 11 million people at more than 50,000 organisations worldwide achieve better outcomes.

Product

In an age of uncertainty, growing competition and rising workplace stress and anxiety, people expect more from their employers, not just a job and a workplace. Investors in People has been working hard on expanding and diversifying its product offering by developing new solutions to further support and equip organisations of all shapes and sizes.

When giving companies the tools to improve, it builds a picture and pathway based on meetings, comprehensive surveys, interviews and sharing of knowledge. In socially distanced times, Investors in People has quickly transitioned services to take advantage of online tools to continue giving customers what they need.

To help customers drive change programmes, Investors in People has invested heavily in a strong digital product portfolio to better deliver data, analysis, documentation creation as well as progress tracking.

Furthermore, as Covid-19's impact becomes more understood, Investors in People has new schemes and products in place to help companies tackle the emerging dynamic of the labour market amidst societal changes.

Achievements

Investors in People is a benchmark for brand awareness within UK businesses: today more

Brand History

1990 The UK Department of Employment embarks on creating a national standard of best practice for employee training and development.

1991 The first 28 Investors in People organisations are celebrated.

2008 An extended framework recognises different levels of success and progress, encouraging more routes for continuous improvement.

2015 The new Standard, a high-performance model exploring the full capability of an organisation and its people, is launched.

2017 Investors in People becomes a Community Interest Company, mandated to improve the working lives of people in all organisations and communities.

2019 Investors in People unveils 'We invest in wellbeing', helping organisations to manage and improve the social, physical and psychological wellbeing of their people.

2020 The pilot of 'We invest in apprentices', a product supporting organisations to better manage their support and investment in apprentices and skills programmes, is launched.

THE INVESTORS™ IN PEOPLE
AWARDS 2019
Winner

DID YOU KNOW?

Investors in People believe a **healthy workforce** is an **organisation's most valuable commodity**

than 1.5 million people work for an organisation accredited by Investors in People in 66 countries, and that is why it received the coveted Social Enterprise Mark for organisations improving both people and the planet.

The social benefits that Investors in People helps to provide are threefold: happy people, competent leadership and more productive businesses. In 2020, Investors in People has been leading the focus on putting people first and building a better normal post Covid-19.

To highlight success, the eponymous Investors in People Awards spotlight great work by successful companies who are growing better

businesses: the event itself is now a Gold Trusted awards programme and shortlisted in numerous categories in the Awards Awards 2020.

Recent Developments

As 2020 unfolded, Investors in People worked closely with its customers and partners to develop new products and tools as attention quickly turned to staff wellbeing in unprecedented times.

The new 'We invest in wellbeing' accreditation uses the latest learnings in data-gathering and insight to springboard organisational efforts towards Physical, Psychological and Social Wellbeing.

Furthermore, helping new generations of workers, the 'We invest in apprentices' programme assists companies closing the skills gap and investing in training.

These complement other initiatives including targeted newsletters, knowledge sharing, advice, and the long-standing 'We invest in people' programmes and accreditation, which continue for customers as usual.

Promotion

In 2020, Investors in People will partner with even more like-minded organisations, influencers, ambassadors and communities.

It has a shared goal with partners throughout the UK, and worldwide, to change work for the better, which it believes is at the root of a more efficient, effective and prosperous society.

Brand Values

Investors in People's brand values underpin the success of the organisation's purpose: those values are to be ambitious, driven, collaborative, empowered and always improving.

As a community interest company, Investors in People's vision is to ensure every community prospers through investing in people. It helps companies put people first by turning organisations into communities, so individuals can fulfil their potential. In turn, companies maximise their collective potential to make positive societal change.

IM, irwinmitchell

Nationally acclaimed, future focused, innovative and supportive, Irwin Mitchell understands that whether it's business or personal, everyone's situation is different. When it comes to legal advice and support with financial planning it's **'the expert hand, with the human touch'**

Market

As one of the largest law firms in the UK, Irwin Mitchell provides a wide range of legal and financial services to thousands of individuals and businesses. In these times of unprecedented change its focus remains the same; to support its colleagues, clients and communities. Irwin Mitchell's track record and expertise, coupled with a reputation as a litigation powerhouse, makes it stand out from the crowd.

DID YOU KNOW?

From humble beginnings back in 1912, **Irwin Mitchell has gone on to support over one million clients**

It understands that consumer needs are changing, combining the latest technology with excellent service to deliver impressive results and build long lasting relationships. This was demonstrated by the way in which it reacted to the Covid-19 pandemic, temporarily closing 15 offices and moving to home working in a matter of weeks, so that support for clients could continue.

As the leading personal injury and medical negligence practice in the UK, Irwin Mitchell supports thousands of families whose lives have been turned upside down by the unexpected. With a national public law team and the UK's leading Court of Protection practice, it works tirelessly to ensure that clients have everything they need. This is strengthened by an in-house asset management division, which provides tailored financial planning and investment advice.

Irwin Mitchell's private client offering specialises in residential property, family, wills and tax, trusts and estate disputes. This is supported by experienced wealth management advisers that help people of all ages to prepare for their current and future financial needs. Its prestigious client base includes high and ultra-high net worth individuals such as business owners and entrepreneurs, corporate executives, investors and multi-generational families.

Irwin Mitchell offers a wide range of commercial services and has expertise in several other sectors including manufacturing, technology, finance, consumer businesses, education, media and sport. Its strength comes from offering more than just legal advice. It understands the current climate and is committed to helping businesses grow while managing risk in a volatile market.

Product

Irwin Mitchell employs more than 3,000 people and has 15 offices throughout the UK. It offers personal and specialist services to national and international organisations and institutions, small and medium-sized businesses as well as individuals.

Achievements

Irwin Mitchell has the largest online market share for personal injury and medical negligence, and the greatest share of voice in legal editorial coverage in the UK media. Its reputation as a leading firm for litigation work has been acknowledged by The Lawyer magazine who named it as the third most active firm in the UK.

It's also recognised in The Times' list of the best 200 law firms in England and Wales and is officially a Great Place to Work, ranking as number one in its industry. Some of its recent awards include Employment Law Firm of the Year, Catastrophic Injury Team of the Year and Excellence in Client Service.

Its responsible business programme is a fundamental part of its commitment to make a real difference and its dedicated charity, the Irwin Mitchell Charities Foundation, has raised more than £2.5m for charitable organisations since 1997.

Priding itself on being diverse and inclusive, Irwin Mitchell was recently named as one of the most inclusive employers in Britain by LGBTQ equality charity, Stonewall. It has also been named in The Times Top 50 employers for women, and has the most female Partners of any UK law firm.

DID YOU KNOW?

More than **250 of its lawyers** are **individually recommended** by the independent **Chambers UK and The Legal 500** guides to law

Recent Developments

In one of the most exciting few days in its 108-year history, Irwin Mitchell rebranded and announced a partnership with England Rugby in September 2019.

The brand relaunch went beyond a new logo and colour scheme, it was about going to market as one. Its masterbrand approach is built around simplicity and promoting its business in an integrated way, so current and future clients can easily see the breadth of the services it offers.

Brand History

1912 The company is founded in Sheffield.

1997 The Irwin Mitchell Charities Foundation is founded.

2005 IM Asset Management is launched.

2012 Irwin Mitchell becomes one of the first Alternative Business Structures (ABS) and the first multiple-licensed ABS.

2014 Irwin Mitchell merges with Berkeley Law, specialists in wealth advice for high net worth individuals in the UK and overseas.

2015 Irwin Mitchell merges with Thomas Eggar, significantly increasing its UK geographic coverage.

2017 Irwin Mitchell Private Wealth and IM Wealth Management are launched. Irwin Mitchell becomes the Official Legal Services Provider of the 2017 World Para Athletics Championships in London.

2019 It is named as the Official Legal Partner of England Rugby.

2020 All 15 offices are able to work remotely.

On the eve of the Rugby World Cup, Irwin Mitchell revealed that it had become the Official Legal Partner of England Rugby with a launch event at Twickenham, an ideal match for its new brand vision.

Through the partnership, which includes the men and women's teams, it has developed a new mentoring programme with England Rugby to help keep young players in the game. The Irwin Mitchell Mentoring Club is a structured, development-orientated programme aimed specifically at adults who support players aged 14-18. It also works closely with England Rugby's in-house legal team and the community member clubs.

Promotion
Irwin Mitchell has seen a year-on-year increase in brand awareness, website traffic, social media engagement and media coverage, thanks to an integrated marketing strategy.

Its 2019 award-winning personal injury advert featured real clients. The 'I am able' campaign shone a positive light on what is possible with a positive mindset and access to the best support, rehabilitation and adaptive equipment.

Due to the popularity of the advert, it was still being used when social distancing started and a campaign promoting what you're able to do no longer felt appropriate. Irwin Mitchell reacted

by producing a new advert, featuring staff members talking about what they were looking forward to when the lockdown was lifted. All of the clips were filmed on mobile phones in houses and gardens and feature a line that encapsulates the brand values – 'we're here, just like we've always been'.

Irwin Mitchell has continued to invest in its partnership with England Rugby and advertised in national newspapers, online and on billboards during the Rugby World Cup to remind the England team as well as their fans that 'we are with you'. With sport returning, its focus is on the mentoring club, enlisting the help of current Red Roses captain Sarah Hunter and former England captain Dylan Hartley, who have become ambassadors for the scheme.

Irwin Mitchell's highly praised UK Powerhouse reports have continued to be published quarterly,

working with Cebr to examine economic growth in 48 towns and cities across the UK. This included taking an in-depth look at the impact of the pandemic, considering which industries were most affected and the impact on regional economies.

This formed a small part of its response to Covid-19, which included a new hub on the website, weekly virtual events, thought leadership round table discussions as well as expert commentary on everything, from advice on furloughing to lockdown workouts and how to cope without a carer.

Brand Values
Irwin Mitchell is 'the expert hand, with the human touch', navigating life's ups and downs and achieving incredible things by putting its clients at the centre of everything it does.

It's committed to positive health and wellbeing, supporting charities, the environment and its local communities – from printing less to raising more funds for great causes or by offering a helping hand through its pro bono work.

Irwin Mitchell's unique and human approach builds the foundations of its entire brand and is underpinned by its values – pioneering, approachable and caring, tenacious, efficient and with integrity.

England Rugby

Official Legal Partner

Liverpool FC is **globally recognised and admired** for its **ongoing success and illustrious heritage**. The Liverpool Way reflects how the club has created **one of the world's greatest footballing families**, playing an attractive style of football on the pitch with a **legion of loyal and dedicated supporters**

Market

Football is the most popular sport in the world (Source: GlobalWebIndex) and Liverpool FC is at its heart, operating on a global stage with fans in every corner of the world. Recent wins in both the Premier League and the UEFA Champions League, the world's biggest annual football competitions, have delighted the club which is proud of both its men's and women's teams.

As a socially responsible club, Liverpool FC plays a proactive role in the community through its official charity, the LFC Foundation and its community team, Red Neighbours. The LFC Foundation aims to create life-changing opportunities for children and young people in Merseyside and beyond.

In addition, the Red Neighbours programme creates events and experiences specifically aimed at improving the lives of those living in and around Anfield, where the club is based in Liverpool. It also works closely with the local community to help alleviate food poverty, encourage physical activity, reduce social isolation for the elderly and create memorable experiences for young people.

Product

Liverpool FC is one of the most popular teams in the world's best loved sport. It has a huge global following of 487 million as well as a global TV audience of 870 million (Source: Nielsen), in addition to 306 official supporters clubs in 99 countries.

Achievements

Founded in 1892, Liverpool FC is one of the world's most decorated football clubs, having won 19 League Titles, seven FA Cups, eight League Cups, six European Cups, three UEFA Cups, four European Super Cups, 15 Charity Shields and the FIFA Club World Cup. In June 2020, Liverpool FC ended a 30-year wait to win the League again, becoming champions of the Premier League for the first time.

The Kop is famous for being the '12th man', roaring Liverpool FC on and has seen many memorable moments. It is one the loudest stands in football, making Anfield a feared ground for any opposition.

The fans are very important to the club and it has been widely recognised for its efforts to enhance the football fan's experience. In 2019 it won the Best Tour and Museum Experience at the Get Your Guide Awards as well as the Visit England Accolade of Excellence in the 'Welcome' category. It also received three awards at the 2019 Women of the Future Awards as well as being recognised in the Football Business Awards.

Liverpool FC's players also hold some of the most prestigious accolades in world football including Football Writers Player of the Year 2019/20, African Footballer of the Year 2019 and UEFA Best Player in Europe 2019.

Recent Developments

Anfield Stadium has seen the transformation of the main stand into one of the largest all-seater single stands in European football. Approximately 8,500 seats have been added, taking the overall capacity to 54,000, enabling more fans to add their voice to the Anfield atmosphere.

The development of a new training ground in Kirkby is currently underway. This £50m project will see the club bring its first team and academy football training operations and facilities together on one site. This development will not only provide first-class amenities for its players and staff but will also greatly improve sports facilities for the Kirkby community.

During lockdown in 2020, when the Premier League was postponed, Liverpool FC donated £90,000 to the North Liverpool Foodbank, and continue to prepare and deliver 1,000 meals per week in its Anfield kitchen, which now totals over 26,500 meals donated to local families in crisis.

DID YOU KNOW?

Anfield Stadium is the **most Instagrammed** location in the UK behind Big Ben

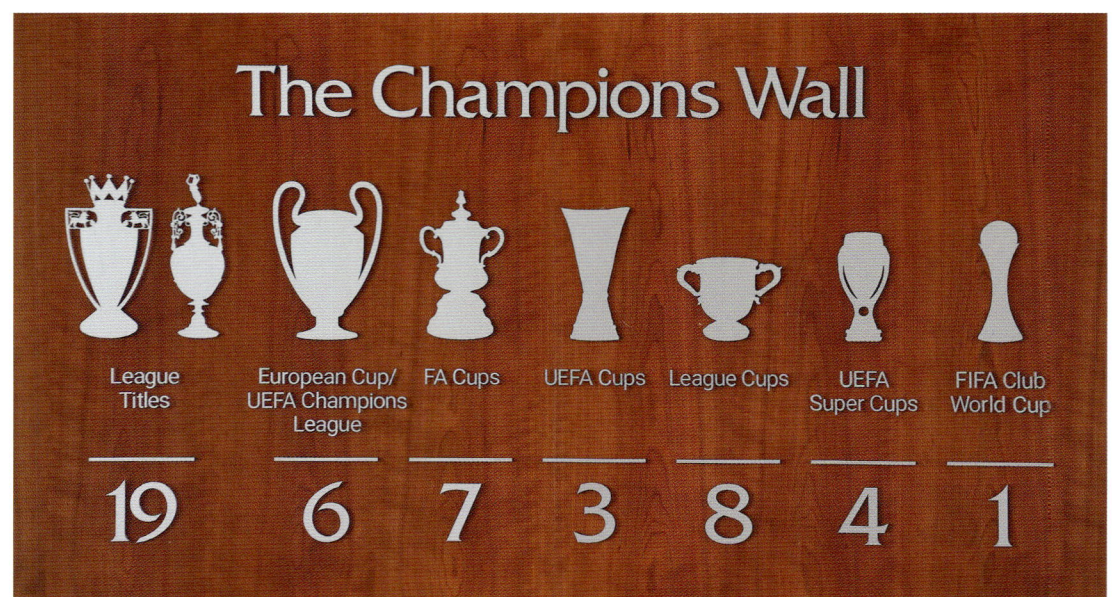

The Champions Wall

League Titles	European Cup/ UEFA Champions League	FA Cups	UEFA Cups	League Cups	UEFA Super Cups	FIFA Club World Cup
19	6	7	3	8	4	1

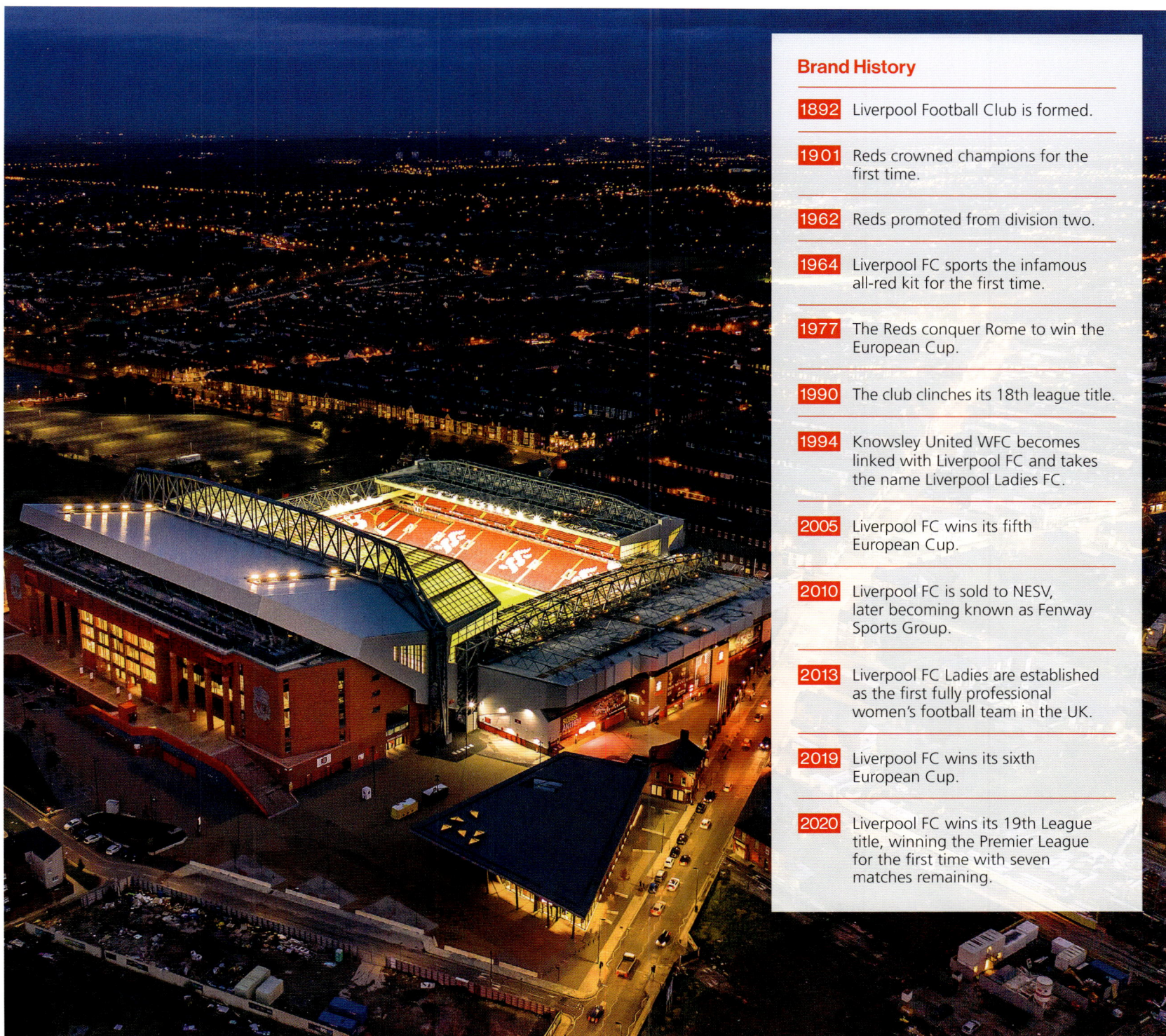

Brand History

1892 Liverpool Football Club is formed.

1901 Reds crowned champions for the first time.

1962 Reds promoted from division two.

1964 Liverpool FC sports the infamous all-red kit for the first time.

1977 The Reds conquer Rome to win the European Cup.

1990 The club clinches its 18th league title.

1994 Knowsley United WFC becomes linked with Liverpool FC and takes the name Liverpool Ladies FC.

2005 Liverpool FC wins its fifth European Cup.

2010 Liverpool FC is sold to NESV, later becoming known as Fenway Sports Group.

2013 Liverpool FC Ladies are established as the first fully professional women's football team in the UK.

2019 Liverpool FC wins its sixth European Cup.

2020 Liverpool FC wins its 19th League title, winning the Premier League for the first time with seven matches remaining.

The LFC Foundation works in partnership with the global children's charity, Right to Play, on programmes both at home and oversees that use sport and play to help provide vulnerable children with the tools and skills they need to overcome the impacts of poverty, conflict and disease.

LFC's retail store and shop-in-shop footprint currently spans 297 locations globally, across the north west of England as well as in Ireland, Thailand, Dubai, Vietnam, Malaysia, Indonesia and Singapore.

At the start of the 20/21 season, Liverpool FC registered record-breaking sales for all three of its new Nike jerseys – home, away and third kit. The 20/21 home and away shirts saw significant sales, 110% higher than 19/20, while the third kit achieved record sales across the official online store compared to previous third kits. On the day of home kit reveal, the club's online store experienced its most popular day, with traffic to the site and purchases made significantly higher than ever before.

Promotion

Liverpool FC works with leading-edge commercial partners around the world providing unparalleled commercial opportunities, due to the global recognition of the Liverpool FC brand. Its sponsorship partners include Standard Chartered, Nike, AXA and Expedia.

The club regards its online presence as the new era in fan engagement and has been successfully adapted to the demands of its followers with its globally published content and comprehensive e-commerce offering. In addition, the official club app connects with fans near and far and the Digital Match Centre provides interactive and premium match day content. It was an immediate success, attracting one million unique users within its first four weeks.

Liverpool FC had the most engaged social media fanbase in the world (Source: Blinkfire Analytics 2019) with 722 million social media engagements in 2020. As the most visited Premier League club website (Source: Similarweb), its own digital channels continue to grow.

Brand Values

The Liverpool Way is a beacon that drives the way in which the club conducts itself and is based on four core values: Ambition, knowing that dreams are achievable; Commitment, putting heart and soul into everything; Dignity, earning respect through honesty and integrity; Unity, working together and believing in each other's ability and expertise. It is these values that allow Liverpool FC to define itself as the world's greatest football family.

Marshalls

Creating Better Spaces

Marshalls is the **UK's leading manufacturer of hard landscaping products**, and has been **supplying superior natural stone and innovative concrete products** to the construction, home improvement and landscaping markets **since the 1890s**. Marshalls **strives to create products that improve landscapes** and create better environments to **develop happier and healthier communities**

Market

A global leader in creating better spaces, Marshalls strives to improve environments for everyone, from integrated landscapes – promoting wellbeing – to spaces that are created using fairly traded stone. It also innovates with products that alleviate flood risks as well as protective landscape furniture. Working in the public sector in addition to domestic and commercial markets, Marshalls provides a 360 degree service – from planning and engineering, to guidance and delivery. Marshalls is committed to producing new products that better any existing market offering, and to make them from the best materials it can source.

Product

Marshalls domestic customers range from garden designers and professional landscapers to DIY enthusiasts and driveway installers. Designed to inspire, Marshalls extensive product ranges combine quality, elegance and durability featuring both traditional and cutting-edge designs, with products to suit every taste and style. In the public sector and commercial market, Marshalls works with a diverse commercial customer base, including local authorities, architects, specifiers, contractors and house builders. Over the years, Marshalls has paved every location on the London Monopoly board, including Trafalgar Square twice. Marshalls' customers benefit from unrivalled technical expertise, manufacturing capability and an enviable product range. This includes superior natural stone, innovative concrete hard landscaping products, water management solutions, rail products, landscape furniture and protection products as well as natural stone cladding and facades.

Achievements

Marshalls was the first organisation to achieve verification against BRE Global's newly launched Ethical Labour Sourcing Standard (BES 6002) in 2017. It continues to focus on being a successful and profitable business whilst minimising its impact on the environment. Striving to be innovative, Marshalls responds to market challenges and opportunities and leads the way in its sector.

Marshalls has remained a signatory of the United Nations Global Compact since its acceptance in 2009. It is committed to aligning operations and strategies with the 10 universally accepted principles in the areas of human rights, labour, the environment and anti-corruption. Marshalls has also retained the Fair Tax Mark for more than five years in recognition of the business' commitment to transparent tax processes and it is also recognised as a Living Wage Employer. Furthermore, The Carbon Trust has reaccredited Marshalls three times. Since 2009, it has reduced its relative carbon footprint by almost 16%.

Recent Developments

Last year, Marshalls revisited its Future Spaces project, which was set up to foresee how commercial, public and domestic spaces might adapt and evolve over the next 10 years. Intensive research was undertaken, with the aim of the Future Spaces project being to predict how changing lifestyles, technology and economic conditions might dictate the look, feel, colour, shape, textures and materials used to create those spaces. The updated report highlights the visions that came true and those that were not predicted.

Brand History

1890 Solomon Marshall begins quarrying in Halifax, and in 1904 establishes S. Marshall and Sons Ltd.

1947 A second production site opens manufacturing lintels, steps and fence posts.

1964 Marshalls becomes a plc, with shares quoted on the London Stock Exchange.

1972 New product development sees the introduction of block paving and 'Beany Block'.

2011 A European venture is announced, Marshalls NV.

2012 Marshalls becomes an official supplier to the London 2012 Olympic Park.

2014 Accreditation by the Living Wage Foundation is achieved.

2017 Marshalls acquires precast concrete manufacturer, CPM.

2019 The Fair Tax Mark is awarded to Marshalls for a fifth year.

2020 The 'digital by default' strategy is put in place.

Sustainability remains at the heart of everything Marshalls does, and the company continues to be at the forefront of sustainable business. Marshalls has become an industry leader in the fight against modern slavery, going way beyond the statutory publishing of a statement. Last year the company rolled out a training programme across its logistics operation to enable its people to spot and report suspicious activity. This programme has been shared with other businesses and continues to contribute to successful prosecutions. Together with anti-slavery partner, Hope for Justice, Marshalls has made good progress in preventative education work with employees, suppliers and those in and around overseas supply chains, especially in Vietnam and India. In 2018, Marshalls became a Patron Partner of CRASH, sharing practical skills, building materials and donations to help homelessness charities and hospices with their vital construction projects. Marshalls also became the first in the construction sector to join the Co-op's Bright Future programme. It offers the opportunity of a paid work placement or a job to those who have been rescued from modern slavery in the UK.

DID YOU KNOW?

Over the years, **Marshalls has paved every location** on the London **Monopoly board**

Promotion

Marshalls is in the midst of a digital transformation, combining digital trading, digital marketing and digital business, all of which is focused on the customer experience. This strategy places the customer at the core and seeks to create an integrated experience across all platforms. Over the past year, Marshalls has invested heavily in its domestic website with a phased upgrade, building towards the launch of e-commerce in May 2020. Marshalls' strategic direction is 'digital by default', which seeks to define digital as intrinsically a core part of the company's culture.

Marshalls continues to lead the way in thought leadership. Content centres operate around a show and tell model where the business seeks to inspire others by sharing best practice. Through ethical sourcing, landscape protection and intelligent design, Marshalls understands the benefits of sharing ideas and ways of working with others, even those it competes with.

Brand Values

Marshalls' people understand and operate in The Marshalls Way; doing the right things, for the right reasons, in the right way. This echoes across all corners of the business and through thought leadership, promotion and relationships. The business also seeks to encourage others to operate in the same way. Marshalls' aim is to be the supplier of choice for every landscape architect, contractor, installer and consumer. The brand also strives to remain synonymous with quality, innovation and superior customer service.

Menzies
DISTRIBUTION

Menzies Distribution is a **logistics business providing smarter, more agile and more sustainable** supply chain solutions for businesses. **By applying new and innovative business models**, Menzies is seen as the **positive disruptor in the logistics space** and is revolutionising supply chain process and performance across a variety of markets

Market

Menzies Distribution provides smarter supply chain solutions to a variety of market sectors across the whole of the UK and Ireland, with services including stock replenishment, click & collect, returns and parcels delivery to sectors including; retail and grocers, healthcare and pharmaceutical, field service engineers and travel, as well as acting as a neutral consolidator for parcel carriers across Scotland. Menzies also plays a critical role in the newstrade end-to-end supply chain, providing primary trunking and final mile logistics for newspapers, magazines, and other newstrade products. During 2020, Menzies Distribution responded to rapidly changing needs, working with the NHS to supply vital PPE, it also helped retailers keep their shelves stocked when consumer demand for certain goods saw exponential increases in the face of the Covid-19 crisis.

Product

Menzies Distribution deploys new business models for organisations who are looking for better routes to market. Utilising its depth of industry knowledge and expertise, Menzies Distribution is making supply chains smarter, more flexible and sustainable. Its fundamental understanding of what drives value allows it to develop solutions that keep businesses going and growing.

Menzies Distribution operates 24/7, 364 days a year from 60 UK logistics hubs, including its Coventry National Distribution Centre. Using a national footprint 'hub and spoke' structure, Menzies creates bespoke supply chain solutions aligned to the specific needs of individual customers. This system allows for four key benefits; speed, precision, scaleability and excellent service, even in the most challenging of times.

Achievements

In 2020, Menzies Distribution was named as one of the UK's top-performing private companies in The Sunday Times Top Track 100, for the second consecutive year. This ranks Britain's top 100 private companies by fastest growing sales figures over the last three years. Menzies Distribution has risen

DID YOU KNOW?

During one weekend in lockdown, **10 million items of PPE were delivered to more than 1,000 different frontline settings** – all picked and packed to individual site level

four places from its strong position the previous year, and now ranks at number 55 in the table. The 2020 list takes Covid-19 into account and highlights how the UK's biggest private companies have supported the country during the crisis, how it has impacted their industries, and how they are adapting.

Menzies Distribution was Highly Commended in the 2020 NMA awards in the 'sustainability strategy of the year' category. Furthermore, it holds position eight in Motor Transport's Top 100 Logistics Companies and was recognised at the GREENFLEET Awards. It has also received; an IoC Clean Air Award, Driver of the Year award, Sustainable Logistics Company of the Year in Corp 2020, a Last Mile Innovator Award and its Linwood based Customer Service Centre has achieved the CCA Global Service Excellence Award.

Recent Developments

Menzies Distribution's national capability and time critical delivery expertise has aided its growth and diversification into adjacent markets. In 2020, the business rose to the challenges brought by the Covid-19 crisis, becoming a key supply chain partner in the distribution of critical PPE. Menzies Distribution commenced deliveries, utilising its fast and

Brand History

1833 Menzies is established when a Victorian entrepreneur builds up a small newsagent business into a national chain, eventually working with publishers to get their products to market and as a wholesaler to retailers.

1914 World War I brings opportunities for expansion, with the constant need for news distribution.

1965 The company now encompasses 90 wholesale warehouses, 350 railway bookstalls and 161 shops, with a turnover of almost £50m.

2013 The business begins to diversify as circulations decline.

2018 Menzies Distribution becomes an independent business, when it is purchased by private equity investor, Endless LLP. It also launches Highland Parcels – a flat rate parcel delivery service tackling the postcode penalty in the Highlands and Islands.

2020 Menzies Distribution's national network and time critical logistics expertise see the company handle complex supply chain solutions and respond rapidly during the Covid-19 pandemic. Menzies Distribution is providing routes to market for many organisations, including; UK Flooring Direct, American Golf, Office Depot, Bunzl, AG Barr, Flying Tiger, Nisbets, NHS Scotland, Holland & Barrett, Amazon, Yodel and many more.

far-reaching network to get supplies to the front line where urgently needed in GP surgeries and care homes.

Another affected by lockdown was retail convenience business, One Stop. The rapid change in consumer buying habits and a surge in demand saw Menzies Distribution mobilise its delivery service for the retailer at incredible speed. Ensuring that the store chain could continue to provide essential supplies to its local communities was paramount.

Additionally, in these extraordinary times, Menzies Distribution has been working with some of the leading players in the UK parcel industry, pooling resources and expertise to manage the nationwide collection and delivery of Covid-19 home testing kits into testing laboratories.

Promotion
2021 is an exciting year for Menzies Distribution, which will see the emergence of a strong, new brand proposition with multi-sector appeal and resonance.

Brand Values
There are three pillars that support Menzies Distribution's brand proposition. These are defined as; Smart – applying new and innovative business models to partners' and customers' supply chains that revolutionise process and performance; Agile – investing in talent and technology to create smarter, more agile supply chains; Sustainable – being a force for good, and the positive disruptor within the industry, proving that you don't need to compromise between people, the planet and profit.

Menzies Distribution has both an employee wellbeing programme and a CSR committee that oversees its work in supporting five nominated charity partners.

A three-fold sustainability strategy is also in place which is built on its fleet, recycling and reuse, and energy. Menzies Distribution's network is powered entirely by energy derived from renewables and the organisation was highly commended in the NMA awards for Sustainability Strategy of the Year which includes a spectrum of initiatives from zero emissions to carbon offsetting.

OLYMPIA
London

The home of inspirational events, **Olympia London first opened its doors in 1886**.
A London architectural, **cultural and events landmark**, it's one of the capital's busiest venues,
annually welcoming over **1.6 million visitors** to more than **200 events**
and contributing **£1.2bn** to the economy

Market

The events sector contributes £70bn to the UK economy – £11bn from exhibitions alone – and has been hit hard by the prolonged shutdown during the pandemic in 2020. As one of the key players in the industry, Olympia London is not only one of the most established venues in the UK, it is also one of the capital's preferred events venues, thanks to its world-class offerings and location. It is only 25 minutes from Heathrow airport and reachable by various public transport connections in Kensington. Combining multiple spaces to form 45,000 sq ft, this iconic venue hosts more than 200 events a year, welcoming 1.6 million guests and annually contributing £1.2bn to the UK economy.

Product

Showcasing unrivalled heritage and architecture, Olympia London's Victorian Grade II listed buildings offer clients more than event spaces. It comes with 134 years of expertise in running events in elegant surroundings to create an atmospheric experience. Its skilled events management and operational teams have built strong relationships with its clients so they can successfully deliver internationally renowned shows.

From award-winning operations to marketing and sustainability; the results have been seen in increased footfall which had risen to 1.6 million annual guests in 2019.

Achievements

Known as 'the home of inspirational events', Olympia London first opened its doors in 1886.

Established as one of London's architectural, cultural and events landmarks, it is a prime choice for a wide range of exhibitions, conferences and live events. Holding a strong link to the capital's history, it has survived two world wars and seismic political changes, whilst hosting centennial events such as the Ideal Home Show and the London International Horse Show.

Olympia London's elegant Victorian arches have also seen inspirational personalities such as Vivienne Westwood hold her first catwalk show as well as performances by Jimi Hendrix and Pink Floyd; and in 2019 it welcomed SKEPTA and a Burberry catwalk show.

DID YOU KNOW?

All monarchs from **Queen Victoria to Queen Elizabeth II** have **attended** an event at **Olympia London**

Over the years, the venue has been recognised with an array of accolades and in 2019 achieved Superbrand status for the third consecutive year. It was awarded Best Use of Social Media in the UK events industry as well as being recognised at the Gold Green Tourism Awards. A sustainability leader, the venue was also shortlisted at the

Business Green Leaders Sustainability Awards and is among the top five global event businesses recognised in the Sustainable Development Awards, organised by the Global Association of the Exhibition Industry – the only events business recognised from the UK.

Recent Developments

In 2019, the venue was granted planning approval for a £1bn investment plan, set to transform and elevate Olympia London's world-class offering into a destination for not just events, but also hospitality, creativity and entrepreneurship. This development plan is turning the 14-acre site into a cultural destination, conceptualised by the award-winning Heatherwick Studio and architects SPPARC. The transformation is expected to create 5,400 new jobs locally once it is completed and add an extra £9m per year in consumer spending to the Hammersmith and Fulham economy.

Working closely with English Heritage to preserve the original architecture of the exhibition halls, the project will simultaneously bring new features to London, such as a 1,500-seat performing arts theatre; a 4,400-capacity music venue, two hotels and 600,000 sq ft of office and creative space. In addition, there will be 2.5 acres of new public

Brand History

1886 Architect Henry Edward Coe reveals Olympia London's elevation, showing the iconic 170 ft clear roof span. On Boxing Day, Olympia London opens its doors to the public with the Paris Hippodrome Circus.

1888 The First Great Horse Show takes place and remains one of Olympia London's calendar highlights as The London International Horse Show.

1908 Olympia London hosts the first Ideal Home Show, which is still held at the venue today.

1955 Olympia London hosts the first Boat Show.

1967 Jimi Hendrix, The Animals and a young Pink Floyd play Olympia London.

2012 Olympia London celebrates 125 years with specially commissioned works of art, including pieces by artist Peter Blake.

2013 Following a multi-million-pound revamp and separation from Earls Court, the business is rebranded as Olympia London.

2019 A £1bn project to transform Olympia London into a destination for events, culture and business is approved by Hammersmith & Fulham Council. Conceptualised by British designer Thomas Heatherwick, it is the biggest investment in the venue to date.

spaces such as gardens, galleries as well as more than 40 restaurants and eateries, accessible for all to enjoy.

Promotion

Olympia London may have a 134-year history however, the current brand is fairly young, having been launched seven years ago after separating from the neighbouring venue, Earls Court. It has since grown exponentially, reaching Superbrands status in 2017, and owns the fastest growing social media audience in its sector with an impressive 13% growth rate in 2019. In the same year, its inspirational events were promoted using a creative digital campaign across social media as well as posters at London's busiest tube stations, achieving more than 22 million views. The brand has also sponsored a range of industry initiatives

including the 30 Under 30 awards to celebrate up and coming talent.

Brand Values

Reflecting a strong set of values, which focus on care, commitment, passion, trust and respect, Olympia London holds sustainability at the core of its world-class offering. This encompasses grassroots initiatives which champion the environment, community and education.

For more than a decade, Olympia London has sent no waste to landfill with 98% being recycled and the remaining 2% converted into renewable energy. More recently, single-use plastics such as straws and cutlery have been eliminated from the venue. Olympia London also continues to focus on sourcing food locally with its catering

partners. This helped to reduce food waste by 17% in 2019, along with distributing surplus food to those in need within the community.

Engaging with the local community is another outcome of its values, with initiatives that support local charities and causes, for example, offering the venue to Hammersmith & Fulham Foodbank during the Covid-19 pandemic as a food distribution centre.

Over the course of its 134 years, the 'home of inspirational events' has created lifelong memories for millions of people. Keeping true to its brand values and building towards a solid vision for the next 130 years, Olympia London continues to inspire and delight with its rich heritage and bright future.

openreach
Connecting you to your network

Openreach builds and maintains the UK's digital network. It connects families, schools, hospitals, libraries, businesses, broadcasters and governments to the world. **Its mission is to build the best possible network with the highest quality service** to ensure **everyone in the UK can be connected**

Market

As an open, wholesale network provider, Openreach's customers are retail Communications Provider businesses like BT, Sky, Talk Talk, Vodafone and Zen.

Its network supports more than 650 of these businesses who, in turn, use Openreach's products and services to provide their customers with landline, broadband, TV and data connections.

The vast majority of Openreach products and services are regulated, meaning prices, terms and conditions are the same, no matter who buys them.

The company employs more than 35,000 people, in communities all over the UK and it's in the middle of a £12bn project to build the next generation of ultrafast, ultra-reliable 'Full Fibre' broadband.

This new network offers a faster, more reliable and future-proof broadband service, capable of delivering download speeds 15 times faster than today's UK average. The ambitious nationwide build programme is currently reaching 39,000 premises every week – with 560 locations included in the plan so far.

DID YOU KNOW?

Openreach is **building Full Fibre broadband** to another home or business **every 20 seconds**

Product

Openreach's strategy is all about delivering better service, broader coverage, and faster broadband speeds to people throughout the UK.

Its wholesale products include: Standard, Superfast and Ultrafast broadband; dedicated high-speed business lines (known as Ethernet and optical services); and access to its UK-wide network of ducts and poles.

Achievements

Over the last decade, Openreach has made Superfast broadband available to more than 28 million homes and businesses. This mainly used its Fibre-to-the-Cabinet (FTTC) technology, and the investment has put the UK in a strong position, with more than 96% of homes and businesses now able to order superfast speeds.

However for Openreach, Ultrafast Full Fibre broadband is the future. The company has already made this technology available to 3.5 million homes and businesses, and it's continuing to accelerate the build.

Openreach ultimately wants to be the UK's largest Full Fibre broadband provider, reaching at least 20 million UK homes and businesses by the mid-to-late 2020s.

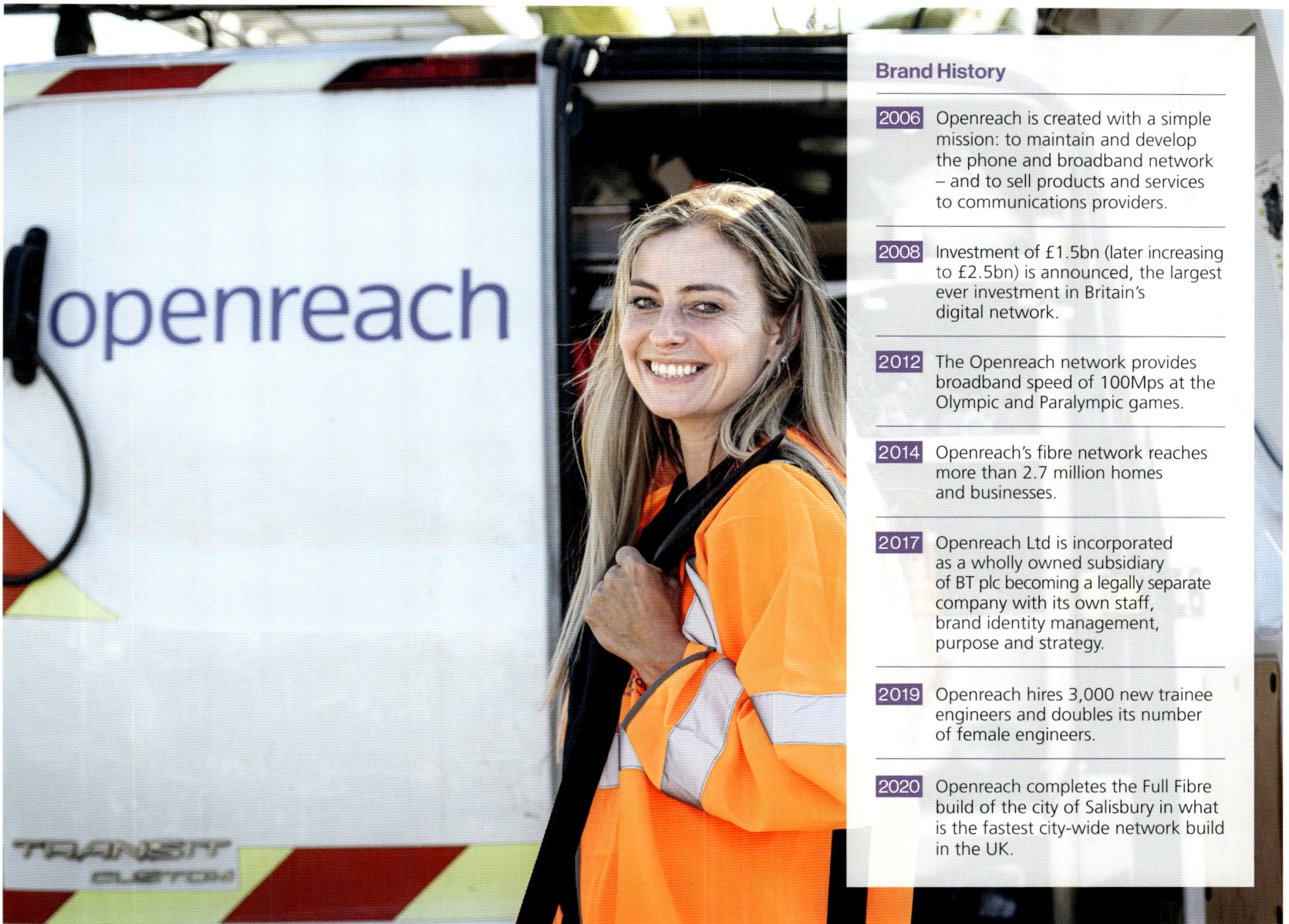

Brand History

2006 Openreach is created with a simple mission: to maintain and develop the phone and broadband network – and to sell products and services to communications providers.

2008 Investment of £1.5bn (later increasing to £2.5bn) is announced, the largest ever investment in Britain's digital network.

2012 The Openreach network provides broadband speed of 100Mps at the Olympic and Paralympic games.

2014 Openreach's fibre network reaches more than 2.7 million homes and businesses.

2017 Openreach Ltd is incorporated as a wholly owned subsidiary of BT plc becoming a legally separate company with its own staff, brand identity management, purpose and strategy.

2019 Openreach hires 3,000 new trainee engineers and doubles its number of female engineers.

2020 Openreach completes the Full Fibre build of the city of Salisbury in what is the fastest city-wide network build in the UK.

The build is happening across rural and urban areas of the UK, with Openreach also working to support government on a range of public and private connectivity programmes.

Openreach is one of the country's biggest employers of apprentices, and over the last two years it hired a total of 6,500 new trainee engineers – the biggest recruitment drive in its history. Armed forces veterans and reservists also form a large part of the Openreach workforce. In fact, Openreach has recruited more than 3,000 former service men and women since 2011, making it the biggest private sector employer of ex-service people.

In 2020, Openreach came 15th in The Sunday Times list of 25 Best Big Companies to Work For. The results of the comprehensive survey recognised Openreach as a company that promotes wellbeing, provides good benefits and fair pay, and has a high level of employee engagement.

Recent Developments
Through the coronavirus pandemic, Openreach has shown its resilience in a number of ways.

Its engineers are designated 'key workers' and have been out making sure hospitals, schools, police and fire stations – not to mention residents all across the UK – stayed connected to the internet. The company has also focused its efforts on maintaining its Full Fibre build programme with engineers surveying, planning, digging and laying fibre in a safe manner. As a result, its Full Fibre build targets have not been impacted.

Openreach's core asset is its network – and despite the surge in network traffic during the pandemic – the company was able to provide confidence that its network was coping with a massive surge towards homeworking and online schooling.

Promotion
The Openreach brand has transformed. From the way it talks, to the way it acts, and this has allowed the digital network business to build relationships with all its customers equally.

As a wholesaler, it has predominantly expected its customers to talk to consumers. However, the brand has evolved to be more outward facing and proactive in its marketing approach to encourage uptake of Full Fibre in particular. This included an Ulster Rugby campaign earlier in the year which leveraged a powerful sponsorship property to resonate with the communities across Belfast and beyond, pushing Full Fibre messaging and its associated benefits.

Openreach is working hard to build diverse and inclusive teams which reflect the communities it serves all over the UK. This year, it refreshed its diversity and inclusion strategy to develop a set of goals and focus areas to achieve that. Central to the strategy is the launch of its new Pride, Gender Equality and Ethnic Diversity networks, which are made up of people from all levels across Openreach.

Protecting the environment is another major focus for Openreach. It is undertaking a vital leadership role, communicating the benefits of its experiences to help design policy measures that support corporate electric vehicle uptake, such as stimulating supply chains and investing in charging infrastructure. This is a partnership between The Climate Group, BT and Openreach.

Brand Values
Openreach works tirelessly to connect the nation through its Big Bold Plan. It's focused on providing the best possible service levels to every consumer and business in the UK; on delivering broader coverage of its network to ensure it's available to as many people as possible; and on upgrading customers onto faster speeds to meet the country's ever-growing demand for data.

P&O FERRIES

'**To the Sea**'. Three simple words that **symbolise a new way to look at a centuries-old and beloved means of transport** from the market leader P&O Ferries. In a world that is adapting to a new normality, **P&O Ferries is putting a stake in the ground with its new brand positioning,** reconnecting people with a more **liberating and authentic way of travel**

Market

P&O Ferries is a leading pan-European ferry and logistics company, last year sailing 27,000 times on eight major routes between Britain, France, Northern Ireland, the Republic of Ireland, Holland and Belgium. Together with its logistics business, P&O Ferrymasters, the company also operates integrated road and rail to countries across the continent including Italy, Germany, Spain, Romania, Turkey, and facilitates the onward movement of goods to Britain from Asian countries via the Silk Road. P&O Ferries is part of DP World, the leading provider of smart logistics solutions, enabling the flow of trade across the globe.

Facing ever-increasing competition from low-cost airlines and in an unprecedented pandemic affecting all forms of travel around the world, P&O Ferries has not just maintained its market leadership but remains one of the most loved travel brands in the UK.

DID YOU KNOW?

The sea, **once it casts its spell, holds one** in its net of wonder **forever***

*Jacques Cousteau

Despite competing against bigger marketing budgets from airlines and global travel operators, P&O Ferries remains the fourth most popular travel brand in the UK. According to the latest YouGov data, it achieved higher scores than big industry players such as British Airways Holidays, Virgin Holidays and TUI.

Product

There are a variety of routes, ships and travel experiences available within the P&O Ferries

offering, underpinning the brand's vision of what travel should feel like and mean for its customers. There are options for every kind of travel and traveller, from a 90-minute Dover to Calais crossing or a quick trip across the Irish Sea from Cairnryan to Larne to an overnight journey to the Netherlands from Hull, where customers can book an upgraded cabin and travel across the North Sea in comfort and style.

Depending on the route, customers can enjoy a range of ever-evolving experiences, from complimentary champagne in the Club Lounge to delicious meals in The Brasserie Restaurant, Starbucks coffee on the sundeck or cocktails and live jazz in The Sunset Bar.

Achievements

2020 has been another award-winning year for P&O Ferries. At the Globe Travel Awards, the company was voted Best Ferry Company for the 13th year in a row. P&O Ferries also had another

FINALLY
YOU'RE FREE

P&O FERRIES

poferries.com

Out of Europe.

Into Europe.

Out of Europe.

Into Europe.

Out of Europe.

Into Europe.

Out of Europe.

Into Europe.

Out of Europe.

Into Europe.

Out of Europe.

Into Europe.

We do it every day.

P&O
FERRIES

poferries.com

Brand History

1837 The 'Peninsular Steam Navigation Company' is founded.

1840s 'Peninsular & Oriental' (P&O) is awarded the Royal Charter for mail delivery to British India.

1850s P&O Ferries operates the largest steamship in the world, the Himalaya.

1887 P&O Ferries celebrates the Jubilee by launching its largest and grandest steamers at 6,000 tons each.

1904 P&O offers its first pleasure cruise.

1924 The brand is the largest shipping company in the world.

1964 P&O Ferrymasters is born.

2000 P&O Cruises becomes an independent company.

2012 P&O Ferries launches its latest ship, Spirit of France, sister to the Spirit of Britain, creating the biggest and most luxurious service on the Channel.

2018 P&O Ferries announces plans to increase capacity on the Zeebrugge-Teesport route by almost 25% in order to create a gateway to Scotland via the north-eastern port.

2019 DP World acquires P&O Ferries and World Duty Free is welcomed onboard, offering a range of premium products from world leading brands.

DID YOU KNOW?

P&O Ferries carried the first pet, a pug named Frodo, from Calais to Dover in 2000 under the new pet passport scheme

impressive result at the British Travel Awards, holding on to the titles of Best Ferry Operator / Best Mini Cruise Operator and Best Ferry Booking Website – both of which they have won year-on-year since these categories were introduced.

Recent Developments
P&O Ferries has excelled at navigating the extremely challenging situation the world has been facing this year, quickly introducing a new safety charter with an array of preventive measures on its ships. It also supported customers through these uncertain times with flexible ticket options, amendment guarantees and continuous live sailing updates and news.

The situation hasn't stopped the company's plans to continuously improve the brand experience either, both onboard and online. The award-winning website and app have seen a relaunch this year, significantly improving the end-to-end user interaction with the brand and products. In a first for the category, P&O Ferries has taken the initiative to partner with World Duty Free, enhancing the overall offering by introducing an array of premium products across all routes.

Promotion
P&O Ferries will be repositioning the brand in the travel and leisure sector and inviting new and old customers to reconsider what it means to travel by ferry with the launch of the 'To the Sea' campaign. It is a rallying cry for those who believe in a different kind of travel to join the P&O Ferries movement. The campaign is highly relevant to both the new way of travel which has been shaped by younger travellers, but also acknowledges how the recent pandemic has shocked the travel market and rapidly changed consumer behaviour.

The campaign marks the start of a new chapter for the brand with a renewed sense of purpose and focus, presenting P&O Ferries as the most liberating form of transport in a modern post-Covid-19 world.

Brand Values
Travelling on a P&O ferry gives customers the freedom to create their kind of trip, bring along any kind of vehicle, all their friends, family and even their pet – all with no baggage restrictions – enabling customers to do more and visit more places whether it's on the path well-trodden or off the beaten track.

It is a way of travel reminiscent of times when going on a trip was more of an adventure, and the journey was as important as the destination.

P&O Ferries believes in a different kind of travel and is ready to help shape the way we travel tomorrow.

19 65

PIZZA EXPRESS

Since 1965, when Peter Boizot opened the **first PizzaExpress restaurant in London's Soho**, the same values of **'great food, evocative music, and distinctive design'** have remained central to the brand's DNA. As the **one recipe that has never been changed,** **this powerful vision has created an iconic brand**

Market

PizzaExpress has a long history of success and whilst the UK-wide lockdown hit the hospitality industry particularly hard, the brand remains resilient. 2020 sees the sociable pizzeria continue to roll out its FutureExpress programme that is designed to enhance not only its physical estate, but the overall customer experience.

PizzaExpress continues to work closely with industry bodies such as UK Hospitality to help professionalise and promote the restaurant industry, instilling the belief that hospitality is and will remain a viable and attractive career option.

As dietary requirements continue to evolve, the brand constantly innovates. Demand for the vegan menu grows year-on-year and this year, the lighter Leggera range achieved endorsement from Weight Watchers.

PizzaExpress' Dough Balls continue to be a crowd-pleaser, having celebrated 50 years on the menu. New recipes are in development to take this icon into the future.

Achievements

Industry awards have recognised the innovative menus PizzaExpress provides. This has included the 2018 FreeFrom Eating Out Awards and the

PizzaExpress has also won marketing awards for its use of technology and launched its new app in 2018, which offers exclusive rewards for customers, and achieved the number two slot in the iTunes free app charts, second only behind WhatsApp.

Building upon Peter Boizot's original vision, the brand has been closely associated with charitable causes, continuing the founder's original aim, to raise funds for the Venice In Peril charity. PizzaExpress also works with Macmillan Cancer Support, with one simple goal: to bring people together so that no-one faces cancer alone. Fundraising activity has seen teams and customers

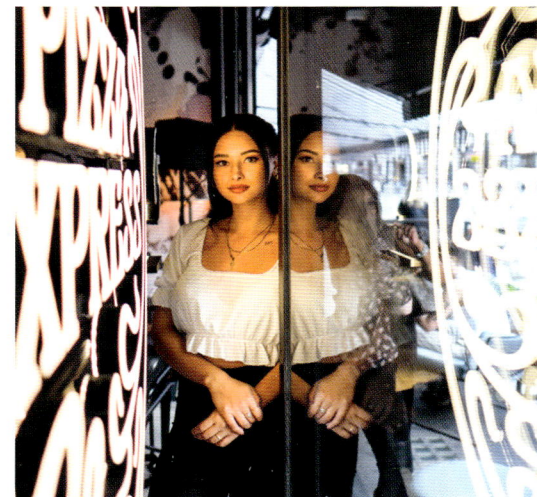

Product

PizzaExpress continues to adapt in line with consumers' ever-evolving tastes, needs and dietary demands, leading the industry with its innovative menus.

The team at PizzaExpress works tirelessly to source the finest ingredients for favourite recipes customers know and love. This year saw the return of the Calzone following overwhelming demand from customers, along with the launch of the online Homemade Favourites series, featuring iconic recipes for fans to make themselves at home during the lockdown period.

PETA Vegan Food Award for the Vegan Giardiniera pizza in 2017. Furthermore, the brand was awarded the Best Restaurant Chain for Vegans in the 2019 Viva! Awards.

As part of its FutureExpress rollout, the distinctive new design at PizzaExpress Langham Place has been shortlisted in the 2020 Restaurant & Bar Design Awards.

PizzaExpress has also been recognised by the Good Housekeeping Institute as the UK's 'favourite high street restaurant' and by Which? magazine for being the 'healthiest and tastiest pizza on the high street'.

raise more than £2m for the charity over the past two years through initiatives such as Go Green Week.

Recent Developments

PizzaExpress has continued to invest and innovate to ensure it remains relevant for the future.

The first phase of its FutureExpress transformation programme saw 25 new format pizzerias launched, with excellent results. Starting with Langham Place, Oxford Circus, the brand rolled out physical transformations across selected 'test and learn' sites at pace. The first quarter of 2020 saw several

DID YOU KNOW?

The iconic **Dough Ball** has been **on the menu** for **50 years**

iconic big seater locations undergo an extensive refurbishment, including pizzerias on The Strand, Bankside and Abbey Road.

With the global pandemic driving the need for brands to adapt quickly, PizzaExpress launched a series of interactive online initiatives, including the Homemade Favourites series, which saw the exclusive release of some of its iconic recipes, including the Margherita, Dough Balls and Fiorentina, for customers to make themselves at home.

As the nationwide lockdown gradually lifted, the brand undertook a series of 'test and learn' reopening trials across its estate. As part of these plans, PizzaExpress introduced robust measures to ensure the safety and wellbeing of its teams and customers. These included a physically distanced layout, hand sanitiser stations, enhanced hygiene procedures and cleaning measures, along with regular health checks of team members. A new digital menu, as well as cashless payment, were also introduced to assist and reassure customers, with the brand's online booking service providing an easy way to reserve a table. The new digital Piccolo Corner provided fun and educational activities to entertain the whole family by scanning a QR code that unlocked a world of colouring, quizzing and playing along with the Piccolo orchestra.

Promotion
PizzaExpress remains at the forefront of technological advances, tapping into customers' stories and encouraging loyalty by creating unique experiences and content through its pizzerias, retail and delivery as well as via its owned media channels.

The 2019 Christmas Connections film depicted families and friends explaining what matters to them most at Christmas, with the brand asking people to make more time for each other. The emotive video achieved millions of views and more than 20 pieces of mainstream media coverage.

The Hunt was also launched in 2019, in celebration of the Dough Ball's 50th birthday, offering fans throughout the country the chance to get their hands on a Golden Dough Ball worth £1,000, which grabbed numerous headlines.

This year also saw the launch of Langham Lates, in partnership with Leah Weller, a monthly DJ residency in the Langham Place pizzeria, which increased footfall and supported a significant year-on-year sales uplift.

Brand Values
PizzaExpress still works to its founding principles of 'bringing people together for great times through a shared passion for food, drink, music and people'. Pride is taken in offering a high standard of hospitality in all the brand's restaurants. It continues to be a stalwart of British life; the perfect place for a first date, a Mother's Day celebration, a quick bite to eat, or a regular gathering of friends. PizzaExpress continues its mission to be the world's most sociable pizzeria and remains the nation's favourite pizza to this day.

Brand History

1948 Peter Boizot travels through Europe, eventually arriving in Rome.

1965 On his return to the UK, Peter discovers that, unlike in Italy, great tasting pizza is nowhere to be found. This inspires him to open the first pizzeria in the UK.

1965 The inaugural PizzaExpress opens its doors in London's Soho – a radical venture at the time.

1967 Renowned Italian designer, Enzo Apicella, joins forces with Peter to open a second restaurant on Coptic Street, in London's Bloomsbury. He then goes on to design a further 85 PizzaExpress restaurants.

1969 Embracing his passion for jazz, Peter launches the PizzaExpress Jazz Club in Dean Street, Soho.

1970 PizzaExpress brings Peroni to the UK.

1971 PizzaExpress launches the 'Pizza Veneziana' initiative, providing a donation to the Venice In Peril fund from every pizza sold.

1986 Peter Boizot is awarded an MBE.

2003 Gluten-free pizzas launch on the menu for the first time.

2006 PizzaExpress introduces the children's Piccolo menu.

2014 PizzaExpress wins Best Restaurant Chain in the FreeFrom Eating Out awards, reflecting the brand's continuing commitment to special dietary requirements.

2017 PizzaExpress launches its first vegan pizza, the award-winning Vegan Giardiniera.

2018 The brand now has restaurants around the world and launches a dedicated vegan menu.

2019 PizzaExpress embarks upon its brand repositioning strategy, FutureExpress.

2020 PizzaExpress celebrates its 55th birthday.

Rolls-Royce is **recognised around the world as a global engineering giant,** delivering cutting-edge power solutions. The company serves the **Civil Aerospace, Defence, and Power Systems** markets with **pioneering products that focus on efficiency, reliability and increasingly, sustainability**

Market

Rolls-Royce's knowledge is built on years of delivering solutions for highly complex power needs, that require long development cycles. Its markets are linked to growth in the overall global economy, or in global security and defence budgets. Rolls-Royce has customers in more than 150 countries, with more than 400 airlines and leasing customers, 160 armed forces, 4,000 marine customers including 70 navies, and more than 5,000 power and nuclear customers. The company's underlying revenue in 2019 was more than £15.4bn, half of which came from services.

Product

As one of the world's largest aircraft engine manufactures, with a fleet of more than 13,000, Rolls-Royce is best known for its jet engines. Although there has been an unprecedented impact on its Civil Aerospace business by Covid-19, Rolls-Royce is still positioned to capitalise, once the world recovers, through its engine portfolio for large commercial aircraft, regional jets and business aviation. Its highly successful Trent

engines are in service on the Airbus A330, A340, A350 and A380, alongside the Boeing 777 and 787 Dreamliner and recently Rolls-Royce launched the Pearl 15 engine for Gulfstream Business Jets, reaffirming its position as a leader in the business aviation market.

In Defence, Rolls-Royce is a market leader in aero engines for military transport and patrol aircraft with strong positions in combat and helicopter applications. It has more than 16,000 engines in service across 150 military customers including naval markets. It has been the industry leader

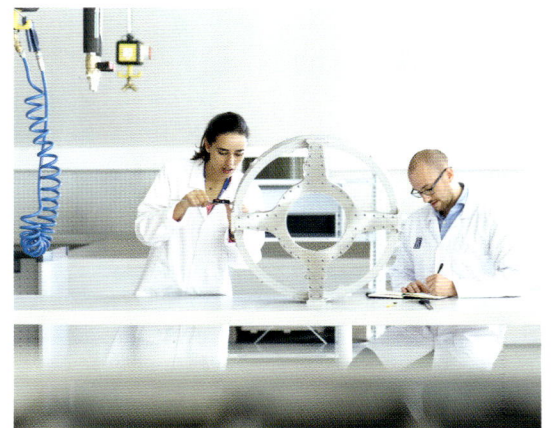

DID YOU KNOW?

Rolls-Royce has been the sole **provider and technical authority** for **nuclear power** to the **Royal Navy** for more than **50 years**

in Short Take-Off and Vertical Landing technology for more than 60 years, with its latest technology being used on the F-35B Lightning II fighter. Rolls-Royce recently announced its collaboration with the Royal Air Force, BAE Systems, Leonardo and MBDA on the development of the next generation of air power – Project Tempest.

The Power Systems market is a key focus for Rolls-Royce in enabling the company to play a crucial role in reaching net zero carbon by 2050. Through its German product brand MTU, whose engines power trains, super-yachts, ferries, mining trucks, tractors and power generation; Rolls-Royce is now positioning itself as a systems integrator. The investment in microgrids, electric and hybrid-electric power is helping the company take a strong position in reliable low carbon power generation.

As one of the largest employers of nuclear designers, engineers and scientists in the UK,

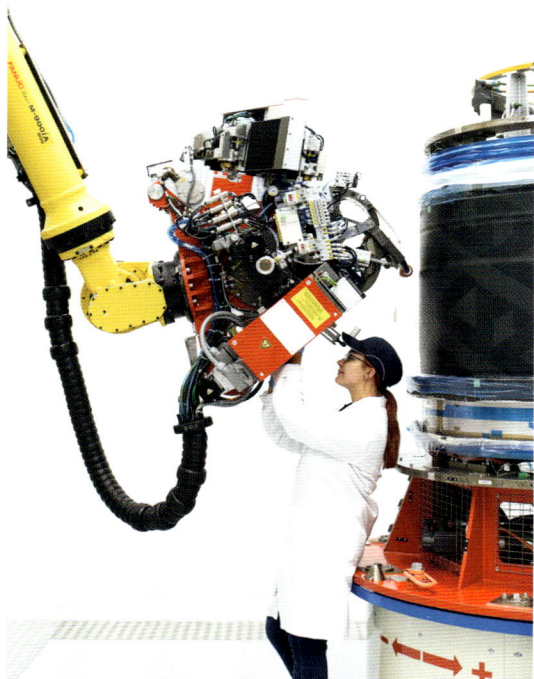

Rolls-Royce also has vast experience in developing nuclear energy power solutions. It has been the sole provider and technical authority for nuclear power to the Royal Navy for more than 50 years and is now utilising this experience to help develop small modular reactors for the civil nuclear market.

Achievements

Rolls-Royce has been recognised with Industry Leader, Industry Mover and Gold Class awards for the Aerospace and Defence sector in the Dow Jones Sustainability Index. It is also listed in both the DJSI World and DJSI Europe indices.

Recent Developments

Supporting the growing demand for cleaner, more efficient and sustainable power, Rolls-Royce's strategy is built around three pillars: improve the gas turbine; promote sustainable fuels; and be at the forefront of developing innovative power technologies. In Civil Aerospace, the UltraFan® gas turbine design will deliver more thrust, more efficiency and more reliability than ever. Rolls-Royce is also leading the way in developing hybrid/electric aircraft power systems through the growth of its electrical division as well as partnerships, to accelerate its capability. This championing sustainability focus will be vividly demonstrated when the company attempts to break the world speed record for an all-electric flight in 2021. In the Industrial sector, Rolls-Royce is continuing its pioneering

Brand History

1904 Henry Royce meets Charles Rolls, whose company sells high-quality cars in London.

1914 At the start of World War I, Royce designs his first aero engine, the Eagle, which goes on to provide half of the total horsepower used in the air by the Allies.

1940 Royce's Merlin powers the Hawker Hurricane and Supermarine Spitfire in the Battle of Britain.

1950 Rolls-Royce enters the civil aviation market with the Dart.

1976 Concorde, powered by the Rolls-Royce Snecma Olympus 593, becomes the first and only supersonic airliner to enter service.

1999 Rolls-Royce acquires Vickers for £576m, transforming Rolls-Royce into the global leader in marine power systems.

2003 BMW takes over responsibility for Rolls-Royce cars.

2011 Trent 1000 engines power the new Boeing 787 Dreamliner into service.

2012 Rolls-Royce opens a new 154,000 sq m aero engine build facility in Singapore.

2015 The two Rolls-Royce marine gas turbine engines that power the Royal Navy's new aircraft carrier, HMS Queen Elizabeth, go into operation for the first time.

2017 Rolls-Royce launches R² Data Labs, a development hub for new data-led services.

2019 Rolls-Royce collaborates with Sunseeker International to build its first production yacht with hybrid power.

2020 Rolls-Royce announces a breakthrough in artificial intelligence management.

tradition with the development of microgrid systems, modular reactors and sustainable fuel technology.

Digitalisation is another major element of Rolls-Royce's strategy. Building on 30 years of delivering performance data analytics for its TotalCare® aircraft engine maintenance programme; Rolls-Royce is now using digital twin and AI technologies to deliver further improvements in its capability and services. Spearheaded by its R² Data Labs division, Rolls-Royce is creating a 'digital first' culture that will enable new opportunities for growth. This includes its 'Helping you prepare' campaign,

providing access to its digital learning solutions and network of digital partners to help benefit more than 20,000 people affected by the Covid-19 pandemic.

Promotion
The company vision is to 'pioneer the power that matters'. Through a global network of 29 University Technology Centres, Rolls-Royce is at the forefront of scientific research, delivering leading-edge technologies that will contribute to a low carbon economy.

Rolls-Royce is going through an exciting time, transforming from an engineering company,

focused on civil aerospace, into a global power group, helping to lead the transition to a net-zero economy. Through this journey, Rolls-Royce is continuing its long-held tradition of creating new, market-shifting opportunities – for itself and its customers.

Brand Values
Rolls-Royce exists to be the 'Pioneers of Power'. The company vision is to pioneer cutting-edge technologies that deliver clean, safe and competitive solutions to meet the planet's vital power needs.

ROYAL LONDON

For more than 150 years, **Royal London has been committed to improving people's lives** in the UK. Offering products and services across **pensions, protection and wealth management**, it continues to develop and innovate to **help people navigate life's challenges**, as well as plan for the future

Market

Royal London is a purpose-led business that aims to always put the needs of its customers first whilst starting to positively impact society. It is the UK's largest mutual life insurance, pensions and investment company, with assets under management of £139bn, 8.6 million policies in force and 4,348 employees (figures quoted are as at 30 June 2020). Operating in both the UK and Ireland, Royal London offers award-winning products and services to help its customers protect today and invest in tomorrow.

Putting its customers first is in Royal London's DNA. As a mutual, it is customer-owned and Royal London's people are also members of the organisation. As members, its people work solely for the benefit of other customers and members to secure a better financial future for its customers, their families and their communities.

Product

A focus for Royal London is to improve access to products, challenging industry practice and improving customer outcomes and one example of this is the Diabetes Life Cover product. Royal London identified that people with diabetes can often struggle to find competitively priced life insurance and so it designed cover especially for them. The specialist cover, available through independent financial advisers, makes it easier for people with diabetes to secure life assurance and rewards them with lower premiums for better management of their condition.

Royal London also sells life insurance products directly to consumers who can't access or don't want financial advice. Its Over 50s life insurance policy covers the whole of the customer's life and pays a lump sum when death occurs. Royal London offers its Over 50s guaranteed acceptance with no medical for UK residents aged 50-80 years old.

Believing good protection is about more than just money, all protection plans bought through an independent financial adviser come with

DID YOU KNOW?

Royal London's **two founders** were in their **early 20s** when they left their jobs to **start Royal London**

Helping Hand. This is a comprehensive support service, provided by third parties. It gives customers access to tailored and personal support, such as a dedicated nurse should they experience illness, injury or bereavement and is available from day one of a customer's plan.

Achievements

Royal London has been recognised with a clutch of recent awards including Best Pension Provider 2019 by Money Marketing and Best Online Services 2019 by the Cover Customer Care Awards.

In the Financial Adviser Service Awards, Royal London was Company of the Year 2019 for the second consecutive year and Royal London Asset Management (RLAM) has also received a five

star rating, for the fourth consecutive year in the same awards. In addition, Royal London's Over 50 Life Insurance has a five Star Rating for features and benefits from Defaqto (Source: Rated by Defaqto for features and benefits, July 2020).

Recent Developments

As a purpose-led organisation and brand, Royal London is building increasingly strong and meaningful relationships with its customers. It has developed a social impact strategy, after extensive people engagement and research, both internally and externally with its customers and other partners. Royal London is fully committed to creating positive change, encompassing its relationship with colleagues, customers and communities, as well as wider society and the environment. There are three themes at the core of its social impact agenda where Royal London's specialist expertise enables it to make a real difference. These are – building financial resilience; taking on the long-term savings challenge; and strengthening responsible business.

During 2019, Royal London developed 10 commitments, each linked to one of the social impact themes and relevant to specific aspects of its business. The 10 commitments outline what Royal London is doing to make progress against its social impact agenda and how it plans to make a positive difference.

Promotion

Royal London is one of the largest TV advertisers in the country promoting its brand, products and services*. Another way in which it communicates with its audience is by producing informative documents, such as its Good With Your Money Guides. The guides aim to help people increase their financial knowledge about pensions, life insurance and more.

Sponsorship is also key, Royal London has sponsored the England and Wales Cricket Board since 2014. It is proud to help bring one day cricket to players and fans at an international and domestic level. The brand's multi-year deal makes it title

Brand History

1861 Joseph Degge and Henry Ridge found the Royal London Life Insurance and Benefit Society in London.

1904 Royal London grows exponentially in the following years with 4,500 agents operating from more than 300 district offices with assets of nearly £1.5m.

1908 In a Special General Meeting, members vote 8,817 to 1,014 to convert from a Friendly Society to a Mutual Company.

1914-1918 Royal London begins to employ women after 147 male Royal London employees are killed in WWI.

1936 Royal London expands rapidly, issuing nearly 990,000 policies.

1939-1945 Once again, women join Royal London and this time stay following the war.

1988 Royal London Asset Management is founded as a separate company.

2000 Royal London embarks on an ambitious period of growth, starting with the acquisition of United Assurance Group (a merger between United Friendly and Refuge Assurance) for £1.6bn.

2011 Royal London celebrates turning 150, the same year it acquires Royal Liver. The Royal London Foundation is also launched.

2013 Acquisition of new life, pensions and asset management businesses from The Cooperative results in two million new customers and £20bn in assets.

2019 Royal London's '10 commitments' are announced.

sponsors of England Women's and Men's international one day cricket, known as the Royal London Series. One day domestic cricket is also supported with the Royal London Cup and the Royal London Club Championship, helping to support the development of the 50-over game nationwide, from a local community level through to international.

The Royal London pelican, Gilbert, represents the qualities associated with this bird – a heraldic symbol of generosity, with a royal past. This made getting involved with a pelican colony in the UK the perfect match for Royal London. The brand is partnering with the Royal Zoological Society of Scotland to look after their colony of Eastern White pelicans in Edinburgh Zoo whilst also supporting the conservation work undertaken by the society.

Brand Values

Royal London was founded in 1861 by two young men who wanted to help people avoid the stigma of a pauper's grave. This principle is still at the heart of Royal London, with it being committed to putting the needs of its customer first. Royal London works to help its customers secure their future and shield them financially against life's challenges. It also aims to be a force for social good – through responsible investing, adhering to the highest standard of corporate governance and supporting its people and communities.

As a mutual insurance company, Royal London can distribute and reinvest its profit. When Royal London does well, it aims to boost eligible customers' retirement savings, by adding a share of its profits to their plan each year, known

as ProfitShare. Although Royal London can't guarantee it'll be able to award ProfitShare every year, its continued strength in how it runs its business meant that for eligible customers, it was able to share £140m of its profits with around 1.8 million customers in April 2020. Royal London has now added over £1bn to the value of eligible customers' savings since ProfitShare was introduced in 2007.

Royal London is determined to tackle the big societal issues affecting the financial future of its customers, people and their families. Its social impact approach focuses on the areas where it thinks it can use its strengths to make a real difference in the long term.

*Within top 2% of UK advertisers, by spend, 1st January 2019 to 30th September 2020 – Nielsen, Advertiser TV Spend Report

Royal Mail

The postal service is a **key part of the UK's infrastructure** and Royal Mail is in the **unique position of reaching every household in the UK** with a work force that **stretches across the length and breadth of the country**

Market

The UK Parcels Market is the most competitive in Europe and one of the most competitive in the world, with 15 carriers of scale competing for the billions of items sent within the UK each year. In this dynamic market Royal Mail remains the UK's pre-eminent delivery company with a majority market share maintained by offering the best combination of quality, service attributes and price. It handles more than 13 billion letters and 1.3 billion parcels each year and delivers more parcels in the UK than all its major competitors combined.

Through its various brands, it connects businesses of all sizes throughout the length and breadth of the British Isles and can deliver to every address in the UK each day.

DID YOU KNOW?

The **Warrington parcel hub** is the **size of 4.5 football pitches** and will process more than **600,000 parcels per day**

Product

Whether Royal Mail customers have an item that is urgent, requires proof of delivery on arrival or simply want a standard service, Royal Mail has a wide range of delivery services to suit every need. Ranging from the one-price-goes-anywhere Universal Service stamped products; to guaranteed next day services; to advertising mail; to parcel collections and deliveries for some of the nation's largest retailers and businesses. Customers are also able to send items to more than 230 countries and territories worldwide through Royal Mail's global network of postal partners. Furthermore, with 10,500 Post Office branches, 1,200 Royal Mail Customer Service Points, and a national network of more than 100,000 postboxes and parcel postboxes, Royal Mail has a convenient and accessible network.

Achievements

Royal Mail is one of the oldest brands in the UK, with an illustrious history dating back to 1516. Over its 500-year history it has changed and adapted to the meet the needs of an ever-changing

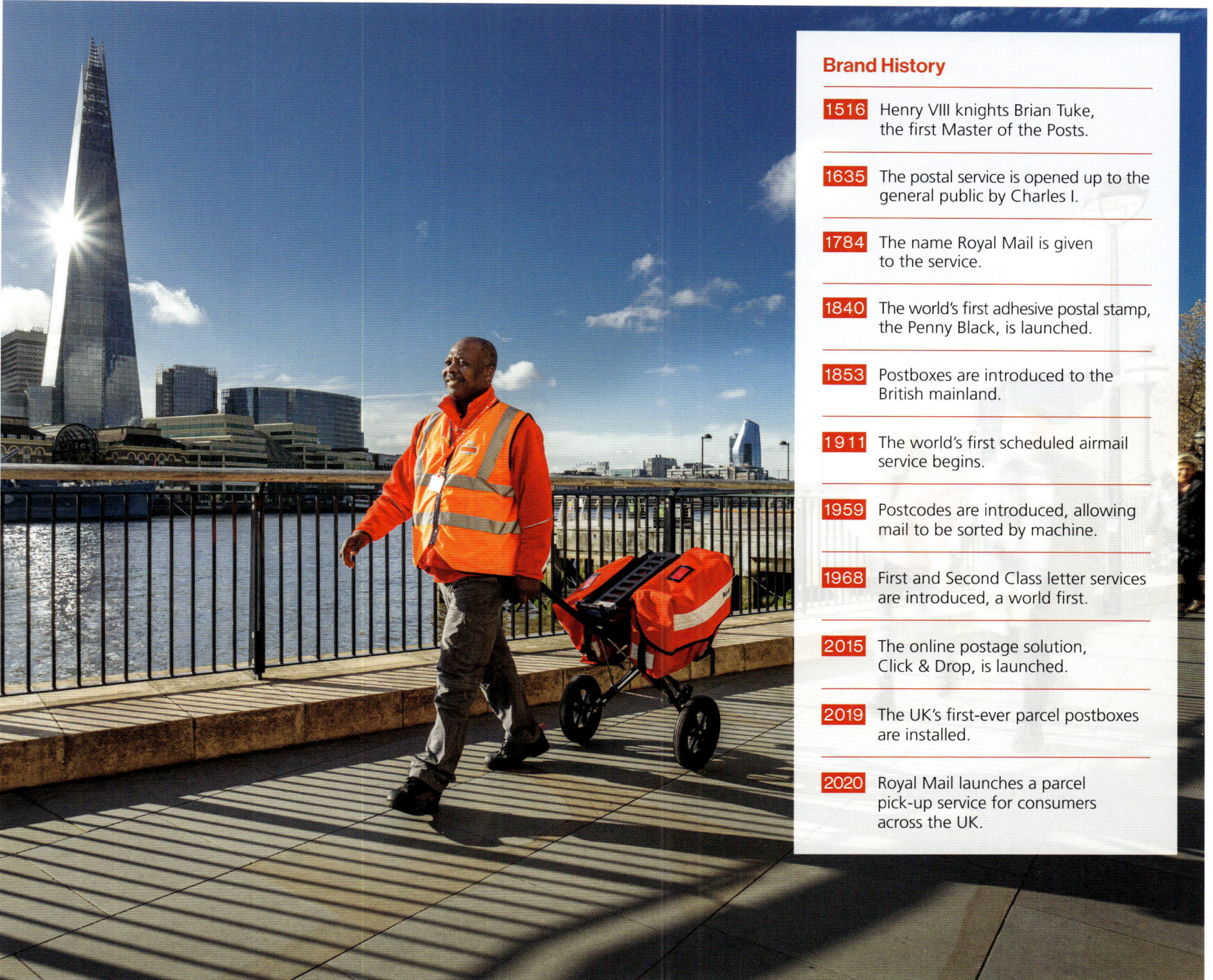

Brand History

1516	Henry VIII knights Brian Tuke, the first Master of the Posts.
1635	The postal service is opened up to the general public by Charles I.
1784	The name Royal Mail is given to the service.
1840	The world's first adhesive postal stamp, the Penny Black, is launched.
1853	Postboxes are introduced to the British mainland.
1911	The world's first scheduled airmail service begins.
1959	Postcodes are introduced, allowing mail to be sorted by machine.
1968	First and Second Class letter services are introduced, a world first.
2015	The online postage solution, Click & Drop, is launched.
2019	The UK's first-ever parcel postboxes are installed.
2020	Royal Mail launches a parcel pick-up service for consumers across the UK.

world. Its most recent innovation being the introduction of parcel postboxes onto the streets of the UK.

Royal Mail's post boxes are a British icon and have been featured over the years both on TV and in film. They have also been used to mark significant moments in recent UK history. Postboxes were painted gold in honour of the 2012 Olympic Games being held in London and for Black History Month in October 2020, boxes were beautifully decorated as a mark of respect to black Britons, both past and present, to mark this special month. These postboxes were located at sites in London, Glasgow, Cardiff and the Belfast box was in fact a parcel postbox.

Recent Development
Royal Mail is investing in its future, focusing on customer service improvements, digital initiatives, network enhancements to support the considerable growth in the market, and new ways of working to deliver an even better service to all its customers. Recent years have seen the launch of new services to offer greater convenience

DID YOU KNOW?

68 million Penny Black stamps were used in their **first year**

and flexibility for receiving customers too, such as inflight delivery options, an app to help consumers manage the sending and receiving of items from their phone, the collection of items from a consumer's home and the introduction of the first UK parcel postboxes. This marked the first major repurposing of the postbox in the last 160 years. There are now plans to install more parcel postboxes across the UK.

Promotion
With the events of 2020, the need for business customers and consumers to access Royal Mail's services quickly and conveniently has never been more important. Royal Mail has invested in a campaign that aims to highlight how Royal Mail has 'postage that fits around you', with access

to services at the customer's fingertips through its app and website. In July 2020 Royal Mail launched a business Instagram page, providing inspiration, support and advice for growing small businesses and marketplace sellers.

Brand Values
Royal Mail has great people, trusted to deliver. The delivery of parcels and letters is a way of keeping the country together and businesses operating, even in the most challenging of times.

Royal Mail always has its eye on the future and that is especially so with the environmental challenges that the world faces. In order to do its part in delivering a cleaner future, Royal Mail is already the greenest carrier in the UK as it deliverers the majority of its items on foot. To enhance this even further, it has set targets to: reduce emissions and improve air quality in the communities in which it operates; and reduce the amount of natural resources consumed in operations through better use of water and waste management processes.

the Luxury Included® holiday

By offering **luxury, innovation and choice**, Sandals and Beaches Resorts has been at the **forefront of the Caribbean all-inclusive travel sector for almost 40 years**. In an industry brimming with new contenders, the **passion, knowledge and experience** of Sandals' **management team and resort staff has maintained its market-leading position**

Market

Sandals Resorts sets itself apart by steering away from off-the-shelf five-star package holidays, placing an emphasis on personal choice and offering customers more for the price of their holiday. Sandals Resorts' holidays include cuisine at multiple 5 Star Global Gourmet™ speciality restaurants at each resort, unlimited premium brand alcoholic and non-alcoholic drinks, tips and taxes, as well as complimentary land and water sports such as golf and scuba diving for PADI certified divers. There are 15 Sandals Resorts created exclusively for 'two people in love' located in Jamaica, Saint Lucia, Antigua, the Bahamas, Grenada and Barbados. Its sister brand, Beaches Resorts, comprises three resorts in Jamaica and Turks & Caicos, catering for families, groups, and couples.

Product

Sandals Resorts launched the Caribbean's first Over the Water Maldivian-style suites in Jamaica at Sandals Royal Caribbean Resort & Private Island in 2016, with more Over the Water additions at resorts in Jamaica and St Lucia thereafter.

In 2019, Sandals Resorts completed a multi-million-dollar renovation of the company's flagship resort, Sandals Montego Bay, including refurbished suites, a new Over the Water bar, and an Over the Water wedding chapel with a glass-bottomed aisle.

Extensive renovations also took place at Sandals Royal Caribbean Resort & Private Island in Jamaica in 2019, including the addition of three new 5 Star Global Gourmet™ dining options including Bombay Club, Spices and La Tavola. Two new room categories were introduced at Sandals Halcyon Beach Resort in St Lucia – the Crystal Lagoon Walkout Swim-up Club Level Suite and the Crystal Lagoon Poolside Luxury Room.

The company's newest resort, Sandals Royal Barbados, which opened in December 2017, features 222 butler and concierge level suites, a rooftop infinity pool, bowling alley and gourmet doughnut shop. More recently,

DID YOU KNOW?

Stay at One, Play at All means you can **stay at one Sandals Resort and enjoy the amenities** of all the others on the same island

a new complimentary live wedding streaming service has been launched for nuptials taking place at Sandals Resorts in 2020 and 2021, allowing brides and grooms to share their special day with loved ones back at home.

Achievements

In 2019, Sandals Resorts received an array of travel trade awards including the coveted Hotel & Resort Operator of the Year, for the 11th consecutive year, at the TTG Awards. Sandals Resorts also won Tour Operator of the Year at the Food and Travel Reader Awards, and Best All-Inclusive Resort Operator for the 11th year at the Travel Weekly Globe Awards, amongst others. The company was also awarded 11 gongs at the prestigious 2020 World Travel Awards including the Caribbean's Leading Hotel Brand 2020, the Caribbean's Leading All-

Inclusive Family Resort 2020, for Beaches Turks & Caicos Resort Villages & Spa and the Caribbean's Leading Resort 2020 for Sandals Royal Barbados.

Sandals Resorts' philanthropic arm, The Sandals Foundation, celebrated its 10th anniversary in 2019. The organisation aims to unite the region with one common goal: to elevate its people and protect its delicate ecosystem under the pillars of community, education, and the environment. The Sandals Foundation has implemented projects and programmes valued at more than US $70m, which have affected the lives of more than 990,000 people to date.

Sandals Resorts is one of the only hotel chains in the world to have nine resorts holding Master Certification from EarthCheck, the world's leading scientific benchmarking, certification and advisory group for sustainability in travel and tourism. Five resorts hold Platinum, one holds Gold and two hold Silver EarthCheck Certifications.

Recent Developments

Expansive renovations took place in 2019 at resorts in Jamaica and St Lucia, including the addition of the Caribbean's longest river pool at Sandals Halcyon Beach Resort. In addition, Over the Water wedding chapels were added at Sandals Ochi Beach Resort and Sandals Montego Bay in Jamaica.

Flagship resort, Sandals Montego Bay, benefited from a new Over the Water bar and the addition of three new restaurants, as well as a complete refurbishment of the swim-up pool bar, originally the first of its kind in the Caribbean.

In 2018, all 18 Sandals and Beaches Resorts eliminated the 21,490,800 plastic straws and stirrers used across the resorts each year.

Recently Sandals acquired the CapEstate Golf Club in St Lucia which is currently being redesigned with the help of pro golfer, Greg Norman. The 18-hole Championship golf course is the second partnership between the two global

Brand History

1981 Sandals Montego Bay, the flagship resort, opens with Sandals Inn in Montego Bay launching four years later.

1986 Sandals Royal Caribbean opens and becomes the only resort in Jamaica with a private island. Three years later, Sandals Ochi makes its debut in 'Butch' Stewart's hometown.

1991-1996 The launch of Sandals Grande Antigua is followed by resorts in Saint Lucia and the Bahamas.

1997 Sandals introduces its first family resort in Jamaica, as Beaches Negril opens its doors. Beaches Turks & Caicos opens in Providenciales, becoming the second family resort.

2002-2008 A further four resorts are opened spanning Saint Lucia and Jamaica.

2009 The Sandals Foundation is announced.

2010 Sandals Emerald Bay, Great Exuma, Bahamas opens.

2013 Sandals LaSource Grenada opens and Sandals Barbados is acquired. Two years later, Sandals Barbados opens following an extensive renovation project.

2016 Sandals opens its first ever, high street retail experience, Sandals Luxury Travel Store, in Chelsea, London.

2017 Sandals Royal Barbados opens.

2018 Sandals launches a tour operation in the UK.

2020 Beaches Resorts announces a new destination, the island of St Vincent.

---

brands – Sandals and Norman – following the development of the golf course in Exuma, The Bahamas.

Promotion

Sandals' marketing activity is upweighted around the group's key selling periods and uses a broad mix of media including TV, print, digital and out of home, with the primary objective of acquiring new customers. The brand's loyal repeat guests are rewarded through the Sandals Select Rewards Programme, giving the most valuable customers access to a wide selection of offers – from room upgrades to free nights. In keeping with the company's desire to support local, Sandals became the proud official sponsor of the West Indies cricket team in 1995.

Looking forward, Sandals will focus on growth throughout Europe; particularly in France, Germany and Italy. To achieve this, the company's online offering is being optimised to create an improved user experience and direct booking engines for these markets are being launched.

Brand Values

Sandals Resorts was created almost 40 years ago by Jamaican-born entrepreneur, Gordon 'Butch' Stewart, who wanted to share the beauty of the Caribbean with the world through luxury holidays, designed for couples in love. The Sandals Resorts brand was born in 1981 alongside the opening of the first resort, Sandals Montego Bay, in Jamaica. Now, Sandals is a household name and a world leader in the travel sector, thanks to the company's focus on innovation, service and high quality product.

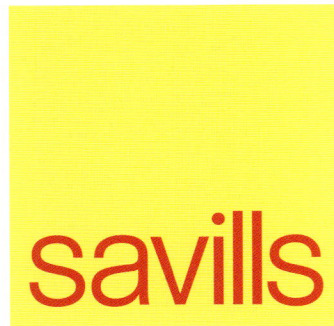

Savills plc is a **global real estate services provider with more than 600 offices** and associates throughout the Americas, the UK, continental Europe, Asia-Pacific, Africa and the Middle East. Its **38,000-strong workforce combines entrepreneurial spirit and a deep understanding of specialist property sectors** with high standards of client care

Market
Savills has an international network of more than 600 offices and associates. Its 133 strategically located offices throughout the UK, give Savills a substantial national footprint. It is the largest multi-service property advisory business in the country, providing more sector specialisms than any of its competitors across the commercial, residential, rural and energy sectors.

Product
During its 165-year history, Savills has grown from a family firm of chartered surveyors into an international property services group. Servicing all aspects of the residential, rural and commercial property markets, the firm continues to adapt its offer to cater for a diverse and evolving client base.

Achievements
In its continued dominance of market-leading deals, in 2019/20 Savills advised Blackstone on the acquisition of the iQ Student Accommodation platform for £4.66bn from Goldman Sachs and Wellcome Trust, the largest ever private real estate transaction in the UK. It also pre-let 2 Ruskin

DID YOU KNOW?

Savills Global Property Management team manage **350 million sq m of real estate**, the **equivalent** of about **54,400 football pitches**

Square in Croydon to the Home Office; secured the largest leasing deal, at 330,000 sq ft, in London so far in 2020; and brokered and managed the transaction of the largest leasing deal in German history, Deutsche Rentenversicherung Bund, taking 87,000 sq m of space at Berlin's 'Treptowers'.

Savills Student Accommodation team was named Agent of the Year for an unprecedented second year in a row at The Student Accommodation Awards and its Industrial and Logistics team was crowned Industrial Adviser of the Year at the EG Awards. There was also a double accolade

for the residential teams at the RESI Awards, taking home UK Sales Agency of the Year and Letting Agency of the Year.

Savills Cross Border Investment team was honoured for its stand out performance in 2019 as Europe's leading investment sales broker, outshining the competition for the third consecutive year. In addition, Savills is The Times Graduate Employer of Choice for Property for the 14th consecutive year, a position that it has held since the category's inception in 2007. The firm also re-entered the Top 100 Graduate Employers list, in 85th place, the only property company to be ranked.

As a business, Savills seeks to identify and develop the future leaders of its business through a range of inspirational training and leadership programmes, ensuring that Savills strengths and culture continue in the future. Recently, Laura Mackay of the Manchester development team, became a member of the EG 2020 future female leaders programme (bottom left). Now in its second year, the cross-industry collaboration aims to create a wider, more diverse range of views and opinions as well as developing skills in communication and presentation.

Additionally, Katrina Kostic Samen head of Workplace Strategy & Design, was named Inspirational Leader of the Year at the British Council for Offices (BCO) NextGen Awards 2019.

As one of the founding members of 'Changing the Face of Property' in 2014, an initiative run by a number of major property firms, Savills remains committed to developing a culture of inclusivity and diversity within the property profession with six areas of focus: gender, age, disability, LGBTQ, socio-economic and ethnicity.

Recent Developments
In the past 12 months, Savills acquired London-based workplace consultancy and design studio KKS, creating a new workplace centre of excellence, offering a comprehensive end-to-end solution for its clients from inception to completion.

Magazine Cover

◆ How Covid-19 will impact real estate ◆ Sustainable buildings
◆ Global food security ◆ Investing in the life science sector
◆ Could Hyperloops speed up the supply chain? ◆ Repurposing retail

savills

Impacts

THE FUTURE OF GLOBAL REAL ESTATE

Issue 03. 2020

TIPPING POINTS

How climate, politics, demographics and technology are transforming real estate

◆ Is construction ready for new methods and materials? ◆ The economic impact of the US-China trade war
◆ The role of real estate in tackling climate change ◆ New thinking in workplace design ◆ Buildings that
understand your preferences ◆ Water stress and development ◆ Global investment strategies

---

Brand History

1855 Savill & Son is founded by Alfred Savill.

1972 The firm is rebranded as Savills and moves to Mayfair.

1988 Savills is listed on the London Stock Exchange and begins trading as a plc.

1997 A 20% share of Savills is sold to First Pacific Davies – one of Asia's foremost property companies – and the subsidiary is rebranded as FPDSavills.

2000 Savills plc is listed in the FTSE 250 and acquires First Pacific Davies in April.

2004 To coincide with the company's 150th anniversary in 2005, the decision is made to drop 'FPD' from FPDSavills. The rebrand brings all the subsidiaries back under the Savills umbrella.

2012 In the UK, Savills prepares its separate residential and commercial limited operating companies for a formal merger and begins trading simply as Savills the following year.

2014 Savills announces its biggest ever acquisition of US firm, Studley, at £154m.

2015 Savills completes its largest ever UK acquisition, the merger of Smiths Gore.

2017 Savills confirms the completion of its acquisition of Aguirre Newman S.A., the leading independent Spanish and Portuguese real estate advisory firm.

2018 James Sparrow is appointed CEO UK & EMEA and Richard Rees is appointed UK MD.

2019 Mark Ridley, former Deputy Group CEO, succeeds Jeremy Helsby, as Savills Group CEO.

2020 In Germany, Savills announces the proposed acquisition of property and facilities management firms, OMEGA Immobilien Management GmbH and OMEGA Immobilien Service, supplementing the company's strong UK & European property management network.

In the US, Savills completed the acquisition of Macro Consultants LLC, a leading project management firm. The agreement accelerates the expansion of Savills existing advisory and management services platform while enhancing the firm's ability to deliver tier-one project management and consulting solutions to its clients.

In Germany, Savills announced the proposed acquisition of property and facilities management firms OMEGA Immobilien Management GmbH and OMEGA Immobilien Service to supplement the company's strong European property management network and to allow it to service clients in Germany as part of a national or pan-European requirement.

A major strategic goal was achieved in 2019, with Savills largest ever organic growth initiative in a new geography. Its presence in India expanded to encompass nine offices, with a headcount standing at 300 and further growth plans underway.

Promotion

Savills research capability stretches across continents and all sectors of real estate providing clear and useful market knowledge, which adds value to its clients' interests. Not only providing information on the major markets but adding original insights, identifying new emerging sectors and providing bespoke client advice.

Acknowledged as thought-leaders in many areas of real estate, Savills communicates its research findings in published and bespoke reports, via social media, through TV and radio, conferences and seminars, providing an enhanced service for its clients as well raising the company's profile.

Brand Values

Savills attracts the best individuals within its market, and through careful selection and the preservation of a unique culture, provides a global platform from which its talents and expertise can not only benefit clients but also the wider community.

The firm's vision is to be the real estate adviser of choice in all the markets it serves, focusing not on being the biggest company, just the best in the eyes of its clients. Its values capture its commitment not only to ethical, professional and responsible conduct but also to the essence of real estate success; an entrepreneurial, value-embracing approach.

Selco Builders Warehouse is the **UK's fastest growing builders merchant**.
Developing an **ever-growing customer base of professional tradespeople** in the Repair,
Maintenance and Improvement sector, **Selco is truly a business on the march**

Market

The UK builders merchant industry, in general, has faced a mixed period over the last two years.

While sector performance has largely remained resilient, there have been testing periods as a result of Brexit, unusual weather events affecting the work of tradespeople and, of course, the recent coronavirus outbreak.

Selco, however, has been able to continue the strong progression it has seen over the last decade and has established itself as a leading player in the portfolio of businesses of its parent company, Grafton Group.

Selco has continually enhanced its position in the market and posted impressive turnover and profit results. This is the result of a combination of bolstering its online and digital offering, continued branch network expansion, as well as a measured and successful reopening programme after lockdown.

Product

With a customer base comprising professional tradespeople and businesses, Selco's primary aim is to serve the RMI and home renovation market. As such, each of its branches has in excess of 13,000 recognised trade products available –

all at trade prices. From timber to decking and bathrooms to power tools, Selco has an extensive product range, both in branch and through its digital offering. This includes the Click & Deliver and Click & Collect facilities. Additional services available to assist tradespeople with their day-to-day work include sheet-cutting, brick-matching, paint-matching and project lists.

Achievements

Selco's rise to prominence has certainly not gone unnoticed in recent years. The company has won back-to-back Builders Merchant of the Year awards and secured its position on the Best Company list for London in Insider Media's Best Place to Work listings.

DID YOU KNOW?

Selco sells over **13,000 SKUs** from more than **300 different suppliers**

Recent Developments

Innovation and progression have been at the heart of this, the most successful period in Selco's long and distinguished history. Over the last seven years, its branch network has more than doubled in size and now stands at 69 stores, following the 2020 openings of the Orpington and Salford branches.

A significant investment and development in online transactional methods – such as Click & Collect and Click & Deliver – has helped enhance the offering and adjusted the business models to the changing trading habits of Selco's customers.

Over the last 18 months, Selco has broken new ground with innovations to its infrastructure. Its new Lightside Distribution Centre, in partnership with Unipart, serves all branches and provides a 66,000 sq ft headquarters in Oxfordshire

to host a greater volume of stock from more than 100 suppliers, ultimately leading to savings for customers.

In addition, in 2019 Selco became the first UK builders merchant to open a dedicated customer delivery hub. Based in Edmonton, it serves six London branches, with a team of 36 colleagues aided by 17 HGVs. It is responsible for approximately 1,000 customer deliveries and an estimated 420 inbound deliveries per week.

From an HR perspective, Selco is committed to offering exciting career opportunities to all colleagues throughout the business. A £500,000

investment in its Rising Stars programme in 2020, which gives colleagues the chance to progress their careers, is testament to this.

Promotion

With Selco's primary target audience being the professional tradesperson, there is a male slant towards its communications strategy.

Promotion through channels which attract a largely male audience, such as radio stations including talkSPORT as well as trade websites and publications, ensures Selco's key messaging is reaching the desired market.

Brand History

1895 Sewell & Co (Timber) Ltd, a small family business operating a modest timber mill and caravan fit-out business in Birmingham, lays the foundations for Selco.

1938 The company develops itself into a builders merchants.

1982 The company changes its name to Selco and establishes a business model exclusively for the professional tradesperson.

1990 Selco opens its first branch outside of the Midlands in Swansea.

1998 Merchanting and DIY group, Grafton Group plc, purchase Selco.

2002 After continued expansion across the Midlands and South West, Selco opens its first branch in London.

2006 The north west becomes Selco's latest home with a branch opening in Manchester.

2020 After more than a decade of expansion and development, Selco takes its branch network to 69 by opening in Orpington and Salford.

This is supported through local communications as well as PR activities. In addition, digital advertising and social media promotion to a relevant audience, in excess of 75,000, have played increasingly influential roles.

As part of a strategy to strengthen ongoing brand awareness, Selco has also embarked on what is proving to be a hugely successful partnership with the Professional Darts Corporation. This has propelled the brand into the homes of millions of potential customers, through the power of what is still one of most popular sports in the country.

DID YOU KNOW?

Selco is proud to be celebrating its **125th anniversary** in 2020

Brand Values

Selco's entire ethos is based around delivering opportunities to fulfil potential, spanning the business itself as well as customers and colleagues.

Its mantra of 'We've Got It' is able to perfectly demonstrate the company's commitment to providing a platform for tradespeople to secure all their requirements for a day's work under one roof in the quickest, most efficient and accessible way possible, thus making their individual businesses as successful as possible.

At the same time, colleagues are encouraged to maximise their talents by taking advantage of the endless career opportunities on offer as the business continues to grow and go from strength to strength.

Shred-it™

Shred-it is one of the **UK's leading information security companies**. It provides advice on confidential **information protection and secure destruction** and recycling services to organisations of all sizes in the private, public and third sectors. With **more than 5,000 team members** and operating a fleet of over 2,000 trucks globally, the **Shred-it focus is to protect what matters**

Market

Shred-it is one of the UK's leading information security companies operating in a worldwide market. Year-on-year spending on information security products and services has continued to rise as security compliance and risk management become an increasingly critical part of the business landscape. Key drivers for the growth in the market are numerous, but include an increased focus on detection and response capabilities as awareness of security risks and data breaches grows; privacy concerns and stricter regulation such as the EU's GDPR around data loss prevention; and business digital transformation initiatives that reinforce the need to view sensitive data and related systems as critical infrastructure.

Product

Since its founding in 1988, Shred-it has become one of the world's leading information destruction companies, with more than 5,000 team members and a fleet of more than 2,000 trucks globally. Shred-it's fundamental brand proposition is focused on protection. It does this through its team of information protection experts whose one goal is to help organisations comply with stringent privacy laws, legislation practices and procedures via certified state-of-the-art information security products and industry-compliant regulated services.

This ensures that people, customers, businesses and brands as well as the environment are protected by Shred-it.

Shred-it's protection solutions and services, which include secure document destruction, media destruction, branded goods and uniforms destruction as well as recycling services, meet the daily or ongoing needs of today's organisations in the private, public and third sectors. It safely disposes of unwanted or outdated confidential information across all major sectors from local and central government, healthcare, retail, legal, engineering, property, education, to police forces, banks and financial institutions. After paper has been securely shredded, the confetti-sized pieces are mixed with millions of pieces of other shredded documents, baled and recycled into paper products.

DID YOU KNOW?

Fewer than **1 in 5 business leaders** describe their business as **paperless***

*Source: Ipsos 2018

Achievements

Shred-it specialises in providing a tailored information destruction service that helps businesses to comply with legislation and ensures that customer, employee and confidential business information are protected at all times. Shred-it provides a consistent service based on its unique security measures, and has a standard Data Processing Agreement (DPA) which sets out the basis on which the company provides its services and, where relevant, processes data on behalf of a customer. The technical and organisational security measures that are applied when dealing with confidential information are explained in detail in its Security Information policy document. Shred-it's accolades include: ISO 9001, ISO 14001, EN 15713, NAID member, Waste Carrier's Licence (UK), British Security Industry Association Certificate, Fleet Operator Recognition Scheme and it is recognised by the ICO.

Recent Developments

In 2014, Shred-it merged with Cintas Document Shredding to create a new company that operates under the Shred-it brand. In 2015, Shred-it was acquired by Stericycle and is now a wholly-owned subsidiary of Stericycle, a global business-to-business services company,

serving more than 500,000 customers around the world. As an integrated company operating for more than 30 years, Shred-it's focus is to continue developing, delivering and improving solutions to meet the ongoing needs of a diverse customer base, while helping them manage their confidential information and aid compliance with stringent data privacy laws to protect what matters.

Promotion

In an increasingly commoditised market, Shred-it has sought a clear point of differentiation in recent years to distinguish its offering from rivals.

Following market research of its extensive worldwide customer base, Shred-it identified a number of key insights which led to the brand's positioning around the 'We protect what matters' strapline. Shred-it protects people, it protects customers, it protects brands and reputations and it protects the environment. This has enabled the brand to create a message with a clearer focus around the core idea of protection – the brand's red thread and its very reason for existence. This core message is transferable across markets, sectors and channels.

Brand Values

Shred-it has a one team, one goal motto with a customer first approach, to ensure the safeguarding, understanding and managing of confidential information. Shred-it's values around excellence in service provision, depth of experience and sector knowledge, accountability and integrity, together with sustainability and continuous improvement, underpin its leading market position. The values deliver peace of mind and help organisations stay in control through being Shred-it protected. They are encapsulated in the brand's strapline 'We protect what matters'.

Silentnight is the **UK's largest and most trusted manufacturer of branded beds, mattresses and sleep accessories**. With a wide consumer profile, Silentnight's mission is to use its **passion, product knowledge, exceptional quality and sleep expertise** to provide **sleep solutions for a nation of unique sleepers**

Market

The UK retail bed and mattress market is worth around £2.276m (Sources: Global Data Market Report, 2019). Silentnight is the UK's favourite bed and mattress manufacturer (Source: GfK data) and remains well known, with strong brand recall and consideration from consumers, in particular the brand's iconic Hippo & Duck characters.

Product

Silentnight is synonymous with quality and innovation. Founded in 1946 in North Yorkshire, the multi-channel business is celebrated as The UK's Most Trusted Bed Brand (Source: Brand Health check survey, Vision One, August 2019). Committed to working to the highest quality standards for its customers, all its mattresses and upholstered beds are handmade in its UK factory and rigorously tested in its in-house SATRA-approved testing lab.

Over the years, Silentnight has developed a strong core product offering to cater for its mainstream, 'salt of the earth' shoppers. Underpinned by a wealth of research, insight and accolades, products include a wide selection of beds, mattresses and complimentary accessories – resulting in a full sleep solution.

By broadening the wider sleep category, Silentnight prides itself on helping people 'change how they sleep for the better'. The breadth of range includes, heating and cooling products ideal for 'twisters and turners', award winning rolled mattresses for 'convenience seekers', its baby and children's ranges for 'little sleepy heads' and even pet beds for 'four legged friends'. By thinking 'sleepers before springs' the brand offers a benefit-led best in class, customised solution, further enabling Silentnight to increase added value for its customers.

Achievements

Testament to its passion for quality and innovation, over the years Silentnight has been awarded several Which? Best Buys for multiple mattresses across its range. Priding itself on sustainability,

DID YOU KNOW?

One in five UK homes have a **Silentnight product**

it currently holds the award for its Eco Comfort 1200 Mirapocket mattress (held consecutively since 2015). In addition to this, Silentnight's unprecedented focus on sustainability has earned the Eco Comfort Miracoil products, a Good Housekeeping Getting Greener accreditation.

Silentnight is a full member of The National Bed Federation, the recognised trade association representing UK manufacturers of beds and mattresses and is also a member of the Furniture Industry Sustainability Programme, having shown commitment to social, economic and environmental sustainability across its business. Its sustainability

focus has also lead to multiple accolades from the Furniture Makers' Company Sustainability Awards, being awarded the Number One for Sustainability in 2017 and 2018. In addition to this, it is a certified Carbon Neutral organisation, and brand sponsor for leading charitable organisations such as the Marine Conservation Society.

Further critical acclaim has been awarded to Silentnight for its baby and children's range of products, including the Mother & Baby Awards, Mumsnet Best and Made for Mums Awards.

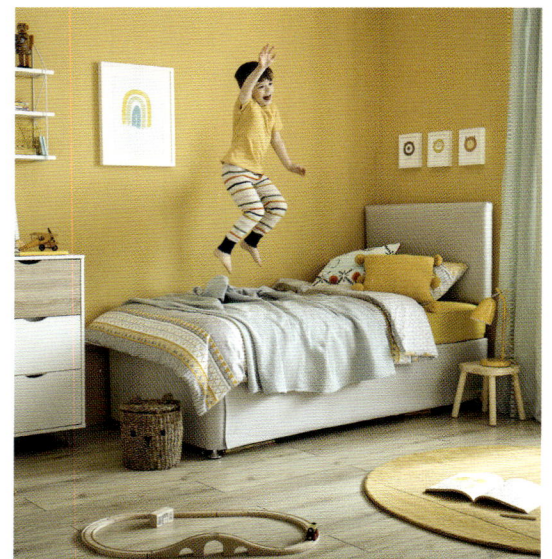

Recent Developments

In a nation of 60 million sleepers, Silentnight knows that one size doesn't fit all, which is why it's committed to delivering market-leading new product innovation, in its drive to give consumers the best sleep experience possible. In 2016, Silentnight launched an award winning new brand, Studio by Silentnight, targeted at the style-conscious, convenience-seeking sleeper. This rolled mattress comes in a choice of comfort options and sizes to suit varying sleeping styles and in 2020, the rolled mattress range was extended further, with three new 'hybrid' additions to the Studio collection.

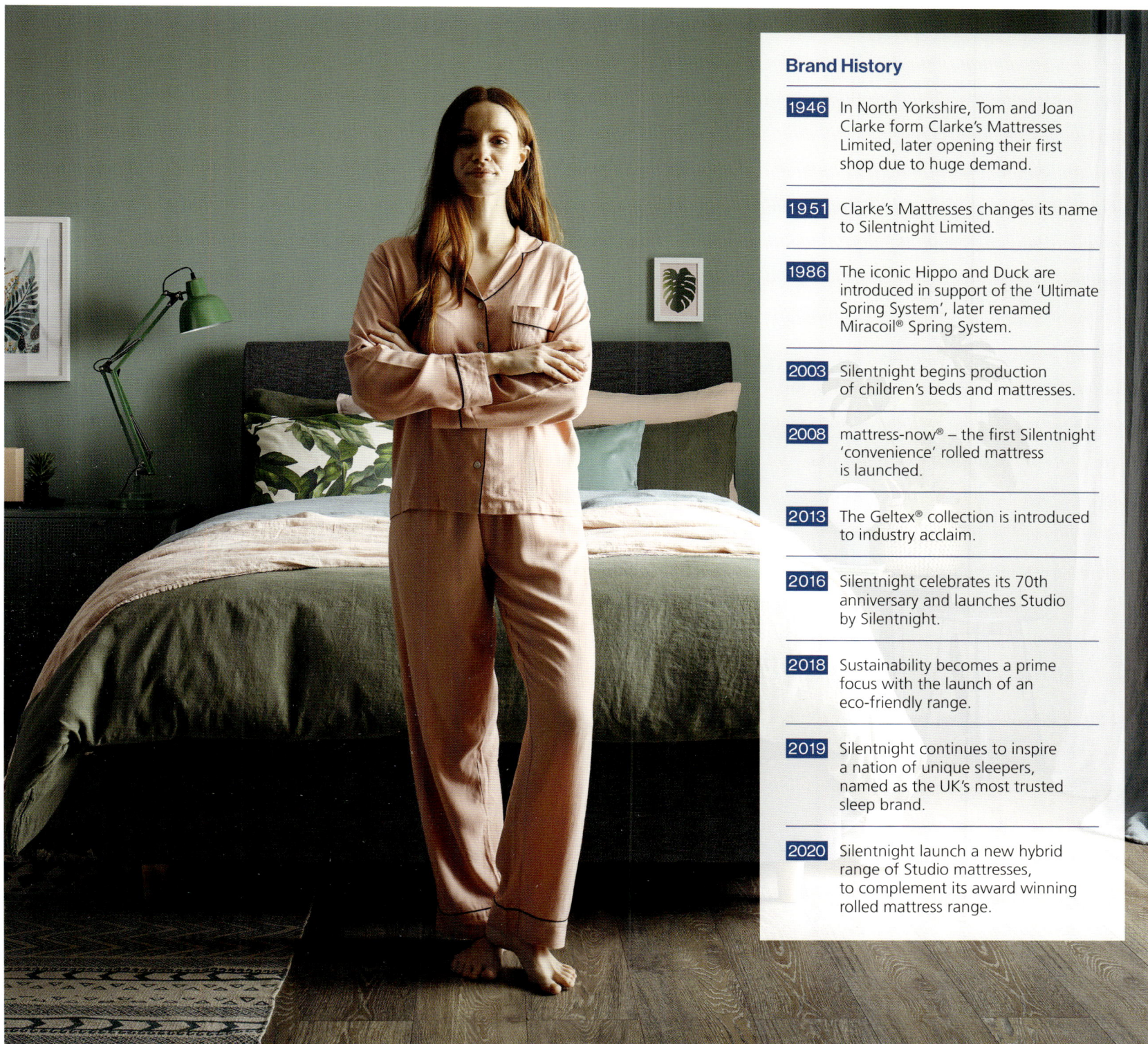

Brand History

1946 In North Yorkshire, Tom and Joan Clarke form Clarke's Mattresses Limited, later opening their first shop due to huge demand.

1951 Clarke's Mattresses changes its name to Silentnight Limited.

1986 The iconic Hippo and Duck are introduced in support of the 'Ultimate Spring System', later renamed Miracoil® Spring System.

2003 Silentnight begins production of children's beds and mattresses.

2008 mattress-now® – the first Silentnight 'convenience' rolled mattress is launched.

2013 The Geltex® collection is introduced to industry acclaim.

2016 Silentnight celebrates its 70th anniversary and launches Studio by Silentnight.

2018 Sustainability becomes a prime focus with the launch of an eco-friendly range.

2019 Silentnight continues to inspire a nation of unique sleepers, named as the UK's most trusted sleep brand.

2020 Silentnight launch a new hybrid range of Studio mattresses, to complement its award winning rolled mattress range.

Another product innovation, only available to the Silentnight Group, is Geltex®. Developed in response to sleepers who twist and turn, Geltex® is a high performance gel-infused foam which offers unparalleled breathability, perfect pressure relief and optimal body support which actively responds to an individual as they sleep.

Promotion

Operating in a dynamic, omni-channel marketplace, Silentnight continues to offer strong promotions via its retail partners. Supporting POS and engaging digital content reaffirms Silentnight's flagship presence nationwide.

Through Silentnight's own retail stores and leading ecommerce platform, the 'UK's most trusted bed brand' aims to be a destination brand for experience, establishing itself as a centre of excellence across all touchpoints.

The successful evolution of Silentnight's digital platforms has further established brand trust and engagement. Using data-driven consumer insight, the brand continues to promote compelling content, remaining relevant by offering a full-service, personalised solution when it comes to sleep, products and advice.

The brand's growing presence on social media has created an ongoing conversation with its audience. Competitions, PR activity and brand advocacy via influencer partnerships has also enabled the brand to realise its mission to 'change how people sleep for the better'. Positive consumer sentiment and strong customer reviews remain fundamental to increasing Silentnight's equity and engagement.

Brand Values

People and sleep come in many forms and too many people are compromising on their sleep.

Silentnight believes everyone, everywhere should get the best out of bedtime and its mission, therefore, is to provide a range of sleep solutions for a nation of 'unique sleepers'.

To ensure Silentnight remains the trusted authority on sleep, it invests in continuous research into sleeping habits, biometric analysis and building the latest scientific developments and technical innovations into its products, all with the goal of changing how people sleep, for the better.

Silentnight's proven expertise is further supported through collaborations with industry leading third parties, including university Knowledge Transfer Partnerships and a long-standing partnership with UCLAN to develop evidence-based products and marketing.

TATA CONSULTANCY SERVICES

The **fastest growing IT services brand of the decade**, Tata Consultancy Services (TCS) has maintained its impressive position among the **top three brands in its sector**. It **continues to grow globally** and is an influential brand in the UK digital economy

Market

TCS has had a presence in the UK for more than 40 years – its second largest market outside India. It is integrated across the UK's regions and industries, from retail and manufacturing to energy and the public sector and employs more than 19,000 people in 60 locations. TCS' UK workforce is young and diverse, with 54 nationalities represented. Women make up 28% of the workforce, much higher than the 17% average in the UK IT sector.

In response to the Covid-19 pandemic, TCS is utilising the technology pillars of Business 4.0™ – agile, intelligence, automation and cloud – to usher in a new era, with innovation growth and transformation being key.

Product

With the ongoing repercussions of the coronavirus pandemic, TCS is helping customers look beyond the products and services they sell, to the purpose behind their existence, defining the blueprint for their transformation journey and layering this approach with resilience and adaptability. The company has also embraced a new transformative operating model, Secure Borderless Workspaces™ (SWBS™) that allows enterprises to fully and seamlessly transition to virtual workspaces. This aided TCS' swift transition to remote working in the face of Covid-19 induced lockdowns, with a suitable cybersecurity framework put in place. This was in addition to all the project

management practices and systems needed to ensure that work allocation, monitoring and reporting continued as normal. The SBWS™ model ensured that neither the quality nor the timeliness of client deliveries was ever compromised.

TCS has, to date, enabled remote working for 95% of its workforce and established cloud-based governance of more than 23,000 projects, enabling high volumes of digital collaboration – 35,000 online meetings, 406,000 calls, and more than three million messages.

In the past year, it has expanded and deepened relationships, deploying impactful solutions, and winning some of its largest deals to date. In 2019, TCS expanded its strategic partnership with Legal and General to help them transform into a digital workspace, leveraging TCS' Machine First™ Delivery Model and design thinking approach. It also partnered with Ageas UK to digitally transform its IT infrastructure and operations to meet changing business priorities and customer expectations. In addition, TCS' long-standing research and innovation programme has resulted in an industry-leading portfolio of patents, products and platforms.

Achievements

TCS' customer-centric world view has driven continual investments in newer capabilities to help customers build value at speed. Its contextual knowledge and innovative models such as MFDM™ are helping TCS' customers in the UK to stay productive, drive superior customer experience and Transform to technology-led operations. As a result, TCS was ranked number one in customer satisfaction in the UK in Europe's largest independent survey of IT service providers, carried out by Whitelane Research in 2020. TCS was also ranked highest for service delivery quality with customer satisfaction at 80% compared to an industry average of 69%.

TCS was named the Fastest-Growing IT Services Brand of the Decade by Brand Finance in 2019 and is ranked second among the 2020 Top 30

DID YOU KNOW?

TCS employs more than **19,000 people** in **60 locations** across the UK

Suppliers of Software and IT Services to the UK Market by TechMarketView 2020.

In addition, TCS won a Gold Stevie® and two Silver Stevie® awards at the 16th Annual International Business Awards, for developing the official mobile app for the Virgin Money London Marathon.

TCS is also ranked in the top 25 Best Big Companies to Work for in the UK and has proven its outstanding commitment to workplace engagement and employment as Britain's number one top employer consecutively since 2018, as awarded by the Top Employer Institute.

Recent Developments

As a brand that has always celebrated wellness and community spirit, TCS has been a major sponsor and partner of marathons and running events for many years. Utilising this spirit, TCS leveraged these sponsorships with leading international running events to create a compelling campaign, This Run, to drive engagement among customers and employees. This cohesive storytelling platform sits above – and lives beyond – the individual TCS running events. It explores the motivations and emotions behind running and celebrates every detail that makes up the running experience. It also celebrates the role TCS technology plays in making the marathon experience more inclusive, more connected and more exciting.

As part of this support, and due to its status as official technology partner, TCS developed Virtual Race apps for both the TCS Amsterdam

Brand History

1968 TCS is founded as India's first software services company. The first UK office opens seven years later.

2004 TCS undertakes the largest private sector initial public offering in the Indian market.

2006 TCS acquires the life and pensions operations of the Pearl Group to set-up its BPO unit, Diligenta.

2009 TCS becomes a top 10 player in the global IT software and services industry.

2013 TCS is awarded the Platinum Big Tick – the highest ranking in Business in the Community's Corporate Responsibility Index.

2014 TCS becomes the world's second-most valuable IT services firm.

2016 TCS wins Company of the Year along with the Highly Commended Award in the Social Responsibility Project of the Year category at the Employee Engagement Awards. It also becomes the Official Technology Partner of the Virgin Money London Marathon.

2018 Tata Group's 150th year and 50 years since TCS was founded, a rare and significant milestone.

2020 TCS launches its flagship event, the TCS Innovation Forum, virtually.

Marathon and Virgin Money London Marathon. Having won several Stevies® at the 2019 International Business Awards, TCS's race app became the linchpin in enabling the virtual race experience, due to the cancellation of the full versions of the races. The virtual marathon took place on 4th October, with an emphasis on the 45,000 runners taking part around the world continuing to raise funds for their respective charities.

Promotion
During the early stages of the pandemic in 2020, TCS launched its flagship event, the TCS Innovation Forum virtually, with only three weeks notice, as a fully digital eight-part series. From June 3rd until September 9th, TCS welcomed 3,218 clients, based in 52 countries across the world, over three times more than its previous physical events. TCS also leveraged its academic partnerships, featuring speakers from Cornell, CMU, Stanford, Rotman Business School as well as Maastricht and Keio Universities. It received extremely positive feedback with more than 95% of clients stating that this event was equivalent to or better than other digital events they attended during the summer. An excellent example of practising its Agile approach to delivering business outcomes.

In October, TCS announced the findings of its global survey, Digital Readiness and Covid-19: Assessing the Impact, revealing that 90% of organisations are maintaining or increasing their digital transformation budgets amid the pandemic. The global survey engaged almost 300 senior business leaders from large enterprises – 97% with revenue above US $1 billion and 44% above US $10 billion – spanning 11 industries across North America, Europe and Asia.

The analysis compared organisations that had more advanced digital capabilities in place prior to Covid-19, referred to as 'leaders', with those who that had fewer, if any, in place, known as 'followers'. The study showed that fewer leaders (64%) have seen their revenue decline, compared to followers (73%). Moreover, leaders had better business visibility and a more confident outlook, with 74% of them expecting revenues to bounce back within two years, compared to 54% of followers.

Brand Values
TCS understands that the UK's skills challenges can be addressed by raising the profile of digital skills and exposing young people to the opportunities of digital career paths at an early age. Now more than ever, TCS is determined to continue its work inspiring young people across the UK.

In 2020, TCS successfully pivoted its CSR flagship STEM programme, Digital Explorers, to a virtual event. The programme gives young people aged 14-19 years-old the chance to experience work in digital industries. With industry experts on live panel sessions and TCS volunteers mentoring more than 1,000 young people, insight into current and future technological trends was provided. To date, TCS' award-winning STEM outreach programmes have inspired more than 500,000 young people to explore a digital future.

Learning and sharing are core values TCS upholds and nurtures, with a range of learning platforms, extensive training programmes and certifications to equip employees to deal with the current crisis, enabled by TCS Talent Development. As a result of these programmes more than 90% of the company's 19,000 employees in the UK and Ireland have been upskilled in a number of topics.

TESCO

Tesco was founded in 1919 when Jack Cohen, fresh from serving in World War I, set up a stall in Well Street Market, Hackney. With a **commitment to offering great value for customers, Tesco has grown over the last 100 years** into the UK's leading grocer. It now has **400,000 colleagues and 6,700 stores worldwide**

Market

Tesco is the UK's largest grocer with a 27% market share (Source: Kantar WorldPanel). Its offering is unparalleled in the grocery market, providing customers with affordable, quality and sustainable products. It serves nearly 50 million shoppers every week in the UK, both online and across a range of store formats.

DID YOU KNOW?

Tesco fulfilled the **first-ever online grocery order**, made by customer Jane Snowball, **in 1984**

In 2017, Tesco acquired Booker, the UK's leading wholesaler. By combining the retail expertise of Tesco and the wholesale expertise of Booker, Tesco positioned itself as the UK's leading food business, accessing new avenues of growth such as the out-of-home market.

Product

Tesco offers an expansive range of groceries, including 16 great value Exclusively at Tesco brands. This is complemented by its clothing brand, F&F; exclusive homeware brands, Go Cook and Fox & Ivy; other general merchandise available in larger stores; as well as Tesco Mobile and Tesco Bank, offering mobile phone and banking products.

Achievements

Over the last five years, Tesco has taken decisive action as part of its efforts to become a stronger, more customer-focused business. 2019 marked the completion of this turnaround, which spanned re-engaging colleagues, resetting relationships with suppliers and a focus on serving customers better. This has not only added value for shareholders but also placed Tesco in a strong position to respond to the impact of Covid-19, one of the most disruptive periods in its 100-year history.

Marketing Week recognised Tesco as its Brand of the Year 2020. Furthermore, in 2019, Tesco was voted by customers as Britain's Favourite Supermarket, for a fifth consecutive year, at The Grocer Gold Awards. Numerous other industry accolades include Grocer awards, for both service and availability in 2019 and 2020. It was also recognised as Supermarket of the Year 2019 at the Retail Industry Awards and Online Retailer of the Year 2019 at the IGD Awards.

Tesco's communications are also multi-award winning. The Food Love Stories campaign was recognised at the Retail Week Awards 2019 and Media Week Awards 2018. It also received the Grand Prix at Thinkbox TV Planning Awards, 2019 and a prestigious Media Lions Grand Prix at Cannes. Furthermore, Tesco's Centenary campaign won Best Paid Social Media at the Digital Drum Awards 2020 and Tesco Magazine was Highly Commended for Best Use of Content at the Marketing Week Masters 2018.

Recent Developments

The outbreak of Covid-19 saw an unprecedented, sudden increase in demand, putting pressure on the whole food supply chain, including stores. Tesco had to rapidly adapt its response, focusing on four key areas: providing food for all, safety for everyone, support for colleagues and support for communities.

The investments and improvements that Tesco had made over the last five years in the online business meant that it was able to quickly ramp up online capacity when the outbreak started. It increased total slots from around 600,000 before the crisis to just under 1.5 million in August, supporting more than 650,000 vulnerable customers. In August 2020, Tesco announced the creation of 16,000 new permanent roles to bolster its exceptional online growth. This is in addition to the 4,000 permanent jobs already created since the start of the pandemic.

Tesco has committed to removing one billion pieces of plastic from its UK stores by the end of 2020. Addressing the key sustainability challenges caused by food production and consumption is a longstanding priority for Tesco – ensuring products are good for customers, good for the planet, and good for the people that produce them.

Food Love Stories

TESCO
Every little helps

tesco.com/recipes

£4 £2.90
£8 £5
£2.50 £1.20
£4.25 £3.50

Prices that take you back.
Hundreds of deals all this month.

CELEBRATING
TESCO
100 Years
GREAT VALUE

Brand History

1919 Jack Cohen starts out by running a market stall in east London.

1929 Jack opens his first store in north London, selling dry goods. The name Tesco is born using the initials of his tea supplier T.E. Stockwell and CO from Jack's surname.

1934 Jack continued to grow the business, opening a new headquarters and the UK's first modern warehouse.

1947 Tesco is floated on the London Stock Exchange.

1955 Tesco reaches the milestone of 500 stores and in 1958 unveils the first supermarket.

1963 Green Shield Stamps are introduced, an early forerunner to Clubcard vouchers.

1968 Tesco opens the UK's first superstore.

1973 Tesco begins selling petrol at large stores.

1992 Tesco introduces smaller format Metro and Express stores.

1995 Tesco Clubcard launches.

2000 Tesco.com is launched, followed by Tesco Mobile in 2002.

2018 Tesco merges with Booker.

2020 Tesco donates a £30 million package of support for local communities tackling Covid-19.

Tesco is also mindful of its customers' evolving needs, launching new plant-based and meat-free ranges, including Wicked Kitchen and Plant Chef, as well as an award-winning Free From gluten, wheat and dairy range.

Tesco launched Clubcard in 1995 to better understand and communicate with its customers, and today there are 19 million households in the UK with a Clubcard. At the end of 2019, Tesco launched the UK's first grocery loyalty subscription service, Clubcard Plus, giving customers benefits including 10% off two 'big shops' in-store each month.

DID YOU KNOW?

Tesco has given **£83m to 33,000 local community** projects through its **'Bags of Help'** grants

In March 2020, Tesco launched Aldi Price Match, a bold new proposition matching the prices on hundreds of Tesco and branded products with Aldi, ensuring customers are getting competitive prices on these products at Tesco and saving themselves a trip.

Promotion

Tesco has a long history of witty and populist advertising campaigns. From the quirky Dudley Moore jet-setting around the globe in search of great quality food to Prunella Scales's long-standing role as loveable customer, Dotty. In recent years, the retailer has seen success across several campaigns. Food Love Stories, one of Tesco's longest-running campaigns in recent history, recognises the important role that food plays in people's lives while reflecting diversity and the different ways we enjoy food. During lockdown, the 'Food Love Stories – Dedications' campaign saw Tesco customers create and dedicate a special dish to a loved one and share it on social media.

In January 2019, Tesco's best performing value campaign in eight years, marking its Centenary year, saw the highest recall in 'value advertising' in the UK (Source: Millward Brown). This year-long campaign, to 'Celebrate 100 years of Great Value' at Tesco, used nostalgic and iconic characters from the past.

Meanwhile, the launch campaign for Clubcard Plus took legendary images and sequences from Casablanca and disrupted them with conversations about Clubcard Plus benefits, bringing to life the idea of 'value that you can't stop talking about'.

Brand Values

'Serving shoppers a little better every day' is Tesco's core purpose, underpinned by three values: No one tries harder for customers; We treat people how they want to be treated; Every little help makes a big difference.

tommee tippee

tommee tippee® is the **UK's number one baby feeding accessories and sleep brand** as well as **one of the top brands of infant products in the global market**. It provides intuitive and stylish products, **loved by babies and recommended by generations of parents**

Market

The UK baby accessories market is estimated to be worth approximately £355m (Source: IRI, Profitero & Company Data, June 2020) and encompasses everything from bibs and bottles, to monitors and harnesses. It does not include nappies, wipes, toiletries, formula milk, baby food or nursery furniture. tommee tippee® is number one in six of the top 10 categories in the baby accessories market, including bottles, soothers and cups (Source IRI, June 2020).

tommee tippee® has just under a quarter of the total market share by value (Source: IRI, Profitero & Company Data, June 2020). Internationally, it is sold in more than 70 countries.

Product

Every tommee tippee® product has been designed around one key principle – to make parents' lives easier. Since introducing the original spill-proof cup, tommee tippee® has earned a reputation for its clever ideas and the quality of its intuitive products that support children on their journey from newborn through to independent sleeping and feeding.

In recent years, significant additions to the product portfolio have included the Closer to Nature® baby feeding bottle, Perfect Prep™ bottle preparation machine and Twist & Click nappy bin. In 2020 tommee tippee® introduced two new product ranges to its extensive portfolio; the Made for Me breastfeeding range and, for the first time, a tommee tippee® sleep range which includes sleepwear and accessories.

Breastfeeding can be a wonderful experience however for many mums, breastfeeding can be a challenge. As every mum is unique, the Made for Me breastfeeding range includes electric, manual and silicone pumps to suit her needs, plus a range of accessories to help support mums to feed whenever and wherever they want.

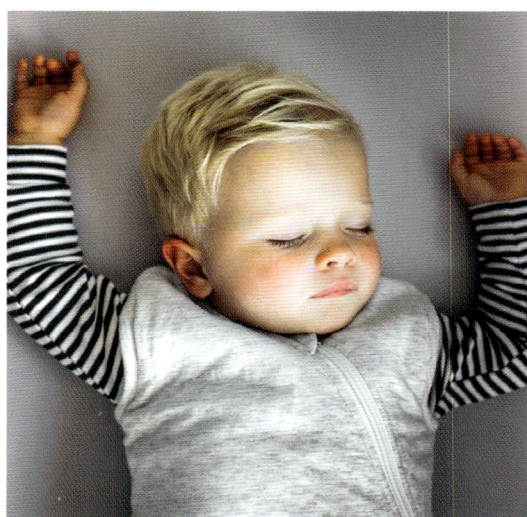

DID YOU KNOW?

Seven Perfect Prep machines are **sold every hour** in the UK*

*Source: IRI & Company Data, June 2020

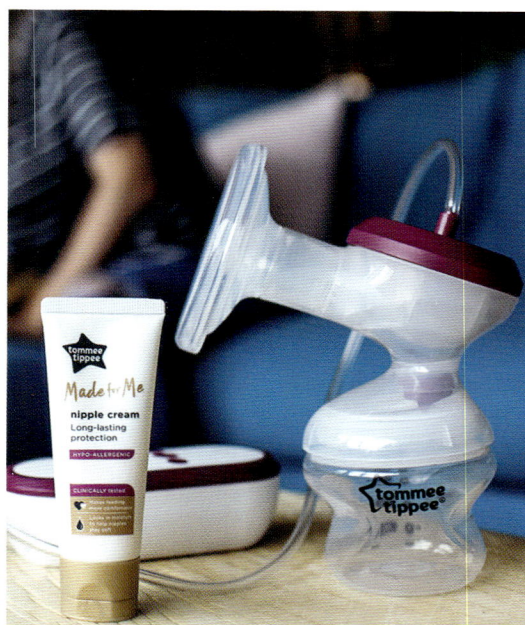

Parents will lose a staggering 44 days of sleep in the first year of being a parent. Following the acquisition of the Gro Company in 2018, tommee tippee® has launched its first sleep range including swaddles, sleep bags, light and sound aids and other accessories, all designed to encourage safer and longer periods of sleep for babies, and parents alike.

These product launches yet again demonstrate tommee tippee®'s ability to listen to its consumers' needs and provide innovative solutions to help them #ParentOn.

Achievements

tommee tippee® continues to impress industry professionals, as well as parents, with products winning an array of awards. Once again, tommee tippee® swept the boards at the MadeforMums awards with 10 awards in total, including Gold 'Can't Live Without' product for Perfect Prep Day & Night, Best Portable Sleeper for the tommee tippee® Sleepee Basket and Best Nursery Accessory for Groegg2.

Recent Developments

As part of its digital transformation strategy, in December 2019 tommee tippee® launched its first direct to consumer e-commerce website in the UK, closely followed by the USA in February 2020. The Magento powered platforms give tommee tippee® greater capability in delivering its purpose of 'helping mums and dads enjoy the roller-coaster ride of bringing up baby'. As well as e-commerce capabilities, the platform also houses an extensive Parent Room containing hints, tips and real parent stories. Exclusive content is also available through the tommee tippee® email club where users can sign up for useful articles, money-saving offers and bespoke content.

Since launch, the websites have seen over three million website sessions, helping more than 1.7 million new mums and dads #ParentOn, but the journey doesn't stop there. The Australian site is set to launch in late 2020 and moving into 2021, tommee tippee® has an ambitious European

Brand History

1965 Manufacturing rights are acquired for tommee tippee® baby products in the UK and Europe.

1986 tommee tippee® introduces Pur™, the first silicone teat to the market.

2006 The launch of Closer to Nature® changes the face of newborn feeding.

2010 tommee tippee® launches in the US and Canada.

2017 tommee tippee® launches in China.

2018 The company acquires the Gro Company and launches Perfect Prep™ Day & Night in the UK.

2019 tommee tippee® launches its first e-commerce site in the UK, followed by the USA in early 2020.

2020 Two new product ranges are launched, the Made for Me breastfeeding range and, for the first time, a tommee tippee® sleep range.

roll out plan. This should see the brand having an e-commerce presence in eight countries worldwide.

Promotion

tommee tippee® is committed to a digital-first approach across all aspects of its business and has invested heavily in a dynamic digital programme. This includes search marketing, programmatic display, social media, email marketing, SEO, Amazon search advertising in addition to other online retailer activity. Since the launch of its e-commerce platforms,

traffic driving has become an even more important part of the marketing strategy and has seen significant investment.

The brand also receives a substantial amount of PR and editorial endorsement from the parenting press and online outlets as well as having a strong relationship with the parenting blog community. After a competitive pitch process, tommee tippee® announced a new agency partner who has been tasked with driving awareness, engagement and advocacy for the brand in the UK, particularly in the influencer channel.

Brand Values

This award-winning brand was launched in the UK more than 50 years ago and was founded with one simple goal – to make everyday life just a little easier for parents around the world.

tommee tippee® is as fully committed to that original goal today as it was in 1965. That is why it works tirelessly to create innovative and stylish products which are designed to look and feel as smart as they are technologically advanced.

TONI&GUY™ OFFICIAL SPONSOR LONDON FASHION WEEK

TONI&GUY has long been **renowned as an innovator within the hairdressing industry, bridging the gap between high fashion and hairdressing.** Toni Mascolo OBE's franchise model has maintained the company's **high education and creative standards**, protected the brand and made **successes of thousands of TONI&GUY hairdressing entrepreneurs worldwide**

Market

In the years since the birth of TONI&GUY, hairdressing has become a sophisticated industry worth billions, spawning some of the most influential and creative artists in the beauty and fashion sector. From individual salons to global chains, competition is fierce with consumers demanding the highest quality and service. Having helped to change the face of the industry, the multi-awarded Superbrand has 650 salons across 47 countries.

Product

TONI&GUY salons aim to offer a consistent level of service, guaranteed quality, exceptional cutting and innovative colour, in contemporary but well-designed salons. All techniques practised by the stylists are taught by highly trained and experienced educators in 20 academies around the world.

The multi-award-winning label.m Professional Haircare range was created by Toni and his daughter, Sacha Mascolo-Tarbuck, in 2005. The brand has a presence in 64 countries globally and boasts more than 80 products and in 2013, label.m became the first product line recognised by the British Fashion Council as London Fashion Week Official Haircare Product. A percentage of sales from label.m products that carry the logo are now donated to support emerging international design talent.

To celebrate 15 years of label.m and its partnership with London Fashion Week, TONI&GUY has collaborated with four designers – IA London, Simon Mo, A-Jane and DB Berdan. Each created a signature, artistic print for one of the brand's four global best-selling label.m limited edition ranges. This highlighted the mutual bond created between a designer and hairstylist as well as the importance of hair as a key part of overall trend inspiration, taking looks from catwalk to client.

Achievements

TONI&GUY has a worldwide brand presence and is recognised for its strong education network.

DID YOU KNOW?

Co-Founder and **CEO Toni Mascolo OBE still cut hair** one day a week, **alternating between London's Sloane Square and Mayfair stores**, until shortly **before he passed away in 2017**

"Education, education, education," was often quoted by Toni Mascolo as it is considered to be the cornerstone of the hairdressing powerhouse. An average of 100,000 hairdressers are trained each year, with more than 6,000 employees worldwide. This philosophy of motivation, inspiration and education is key to the brand's success.

Co-Founder and CEO, Toni Mascolo OBE, sadly passed away in 2017. During his illustrious career, he guided the direction of TONI&GUY and received much recognition for his work. Toni won London Entrepreneur of the Year and received an OBE for his services to the British hairdressing industry in 2008. He was also honoured with an International Achievement Award from the Fellowship for British Hairdressers and an International Legend Award at the Association Internationale Presse Professionnelle Coiffure Awards. Toni was also an Honorary Professor of Durham University and recognised as one of the 10 most successful Italians in the UK.

Undoubtedly one of the most celebrated entrepreneurs in hairdressing, Toni also received the Primi Dieci Award at BAFTA. Toni's daughter, global creative director, Sacha Mascolo-Tarbuck, was the youngest ever winner of Newcomer of the Year at 19 years-old. Additional awards include London Hairdresser of the Year, Hair Magazine's Hairdresser of the Year, Creative Head's Most Wanted Look of the Year, and its Most Wanted Hair Icon in 2009, in addition to Fashion Focused Image of the Year from the Fellowship for British Hairdressing, as well as Hairdresser of the Year.

Recent Developments

For more than 55 years, TONI&GUY's philosophy has been rooted firmly in education, upholding the brand's heritage of educating its teams to the highest levels, with the last year focused on expanding its global education offering digitally and bringing the TONI&GUY expert community together under one platform.

The legendary artistic team, under the direction of Sacha Mascolo-Tarbuck, has received numerous awards over the years, including 75 British Hairdressing Awards. In 2020, Cos Sakkas, TONI&GUY's head of education and international artistic director, received his third nomination for the prestigious British Hairdresser of The Year accolade at the HJ British Hairdressing Awards (BHA).

In 2019, TONI&GUY North Audley Street, London's Sophie Springett and Hayley Bishop, won Avant Garde Hairdresser of the Year at the BHAs. Furthermore, Jim Shaw and Daisy Carter of essensuals Billericay, were awarded Men's Hairdresser of the Year. Jon Wilsdon, TONI&GUY Deansgate, Manchester was recognised as North Western Hairdresser of the Year and Federico Patelli of TONI&GUY Victoria, London received the award for Trend Image of the Year.

Promotion

TONI&GUY.TV launched in 2003 to enhance the in-salon experience. Containing up-to-the-minute content, today it still receives more than 83,000

Brand History

1963 TONI&GUY is launched from a single unit in Clapham, South London by Toni Mascolo and his brother Guy.

1982 The TONI&GUY Academy launches.

1985 TONI&GUY's first international salon opens in Tokyo, Japan.

1987 TONI&GUY's first franchise salon opens in Brighton.

2001 The TONI&GUY signature haircare range is launched. The following year, Toni and Pauline Mascolo launch the TONI&GUY Charitable Foundation.

2003 TONI&GUY Magazine and TONI&GUY.TV are launched in the UK with the brand becoming the Official Sponsor of London Fashion Week the following year.

2005 label.m Professional Haircare by TONI&GUY launches.

2008 Toni Mascolo receives an OBE for his services to the British hairdressing industry.

2011 TONI&GUY becomes Official Sponsor of the British Fashion Awards.

2016 TONI&GUY partners with Samsung to bring the latest window screen technology to 150 salons.

2019 TONI&GUY wins four accolades at the prestigious British Hairdressing Awards.

2020 TONI&GUY celebrates 15 years of label.m and being the official hair partner of London Fashion Week.

views per week in the UK. TONI&GUY Magazine launched the same year to communicate the brand's heritage and philosophy, focusing on key trends in fashion, the arts, beauty and travel. Distributed in salons across the globe, the magazine promotes the inspirational, accessible face of the company. Furthermore, it won Best Consumer Publication in 2011 at the APA Awards.

Fashion has always been a major pillar of the brand. In 2004, the link grew even stronger when it first began sponsoring London Fashion Week. The TONI&GUY Session Team works on more than 80 shows per year in London, New York, Paris, Milan, Tokyo and Shanghai, offering support to key designers including Mary Katranzou, Pam Hogg, David Koma, Paul Costelloe and House of Holland, among many others. TONI&GUY has also been awarded

Consumer Superbrand status for 12 consecutive years and is proud to support the industry, including the British Fashion Awards.

In 2019, the first TONI&GUY Trend Report was launched. The International Artistic Team's collated their inspiration from catwalks across the world. For the first time, the same rules of garment tailoring, shapes, textures and even colours, were applied to hair.

TONI&GUY takes the safety and wellbeing of clients as being as important as their image. During a challenging year globally, TONI&GUY has taken the opportunity to redesign and refresh salons, introducing the necessary measures to make clients' long awaited first visit back to the salon as comfortable as possible. In addition, the 'We Care' campaign was launched, inspiring

clients on how to look after and style their hair at home. TONI&GUY salon experts created tailored How To guides, using label.m products, alongside exclusive product offers.

TONI&GUY was proud to partner with F1's prestigious Paddock Club at British Grand Prix in 2019. It hosted its own TONI&GUY 'PITSTOP' area to look after the hair of attending VIP guests.

Brand Values

TONI&GUY's reputation has been built on an impeccable pedigree and foundation of education, fashion focus and friendly, professional service. It aims to encompass the importance of local and individually tailored, customer-led service, promoting an authoritative, cohesive and – most importantly – inspiring voice.

In 1810 the Reverend Henry Duncan did something revolutionary. He built the Trustees Savings Bank, whose **sole purpose was to help hard working local people thrive**. Seven years ago, TSB was re-born based on his vision, to make banking better for all UK consumers

Market
In 2013 the big five banks controlled more than 85% of all UK bank accounts. Following the banking crisis, TSB was created to bring more competition to UK banking and actively make banking better for all consumers.

TSB exists to serve those people who feel they are underserved by the big banks – the 'Aspiring Middle' of Britain, who work hard to do the best for themselves and their families and to balance the budget, but feel that the big banks don't really care about or understand people like them. The bank's customer-facing purpose is 'Money Confidence. For everyone. Every day'.

Product
TSB is doing what it can to help people confidently make a little bit more of their hard-earned money, be certain that it is safe and deal with life's unexpected changes.

That is why TSB designs its products and services the way it does. The new 'Spend & Save' current account is designed to help people save money as they spend it. TSB's 'Fix & Flex' personal loans and mortgages allow them to take repayment holidays, should life change. In addition,

its award-winning Fraud Refund Guarantee means that customers who are innocently defrauded of their money, are refunded in line with the terms of the Guarantee.

Achievements
Since its re-birth, TSB has successfully grown its customer base while playing a positive role in society.

It celebrates people who help others in their communities. At its heart is a long-term partnership with the Pride of Britain Awards, which is the nation's biggest annual awards ceremony of its kind. It celebrates ordinary people across the UK who've gone to extraordinary lengths to help others.

Bank fraud is a major worry for many customers. In some cases people can find it difficult to get their money back from the banks when they've been innocently defrauded. In fact, they often say they were made to feel like criminals. The Fraud Refund Guarantee positions TSB as market leading for customer protection, and the bank has become the industry source of reference on fraud for the media. This has meant that 100% of innocent victims of fraud have been refunded at TSB.

DID YOU KNOW?

The **TSB Fraud Refund Guarantee** was **The Sun newspaper's top financial innovation** in 2019

As an employer, TSB has smashed the image of stuffy traditional working practises and values. It was one of the first companies to proactively publish and explain its gender pay gap. It also has a strong presence at LGBT Pride events across the country and it is creating an environment where people, whoever they are, are encouraged and enabled to bring their true selves to work.

Recent Developments
It goes without saying that Covid-19 has had a massive impact on our lives, finances and the banking sector.

As a brand that follows the core principle of 'We are people helping people' TSB rapidly put an action and communication programme in place.

Firstly, to inform and guide its customers with relevant, timely and helpful information regarding TSB's products and services, with special attention to customers in vulnerable health or financial situations. For example, repayment holidays for mortgages, credit cards and loans, interest free arranged overdrafts, tailored support for vulnerable customers and bounce back loans to support businesses.

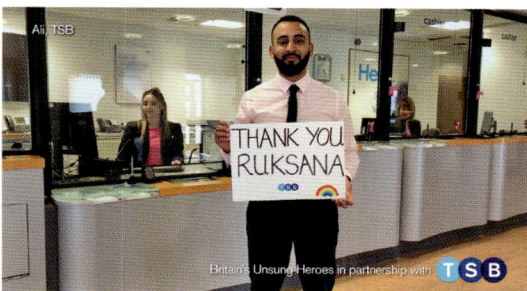

Brand History

1810 The Trustee Savings Bank is established by Reverend Henry Duncan of Ruthwell.

1986 TSB Group plc is founded.

1995 TSB is bought by Lloyds Bank. TSB disappears as a separate brand, living only as part of the name LloydsTSB.

2013 TSB separates from Lloyds Banking Group and becomes an independent entity, tasked by the EU with increasing competition in the British banking sector after the banking crisis.

2014 TSB Bank plc goes public with a successful IPO.

2015 TSB is bought by Sabadell, Spain's fifth largest banking group.

2016 TSB is recognised as Britain's most recommended high street bank.

2017 TSB becomes one of the top 10 'Best Big UK Companies To Work For'.

2018 TSB and Enterprise Nation join forces to help small businesses and entrepreneurs embrace the digital revolution.

2019 TSB announces the UK's first Fraud Refund Guarantee to protect customers.

2020 TSB launches the Pride of Scotland Awards.

Another principal is to acknowledge and recognise the people who are going the extra mile to help others in society. For example, TSB's version of 'Clap for Carers', celebrating the unsung heroes continuing to do extraordinary things in their communities or its colleagues going way beyond the call of duty to help customers.

As society returned to a 'new normal' TSB launched products and services to help people be more confident with their money and make more of life, such as its 'Spend & Save' current account. This helps people save money as they spend it. In addition, TSB's 'Your Money Matters' programme supports people in building better money habits.

Promotion
At the beginning of the Covid-19 outbreak, there was a hunger for clear and factual information. However, as the crisis continued, TSB identified an equally powerful emotional need to see the best in people and feel a sense of belonging, community, kindness and selflessness, which was being demonstrated throughout the country.

TSB's communications programme operated across both dimensions.

TV advertising featured examples of the helpful actions it was putting in place to enable customers to take repayment holidays, protect them from

DID YOU KNOW?

TSB has more than
five million customers

fraud and enable them to talk to TSB online 24/7, so they could deal with any banking queries from the safety of their own homes.

TSB partnered with Channel 4 to create a special TV event to celebrate Britain's unsung heroes.

Later in the year it launched the new Spend & Save current account to help people 'save as they spend'. TSB also continued to partner the Pride of Britain Awards to celebrate the extraordinary

things that have been done by ordinary people in this unprecedented year.

TSB's content programme gave people detailed information about its products and services and how to bank safely, but at the same time recognised the hard work, sacrifice and selflessness that so many amazing people were demonstrating during the crisis.

Brand Values
TSB is a bank which is all about people helping people. Empathy and understanding shone through in a time of need. Its core behaviours of feeling what customers feel and doing what matters to them ensured that it was able to do the right things for its customers and colleagues throughout the crisis.

We have all been through an extraordinarily difficult time but as things get back to normal, TSB is determined to play a leading role in helping people to be confident about their money and make more of life. It's a role it will be proud to play.

What All Marketers Can Learn From The Jungle Book

The secret to great brand storytelling

CHRIS HEWITT
Chief Storyteller
Berkeley Communications

"Many strange legends are told of these jungles of India, but none so strange as the story of a small boy named Mowgli. It all began when the silence of the jungle was broken by an unfamiliar sound. It was a sound that had never been heard before in this part of the jungle. It was a Man-Cub."

So began the dialogue of the 1967 animated adaptation of Rudyard Kipling's The Jungle Book. I can recall it almost verbatim. My childhood memory was to snuggle up with my dad on the sofa and listen intently to the soundtrack, over and over. The entire story was etched into my memory with every turn of the 12-inch vinyl recording.

But why? Why do stories stay with us, seemingly forever?

I couldn't have said so objectively at the time. But now I see. I WAS Mowgli. The skinny lad who loved adventure, to climb, to swing from the trees – to monkey around. And yes, I wanted to 'walk and talk' like Baloo when I grew up.

And that's the point. When we identify with a character within a story, like the Jungle Book, we become that character. We feel something. We experience what Mowgli experiences. It doesn't matter whether it is real or imagined, the very same part of our brain is engaged. That's how we're wired as humans.

The same goes for just about every other story. From The Wizard of Oz, to The Wolf of Wall Street, from The Hunger Games to Harry Potter. Storytelling follows a formula. It is a repeatable pattern within which names, places, dates, situation and characters change, but the structure is largely the same.

The story-formula
So how do most stories flow? First, we encounter a central protagonist, or hero (Mowgli), who has a desire or need to be met (get to the man-village). But there is an obstacle in the way (Sheer Kahn). Along comes a guide or mentor (Bagera and Baloo) who helps the hero overcome challenges along a journey of suspense (Ka the snake, King Louie etc) where things could go either way, until a mostly happy resolution is met (boy meets girl and crosses the water to follow her into the man-village). So, here's the thing. Why can't we apply this very same formula to your brand message? Or your 'about-us' or your next video, case study, media pitch, blog or tweet?

When you are next brainstorming your brand message – let this six-step story framework be your guide.

1. Hero
No that's not you. Most businesses make the mistake of thinking they are the hero by putting themselves front-and-centre of their brand story.

When **we identify with a character** within a story, like the Jungle Book, **we become that character**

They puff-up their attributes by listing numbers of offices, staff, products, even their revenues. No-one cares about you. They care about themselves. So, make your customer the hero of your story. Identify the persona in as much detail as you can – B2B or B2C, it doesn't matter.

2. Mission
What do they want? What is the need to be met? Keep your business out of the story for now and write down the mission the hero customer is on. Spend some time thinking about this. You are showing empathy with the customer by understanding their needs, even if it isn't getting to the man-village. Once you have properly understood and articulated this you can move on to the next stage.

3. Obstacle
What is stopping them achieve their goal? This is where you can inject some drama into your business story by focusing on the primary challenge or concern your customer faces. What is keeping them awake at night? What are they worried about?

What do they fear could happen if they don't act on the problem? This is their Sheer Kahn moment.

4. Guide
Now you enter the stage – your Bagheera moment. But be careful not to over-play your importance. Consider what your credentials are to meet the challenge. What attributes and experience can you bring to the party to help get your customer through the jungle of options ahead.

5. Journey
You shine a light on the pathway ahead and take your customer on a journey of discovery, overcoming obstacles along the way. Highlight the challenges ahead and what might happen – the downside and the upside. This brings a little bit of suspense into your story and keeps the audience engaged.

6. Resolution
The end. Hopefully a happy one. What is the outcome you bring to your customer? Use this moment to highlight the bigger picture and what you stand for as a company. Ultimately, don't you exist to improve the lives of the people you sell to in some way? In what way? What is your bigger picture? Your Why?

It's a wrap
If this framework is the foundation of a blockbusting movie or page-turner-of-a-novel, why can't it work for your business? The short answer is it can.

The key is understanding a simple truth. That your customers and prospects will not change their behaviour until they start to feel something.

People don't remember you for what you say or do, but they do remember how you made them feel. Think about that next time you give a PowerPoint presentation.

The secret to great brand storytelling is the very same as any movie or book you've ever loved.

About Berkeley Communications

Berkeley Communications specialises in creative storytelling for brands. It achieves outstanding results through a storytelling process that is unique and draws upon techniques used by filmmakers, authors and journalists. Its Storytelling Academy exists to inspire sales, marketing professionals and business owners to bring storytelling into the DNA of their organisation. HQ is in the UK with wholly owned subsidiaries in North America and Germany, as well as a network of partners across the globe.

BERKELEY
COMMUNICATIONS

Living In A Box:
The Role Of Digital In The New Normal

The part Digital has to play in a post Covid world

NATHAN MATHAN
CEO, DNA Digital

Welcome to Day Two of the new normal

In what might be the biggest shift in the way we communicate since the invention of the telephone, the developed world now lives in a box and talks to itself through a pane of glass.

While we might reverse this trend to a certain degree after we've learned to contain and mitigate the impact of Covid-19, one thing's certain (and possibly only one thing): its effects are going to be with us for a long time to come.

So why 'Day Two'?

Well, 'Day One' has definitely happened. We've passed through the usual human cycle of reaction to major events: we tried to ignore it, we tried to deny it, we're past the acceptance stage – we know this is here to stay – so now we're firmly in the adaptation stage, which I think of as Day Two.

In Day Two, society is reacting and reforming. The fact that we don't yet know what the world will look like even a year from now means trusted major brands with large followings have an opportunity to play a part in that process by offering people new ways to engage and interact with them.

That's where Digital comes in.

From content to conversation

For the world to function effectively again, we'll need to learn and adopt a whole new set of skills and tools – and we're still figuring out what those skills and tools will be.

It's quite tempting to think that this will mainly impact the world of white collar work and that once we have a vaccine and the restrictions are lifted, things will go back to the way they were before – but that assumption is likely to prove false.

Due to the limitations on travel and presence, people are increasingly doing things digitally that they may have done physically before, and as we become used to doing things this way, it becomes learned behaviour – meaning even when we can go back to doing things the way we did before, we might choose not to.

As people find themselves increasingly deprived of opportunities to spend time with those outside of their households, they'll be looking for ways to meet that basic human need using technology. This means we need to evolve from offering digital consumption to digital dialogue – real, actual talking, not just bite size tweets or status updates.

In short, we need to find ways to replicate the experience of human contact out there in the real world – to see, speak and connect with each other (almost) as effectively as we would if we were in the same room.

What does this mean for businesses and brands?

We need to ask ourselves three basic questions:

1. What do I offer my customers now that is genuinely valuable?

2. How can I offer the essence of that value in the digital space?

3. What digital capabilities are available now or in the near future that can help me achieve that?

And as a bonus question:

4. I need to start writing a plan to do this right now. Where's my pen!?

Imagine you're a hospitality brand that offers a chain of pubs. You may have already pivoted to a restaurant offering – but think about the first question you just read. What do people actually come to pubs for? Isn't a major part of that value about atmosphere and connection with their family and friends? Is there an opportunity for you to offer a form of that connection digitally?

Even **when we can go back** to doing things the way we did before, **we might choose not to**

As a basic example, how about a virtual quiz night app with live quizzes hosted by your brand with features that go beyond a standard Zoom call and allows answer selection, scoring, voting and even digital prizes?

All of this is possible with the digital capabilities we have available to us right now. We just have to think differently.

Enabling technologies

So that's the challenge. This leads us to the question: "What emerging technologies are out there that can help us to do this?" Here are a few examples:

People will still want to have actual conversations, now more than ever. The fact that First Direct bank consistently wins Customer Services awards due to its human led, no "press one to be plunged into a silent telephonic abyss" approach is proof of that. Artificial Intelligence based self-learning conversation technology will help bridge the gap between the cost of provisioning human interaction and expecting customers to consume one-way content.

The near onset of 5G services provides an opportunity for us to deliver richer experiences to mobile devices and previously poorly connected households. This will allow frameworks such as Augmented Reality to hit the mainstream, potentially offering virtual shopfronts or deeper interaction with products that brings us closer to the experience of picking them up and holding them in our hands in our local retail store.

5G connectivity will also allow smoother, higher definition online meeting-based platforms that can be branded and curated by brands to offer specific experiences of the kind as we discussed in our hospitality brand example earlier. This may even lead us back to the Virtual Reality area, which is a technology that gained interest a couple of years ago but was ahead of its time in terms of the hardware and connectivity it needed at that point.

As people are spending more time at home, there is an opportunity to offer services via Consumer AI Assistants such as Amazon Alexa or Google Assistant. This is gaining popularity as the platform becomes more mature. In this way, you're literally being 'where your customers are': at home.

These are just a few examples. Take some time to see what's out there and how it can fit with your offering.

Conclusion

So finally, what does the future hold? Having left my crystal ball in my other suit (which, incidentally, I don't wear anymore as my working life consists of perpetual online meetings in tracksuit bottoms) my honest answer is: I don't know. Nobody does.

What we do know though, is that there's not a single business, from Apple to your local corner shop, that can afford to stay the same.

In that spirit, I hope this article has given you food for thought which will in some small way help you and your business to adapt and thrive in 'Day Three' and all of the days that follow.

The Economic Effects On Consumer Attitudes And Behaviour In 2020

An insight into the rapidly evolving trends in the face of the Covid-19 pandemic

ANDREW O'CONNELL
Managing Director UK, Dynata

The continuing evolution of the Covid-19 pandemic has brought global changes that are evident in every aspect of our personal and professional lives. Dynata's earlier Global Consumer Trend reports – Understanding the Pandemic, The New Normal and The Reopening – first documented many of these changes, which have continued to evolve, reflecting how and where we work, shop, pay and spend our time as well as how businesses and industries have fared during this year of ambiguity. Yet even some of those aspects have stabilised, other parts of our daily lives remain dynamic, including where we live, our confidence in the economy, and even remote learning and job reskilling.

Closer to home, the British economy continues to grapple with both the coronavirus pandemic and the ongoing impact of Brexit. Taken together, these challenges are amplifying economic uncertainty in the UK. While our survey didn't ask specifically about Brexit, it's difficult not to feel its effect in the anxiety expressed in the response of our UK participants.

Baby Boomers express the most concern for their national economy and Gen Z the least

Here's a closer look at some of the most compelling storylines emerging in the Global Consumer Trends: The Economy report:

With a large portion of the workforce working remotely during the pandemic, many of us continue to feel more productive, however work-life balance has experienced a decline since the start of 2020.
Seventy percent of people across the globe feel they are just as, if not more, productive working from home, an eight-point increase since Dynata last asked in April 2020. Yet, despite feeling productive, satisfaction with work-life balance has dropped 10 percentage points since January 2020. Here in the UK, 45% report their work-life balance as "extremely good" or "very good," four points above the global average.

Concern for household finances and national economies remain elevated, though have decreased since the beginning of the pandemic.
Over half of participants expressed concern about their household's financial situation, though this has dropped across most the countries surveyed since April 2020. Consumer anxiety for their national economy has also decreased since the earlier days of the pandemic, with Baby Boomers expressing the most concern and Gen Z the least.

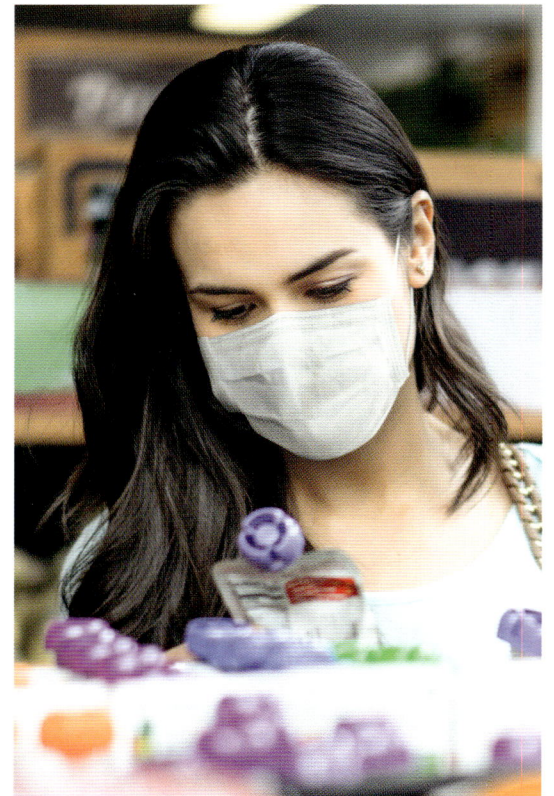

The early stages of the pandemic were marked by increased vacancies in many cities; it appears, however, the flight from those cities may have been a temporary phenomenon. During the pandemic, the percentage of people moving out of London, Paris, New York and Sydney and those that moved into the city is nearly equal – 62% leaving cities vs. 59% moving into cities. And, of those who moved since March, only 55% feel it is a permanent move. Notably, 65% of those in the city centre of London relocated to another residence in the city centre; just 7% left the city for a town or rural location.

Awareness of the Gig Economy continues to grow, though less people report working in it.
More people across all generations are aware of the Gig Economy, yet every generation reports fewer members working in it since January

2020, with Gen X experiencing the largest drop at 17 percentage points, followed by a 14-point decrease for Baby Boomers and Millennials, and 11 points with Gen Z. In January 2020, Brits were the least in favour of the Gig Economy – only 32% defining it as a "good thing," today, that attitude remains stable at 34%.

As children have transitioned from the classroom for remote learning, responsibility for overseeing that learning is not equally distributed between genders.
Seventy-five percent of women with children between 5 - 10 years-old say they were responsible for their child's remote learning, compared to 58% of men; this changes to 42% and 37%, respectively, for parents of 16 - 17 year-olds.

As perhaps expected, more of us are shopping online for essential items during the pandemic, compared to prior offline levels, with the largest growth in the grocery sector.
The grocery sector has grown the most in online shopping as compared to prior to the pandemic, a significant change from prior offline levels – increasing nine percentage points in the UK since Spring 2020 (30% to 39%). And while there are vast differences at the country level in online versus offline spending, little variance exists across genders and generations.

The Dynata Global Consumer Trends report series connects consumer trends with the societal, economical and psychological dynamics that drive them, delivering a unique level of depth and breadth on some of the most important topics in our world today.

About Dynata

Dynata is the world's largest first-party data and insights platform. With a reach that encompasses over 62 million consumers and business professionals globally, and an extensive library of individual profile attributes collected through surveys, Dynata is the cornerstone for precise, trustworthy quality data. Dynata serves nearly 6,000 market research, media and advertising agencies, publishers, consulting and investment firms and corporate customers in North America, South America, Europe, and Asia-Pacific.

dynata

Pivot, Analyse, Repeat

An insight into how agencies and marketing are evolving

DAMON SEGAL
CEO, Emotio Design Group

Okay, so we all know that it has been many months since we locked down and started facing life in a completely new way. We also know there are always winners and losers at times like this in business, with every winner like Peloton and Alphabet, there are 10 losers. The conversations I've had with so many brands have shown me how tough life is for even the biggest of them. Many brands are having to hunker down and carefully manage budgets to see their way through this time. On the flip side, it has been excellent to see how so many have risen to the occasion, navigating the struggles they have faced.

For several years we have spoken a lot about storytelling, and the need for authenticity. I don't think we ever imagined we would see this kind of authenticity or the creation of such extraordinary stories from brands. Stories like how Tesco became one of the first brands to launch a campaign promoting social distancing or how the independent brewer BrewDog turned to making hand sanitiser and giving it away for free to those that needed it. The big question is, will a consumer's loyalty really be driven by the love and trust they find from those stories and for how long. Edleman's 2020 Brand Trust Barometer shows that trust is now the make or break difference for brands. Based on this recent report, there has been an impressive 12% increase from 34% in 2019

Evolving **artificial intelligence** now seems to be becoming **prolific across various marketing platforms**

to 46% in 2020 regarding people's trust of most of the brands they buy or use.

I have been fortunate working in The Academy of Chief Marketers and Superbrands to hear many of those fantastic stories first-hand from our brand members. Also, to gain incredible insight from our Trends and Insights partners, allowing me to stay current with what is important to brands today. This year we have spoken heavily around personalisation and experiential marketing, the latter of which is much harder to carry out right now. Personalisation, however, is coming to the front of the conversation quickly. This topic is driven through the understanding of data, and this understanding comes not only from people looking and paying attention to analytics but also through the evolving artificial intelligence that seems now to be prolific across the various marketing platforms. Platforms like Facebook, Instagram and Google all use AI or Machine Learning algorithms to understand their audiences better; this results in an ability to serve adverts to those most likely to achieve the advertiser's

objectives. This year we have seen a simplification in the approach to campaign structures in order to allow these algorithms to do their job. Although I can see the horror on my daughter's face as she chants "has no one seen films like Terminator!" I would say we have seen significant improvements in campaigns by letting the platform AI's refine their targeting, and to be honest, I don't think the ad engines will be trying to wipe us out any time soon!

We are also finally seeing more sophisticated approaches to cross-device and cross channel tracking, especially with the release of Google's new analytics version 4. Google is preparing for the phasing out of third-party cookies and how they will still track users; the new version will make predictions for the gaps in the data by relying on machine learning.

Video content also remains strong, and the need to be relevant has never been more critical. People are consuming a vast amount of content through channels like YouTube, Netflix and social media. With brands cutting back on budgets yet still needing to engage their audiences in a powerful and meaningful way, it is helpful to know that high production value content is no longer as important as relevance and authenticity. An in-house team can just as quickly now grab their mobile device and record in near cinematic 4K quality, real-time, relevant and authentic content. My recommendation is to make

sure that you are clear on your content strategy and what message and story you are trying to communicate and once you are clear, make sure you pick the right tone and speak human. It is best if you also can produce a good volume of content, so sometimes a little outside help can go a long way.

Over the last 25 years that I've been in digital design and marketing, I have seen our service become more and more commoditised. Agencies have become more driven to give a direct ROAS for every penny spent. It also seems that somewhere along the way, some agencies forgot that people don't just buy from an advert. It is still essential to grow trust and brand awareness in order to drive the cost of acquisition lower, but when budgets are tight agencies often go for the quick wins. Don't forget you also need a long-term strategy if you are to emerge stronger from these unprecedented times (I thought I really should get that word in somewhere!).

Being able to teach somebody how to deliver technically excellent campaigns on a variety of marketing platforms is a relatively quick process. I believe that agencies need to work more as a strategic partner to support and help drive campaigns for brands in a holistic way. Agencies

should not fear educating clients on what they do as working as an extension to a clients' team is where the highest levels of success can be attained. Of course, it works both ways; brands also need to let the agencies in and keep clear lines of frequent communication. This way, they can understand the business's objectives and goals fully and work together to achieve these.

A recent Forrester report commissioned by Google explains that agencies need to embrace the rapid transformation in the world to help brands engage and acquire digital consumers. It is necessary to master technologies to capture the shift in consumer behaviour and deliver on a brand's need for growth.

Ultimately, 2020 has been a severe blip in the road; one of several I have been though over my 30-year career and I am sure like those, this will one day be a distant memory. In the meantime, agencies and brands need to work smarter improving efficiencies in managing budgets and achieving goals.

One client we recently pitched for over lockdown told me that the agency working with them have been very supportive over this period. They followed this with; we remain loyal to our supplier and under no circumstances would we

move to a new agency. It's clear that doing the right thing is always the best policy, it builds that trust and loyalty. Both brands and agencies have had to pivot several times over the past months to survive and thrive where possible, and it's these stories of doing right and maintaining their integrity that will sort the wheat from the chaff over the coming year.

At times like this, I have always looked for motivation in quotes, and one of my favourites for now is 'I can't change the direction of the wind, but I can adjust my sails to always reach my destination'.

About Emotio Design Group

Emotio is an established agency which provides innovative and expert digital and design solutions. After 30 years in design, marketing and development, with 25 of those focused online, it works to maximise clients' objectives through their online presence and brand. Emotio is part of the EDI Collective.

emotio

Superbrands Cover Design Competition Winner

Superbrands UK Volume 21

ASHLEY ZANE
Cover Designer
Superbrands UK Volume 21

The Superbrands Cover is always a challenge as it needs to represent how brand is a key ingredient in the success of an organisation. The elements that are at the core of being a Superbrands – quality, reliability and distinction should also be reflected in the cover design.

Over the last 20 years there have been many executions of the cover from showing an image relating to the number one brand to geometric shapes that carry the colours of all the brands in the annual that year. This year Superbrands decided to open up the challenge of the cover to the world in the form of a competition and this year's winner was Ashley Zane, a Transport Designer, specialising in UX.

Ashley excels at creating unique solutions for challenging project briefs, and is able to research, develop designs and create final visuals. He has experience working in a consulting capacity as well as in research labs and OEM's on UX projects, full vehicle concepts, future ideation projects, and concept artwork. He presents design concepts, leads client briefing meetings, as well as supervising teams of designers. He acts as a catalyst for bringing ideas to the studios, allowing the teams to perform and deliver beyond expectations.

Free hand drawing of Oak tree

Finlarig Castle, photo

Medical Support Vessel Concept

About the Cover

The process for creating the circles involved researching and designing based on Superbrands, the previous covers and where the company could go in the future. I wanted to carry on with the use of multiple colours with a bolder background colour to make them stand out, as a Superbrand should. Using Adobe Illustrator I experimented with various shapes and styles, keeping in mind what it takes to make a Superbrand: Quality, Reliability and Distinction. The idea of using circles as the primary shape is based on the circular economy and company life cycles. These ideas, along with using a flowing strand for each brand, gives a representation of how each brand excels in key areas and that each brand is unique, but also relies on the economy as a whole.

E. AshleyLZane@gmail.com

M. +44 7800 902 261

Each strand represents

a **Superbrands®** company

Appendix

Research and Results Overview 2020/21

Superbrands Expert Councils

Qualifying Brands

Research and Results Overview 2020/21

Results and Relevancy Highlights

STEPHEN CHELIOTIS
CEO, TCBA &
Chair, Superbrands Expert Councils

Since 1995 Superbrands' rankings have provided an overview of sentiment toward brands operating in the UK. Adopting its current methodology in 2006, the research process canvasses the views of UK consumers, business professionals and marketing experts.

This year, 3,233 brands were assessed; 1,610 business-to-business brands across 64 categories, and 1,623 direct to consumer brands across 78 categories. Brands never apply to be considered, each year all the key players within each sector are evaluated to identify the most highly regarded.

The business-to-business brands were assessed by an independent expert council of 20 senior business-to-business marketing leaders, alongside 2,500 UK business professionals, all with purchasing or managerial responsibility within their businesses.

A nationally representative sample of 2,500 UK adults voted on the consumer brands. As a secondary, quality control mechanism, 30 leading experts on the Consumer Superbrands Council also rate the brands, with any lowly appraised effectively vetoed from attaining Superbrand status.

Combining two audiences' perception of the brands ensures the experts' view, typically factoring in considerations such as each brand's purpose, positioning and distinctiveness, are combined with the opinions of prospective buyers, whose awareness and sentiment toward each brand is, naturally, vital.

While all voters bear in mind the three criteria that must be inherent in a Superbrand when casting their votes, namely quality, reliability and distinction, the reality of a sentiment survey is that an individual's perception will naturally be impacted by everything they have seen or heard about each given brand.

Using the Superbrands results to understand a brand's equity or equity shift requires reviewing the detailed sector data over time to uncover underlying changes in performance.

A brand typically has a range within which it fluctuates in the Superbrands ranking over time. This range tends to be determined by fundamentals such as the brand's comparative physical and mental availability. Shorter-term impacts, such as levels of buzz, then influence the brands position within its range in a given year. A deviation to its medium-term range, a de-coupling of movement compared to sector patterns, or an extended period of overall and sector rank improvement or decline, signifies a deeper underlying positive or negative brand equity shift.

Naturally, individuals are keen to explore the overall winners. In that regards the leading Superbrands have been fairly consistent over time, as you might expect. Strong brands do not rise or fall overnight, however with so many brands involved in the process and the voting percentage gaps between each brand small, a tiny voting shift can impact overall rank. It's important therefore not just to monitor the absolute rank but the detail behind it.

For instance, while Rolex, has achieved the number one position in Consumer Superbrands this year, a rise of four places from last year, its underlying performance is essentially, and unsurprisingly, consistent, with its rise merely due to marginal shifts in both its voting percentages and those of the brands around it, rather than any substantive change in perception.

Delving into the data, the percentage of consumers voting Rolex a Superbrand has barely shifted, while its medium-term range shows it's a stalwart of the top 20, having taken the number one spot in 2013 and placing second in 2014, 2015, and 2016.

Generally, steadiness remains common among the leaders, with only three of this year's top 10 not featured in last year's equivalent; two of those were in the wider top 20 last time and the third, Nike, in 22nd, – the sport giant being a regular in the elite group however, having appearing in the top 20 in four of the last eight years.

The best indicator of notable shifts in brand's sentiment is found within a category, for instance through category leadership change or contrasting movement over time, relative to peers. Reassuringly for the existing brand front-runners, only 19 of the 78 categories in Consumer Superbrands witnessed a shift in number one. Even then, some category leadership battles are simply back and forth affairs among close competitors, with changes in leader reflecting a status quo battle; for example, Pedigree regained the helm of the 'Pet Products' category from Whiskas after a one-year gap, while Visa similarly retook the leadership of the 'Financial – General' category from arch rival Mastercard in their tightly fought battle.

The shift in category leader can however reflect fundamental changes too. Spotify taking over the top of the 'Media – Radio & Music Streaming' category from Capital FM is one such instance. Spotify's considerable and consistent improvements in the rankings over recent years, rising 261 places and gaining over 7% more voters compared to last year alone, contrasts considerably to the more traditional brands in this category. Likewise, Netflix replacing the BBC as the number one brand in the 'Media – TV' category is the culmination of data trends seen over recent years, which in-turn reflect wider viewing consumption trends.

Often our data acts as an early warning indicator, but needs additional verification over time, or through additional data sources. Samsung replacing long-term 'Technology – General' category leader Apple in this year's rankings for example could be symbolic of momentous, lasting change in fortunes for the pair. Our historic data certainly shows that Apple's historic advantage over Samsung has waned over recent years. The number of consumers voting Apple a Superbrand dropped a sizeable 5.6% last year, compared to a minus 3.0% average for the category alone and a rise of 1.7% for Samsung. But will this divergence stop, so the brands remain close, will it flip back akin to the Pedigree vs Whiskas battle in Pet Care, or will we see the pattern continue, with Apple trending downwards and Samsung upwards?

Looking at the percentage of consumers voting for a given brand, you can identify noteworthy brand movers quickly. Many of these brands are benefitting from a deeper change in the category, perhaps brought upon by technology or alterations in the market drivers. JUST EAST, for instance, gained the most votes year-on-year of any brand in the survey, with nearly 10% more votes compared to last year. Likewise, rival Deliveroo gained 8% more votes, the fifth biggest gain, reflecting its growing profile as part of that sector's deeper penetration into UK households.

Tesla was another big gainer, picking up just over 9% more votes than in 2019, the third highest rise. Aside from confirming growing awareness of the brand, when contrasted with sector peers, the data suggests environmental considerations are really shifting the sector's winners and losers. On average, brands in the category lost nearly 2% of votes compared to last year, with some dropping considerably more, so Tesla really is a contrast to rivals.

An additional data point to Superbrands, introduced a couple of years ago, is the relevancy index. This sub-index is based on whether consumers believe an individual brand has gained or lost relevance to people today, compared with the past. This sub-index reduces the impact of longer-term goodwill on a brand's scores and focuses consumers' minds on current use. Comparing a brand's performance in both indexes can reveal whether a brand is much loved but increasingly irrelevant, more relevant than in the past but not yet loved, or ideally well-regarded AND deemed to be highly relevant.

As an example, Marks & Spencer remains a relatively strong performer in the overall Superbrands rankings in 41st place, leading 'Department Stores & General Retailer' but places a very lowly 1,364th in the relevancy index. In contrast, Aldi is eighth in the brand relevancy table, the first 'Retail – Food & Drink' brand in that index, but in the core Superbrands ranking places 240th overall or fifth in category behind Tesco, Sainsbury's, Waitrose and ASDA. While perhaps obvious examples, these illustrations show how the data suggests

	Consumer Superbrands Top 10	Business Superbrands Top 10
1	Rolex	Microsoft
2	Visa	Apple
3	Samsung	British Airways
4	Andrex	Visa
5	LEGO	Samsung
6	Apple	Google
7	Coca-Cola	Mastercard
8	Kellogg's	Shell
9	British Airways	PayPal
10	Nike	Emirates

	Brands	Categories	Net Relevancy %
1	Macmillan Cancer Support	Charities	61.25
2	Amazon	Retail – Entertainment & Gifts	61.23
3	Netflix	Media – TV	60.23
4	Google	Social, Search & Comparison Sites	58.94
5	PayPal	Financial – General	58.07
6	Samsung	Technology – General	57.06
7	Visa	Financial – General	55.44
8	Aldi	Retail – Food & Drink	54.09
9	JUST EAT	Services	49.85
10	LEGO	Child Products – Toys and Education	49.34

that Marks & Spencer is much loved but losing relevance however the latter, while lagging in overall positive sentiment, is very much seen as a growing, pertinent brand – note Aldi's core Superbrand ranking over recent years also indicates that sentiment is growing but still has ground to catch up relative to M&S. The ideal scenario is what Amazon has achieved as a brand, placing 15th in the core Superbrands rankings, after a somewhat slow but steady rise, and 2nd in the relevance index.

The Business Superbrands rankings show similar patterns to Consumer Superbrands. A fairly consistent top 20, with only five changes in the top 20 entrants, all of whom, bar Adobe, have been in the top 20 on at least one other occasion over recent years. There are even less changes in category leaders than Consumer

Superbrands, with a mere 13 leadership changes. Here, perhaps even more than among Consumer Superbrands, a category lens is required and the data reviewed over a medium-term period.

Naturally the research is primarily used to identify and reaffirm the leading brands in each category to award those brands the title of Superbrands. Beyond that, a deeper and longer-term look at the core index and associated relevancy index, can reveal much about brand's performance. Whether you are interested in just the overview of which brands are leading in the UK, be that overall or within category, or require a deep dive of the data to understand a given brand's underlying performance, we hope you find the indexes useful and interesting.

It should be noted that the 2020/21 research was conducted prior to the coronavirus crisis.

Superbrands Expert Councils

The Superbrands Expert Councils are made up of highly regarded individuals, with experience spanning the marketing spectrum – from brand marketing to PR and design – in both the B2B and B2C arenas.

It is an enormous privilege to call on their experience and knowledge to create our exceptional panels. In these times of huge change, Superbrands continues to value enormously the expertise that our Council Members bring to the Superbrands voting process. We would like to thank them for generously giving their time to assess the risers and fallers in the UK's rapidly evolving landscape of brands.

STEPHEN CHELIOTIS

CEO, TCBA &
Chair
Superbrands Expert Councils

Since starting his career at Brand Finance, Stephen has provided robust research, trends and insights as well as strategic branding advice to both established and challenger brands across a wide variety of B2B and B2C sectors. Stephen also develops research studies, white papers, and proprietary models for marketing agencies. A regular commentator on CNN, the BBC and Sky among others, Stephen encourages the next generation of marketers as a visiting professor and also a judge for the Marketing Academy scholarship.

STEVE ALDRIDGE (B)

Chief Creative Officer
Wunderman Thompson UK

Steve is a creative champion, successful business founder and effective network leader. His mantra, 'None of us are as creative as all of us' means that under his watch, everyone contributes and their opinions count. Steve nurtures inclusivity and collaboration, building teams that want to work together. He has won more than 250 creative awards, including Agency of the Year three times.

ROB ALEXANDER (B)

Partner
Headland

Rob has had a 20-year career in advertising at TBWA\ and J Walter Thompson, encompassing strategy work for Shell, Vodafone, HSBC, Apple and the 2001 General Election for the Labour Party. Three years ago, Rob moved into the world of corporate and financial communications as a partner at Brunswick, where he led the global campaign planning team. In September 2018 he joined Headland as a partner to help lead campaign strategy and planning.

CHRIS ASHLEY-MANNS (B)

Chief Marketing Officer
Webeo
@chrismanns

An award-winning marketer, starting his marketing career in consumer direct marketing, Chris moved into the B2B agency world working with clients across many industries including fintech, manufacturing, hospitality and automotive. Passionate about B2B marketing innovation, Chris is now CMO of Webeo, the multi-award winning B2B martech solution that empowers personalised, next generation website experiences that enhance CX and website performance. Chris regularly speaks at key industry events.

ALEX BIGG (B)

CEO
Engine | MHP+Mischief

With over 20 years' experience spanning public affairs, issues management, communications and campaign strategy, Alex heads up MHP, one of the UK's leading Public Relations consultancies. In addition, Alex serves as a board member of the Public Relations and Communications Association (PRCA) and sits on the UK management board of the Engine Group.

ANDREW BLOCH (C)

Founder
FRANK.
@Andrew Bloch

Andrew is a non-executive director at FRANK., the PR agency he founded in 2000. He is a board advisor and consultant in the creative and marketing services industry, and involved in a number of businesses, helping them drive growth and deliver value. Andrew has also acted as spokesperson for Lord Sugar for more than 20 years. He is a founding mentor at the School of Creative Arts and a business mentor for The Prince's Trust.

ED BOLTON (C)

Principal (Creative)
Yonder
@YonderConsult

Ed is Yonder's creative lead and is responsible for ensuring that creativity and imagination is at the heart of their work. He is responsible for ensuring the bravest and brightest ideas are being developed for clients in EMEA, North America and Asia. He previously held director roles at the global brand agency Interbrand and the experiential agency Fitch, before setting up and leading the creative offer at BrandCap, which later evolved into Yonder.

CATHERINE BOROWSKI (C)

Founder & Artistic Director
PRODUCE UK
@ProduceUK

Catherine is a practising artist and placemaking specialist with more than 17 years' event industry experience. She created PRODUCE UK as an artistic event-making and placemaking agency and has built a network of cultural programmers, conceptual artists, producers, digital strategists, designers and creatives that specialise in media and creative brand experiences. Catherine has a diverse work portfolio including Argent LLP and the London Design Festival, as well as Hyundai, adidas, British Land, Campari and Discovery Channel.

FRAN BROSAN (B)

Co-Founder & Chairman
Omobono

Fran is co-founder and chairman of Omobono. With offices in the UK and US, Omobono is the creative and technology partner for business brands. It works with global corporates and scale-up businesses, using real-time strategies to help them succeed when facing uncertainty and complexity. Fran is an IPA Advertising Effectiveness Award winner and Fellow of The Marketing Society.

VICKY BULLEN (C)

CEO
Coley Porter Bell

Vicky leads teams and projects for clients as diverse as LEGO, Tesco and Unilever. She believes that the role of her agency is to work with clients to turn the multiple challenges and changes they face into opportunities. She is particularly interested in how learnings from neuroscience can be applied to branding to deliver success. Vicky sits on the Ogilvy UK Board, is a DBA director, a fellow of the Marketing Society as well as a WACL member.

KATE COX (B)

CEO
Bray Leino
@kcox16

With 20 years' experience under her belt, Kate steers the creative communications agency, Bray Leino, to consistently rank among the top B2B agencies in the world, counting a number of B2B Superbrands among its clients. Kate leads a diverse team of specialists to focus on one aim; to drive brand and business success through delivering commercially creative work, which has resulted in an incredible client retention rate.

KIRSTY DAWE (B)

CEO
Webeo
@kirstydawe1

Kirsty is CEO of Webeo, the B2B website personalisation platform that empowers B2B organisations to harness relevance where it matters most. She is a member of the DMA Business Council, has lectured for both the IDM and B2B Marketing and is a regular Superbrands judge. Kirsty is passionate about securing marketing's position on the board through work that combines data-driven creativity with measurable ROI.

SIMON DIXON (C)

Co-Founder
DixonBaxi
@dixonbaxi

Simon has 25 years of international experience having opened studios in the north of England, London (twice), New York and San Francisco. Through DixonBaxi, Simon has forged a reputation as one of the leading practitioners of future-focused branding and design, across all platforms. As well as being a regular international speaker and awards judge, he has featured in the Design Museum's Beazley Designs of the Year, The Tribeca Film Festival and garnered multiple global Gold and Grand Prix awards.

STEVE DYER (B)

Managing Director
Oil the Wheels

Steve has a unique blend of client-side industry knowledge with more than 30 years' B2B agency know-how. He understands industrial / manufacturing decision makers and how to motivate them, because he used to be one! His industrial strength approach to brand marketing has fuelled a recent agency rebrand: Oil the Wheels. A strategic communications marketer, he's a Fellow of the CIM and IDM and has held senior positions on various B2B committees within the DMA.

KATIE EDWARDS (C)

Managing Partner
Publicis.Poke

With more than 20 years' experience in communication agencies Katie has led global brands, launched new brands into the market and steered multiple award-winning campaigns. Working with brands spanning many different categories and business needs including Unilever, P&G, Nestlé, L'Oréal, Pernod-Ricard, Motorola, Orange and many more. Kaite believes that the power of creativity can drive business transformation and solve business problems.

JAMES FARMER (B)

Co-Founder
B2B Marketing
@jamesthefarms

James is passionate about the B2B sector. He is a huge advocate of client-side, vendor and agency space taking centre stage, all geared around customer experience. His personal and business drivers are to continue to enhance the reputation and deliverability of creative commercial thinking within the B2B marketing sector; all to support business growth.

JASON FLETCHER (B)

Executive Creative Director
Gyro UK
@fletchjason

Jason has been helping brands create award winning campaigns for more than 25 years. His passion is for a simple powerful idea that can live and work anywhere. Previous to his current role at specialist B2B agency Gyro, Jason was group creative director at Publicis UK and creative director at TBWA \ London. He has worked with brands including Heineken, Lexus, UBS, EE, Four Seasons, Nissan, Harrods and GSK. He enjoys speaking about creativity at industry events and over a cup of tea.

RACHEL FORDE (C)

CEO
UM UK

With 21 years' experience, Rachel leads UM UK as CEO, having worked across clients including Proctor & Gamble, Universal, Spotify and Just Eat. Since she joined UM, the agency has been voted one of Campaign's Best Places to Work and Shortlisted for Campaign's Media Agency of the Year. Rachel also champions diversity, as an active member of WACL and the NABS 100.

PHIL HAKIM (C)

Managing Director
Flipside

Phil leads the London office of Flipside, a Cannes Lion winning digital transformation company, specialising in the creation of interactive products that solve business problems and enhance people's lives. In his role, he oversees a multi-disciplinary team comprising strategists, designers, UX and UI specialists and engineers to deliver transformative creative technology.

JED HALLAM (C)

Chief Strategy Officer
Initiative

Jed has spent more than a decade helping brands to understand and become part of culture. He's worked in PR, creative and media, and is consistently named by Campaign as one of the UK's top media planners. He joined Initiative in 2018 as chief strategy officer, and since then the agency has tripled in size, doubled revenue, and been shortlisted for agency of the year.

VANELLA JACKSON (C)

Global CEO
Hall & Partners

Vanella has always been passionate about brands and communications. She spent 20 years working in some of the UK's best advertising agencies, including BBH, AMV/BBDO and JWT, prior to her current role, Global CEO, overseeing Hall & Partners. This is a strategic brand consultancy powered by data and insight, with a reputation for being insight inspirers. Its award-winning initiative, The Hub, creates a new vision for the role and impact of data and insight in this new, fast-moving, digital business world.

ROB KAVANAGH (C)

Executive Creative Director
OLIVER UK
@robkav

Rob has been building brands in big agency networks and specialist boutiques in London for two decades. He's no stranger to the transformative power of creative thinking for brands, having picked up precious metal everywhere from Cannes to Campaign, IPA to DMA. As executive creative director at Oliver agency, Rob builds bespoke creative agencies directly with brands and his teams are now the flag bearers for in-house creativity in this fast-growing part of the industry.

STEVE KEMISH (B)

Managing Partner
Junction
@skemmo

Steve is a multi-award-winning marketer and public speaker who has worked in digital marketing since 1997. He has had experience client-side, helped grow a leading email service provider, consulted to numerous clients on digital strategy, and helped build one of the most respected and awarded B2B marketing agencies in the UK. Alongside his decade as a Superbrands Council member, he has chaired the IDM digital council and is a judge for the AEO excellence awards, also co-hosting the business podcast, 'What We've Learnt'.

MARK LETHBRIDGE (B)

Group Chief Executive
Gravity Global
@mtlethbridge

Specialising in brand development, Mark is the founder and CEO of Gravity Global, an award-winning, brand to demand marketing and communications agency. Gravity helps businesses from startups to multinationals achieve fast growth in complex markets. Mark is also the past president of MAGNET that acts for more than 800 brands, setting best practice in global marketing and communications across more than 40 agency locations. Prior to this, Mark founded and was CEO of the AGA Group – a communications group serving global brands.

NICK LIDDELL (C)

Director of Consulting
The Clearing

Nick leads the consulting team at The Clearing, an award-winning independent brand consultancy in London. With over 20 years' experience, Nick has worked with global business and consumer brands from Amex, Guinness and Prada to McLaren and the AELTC. Nick is a regular conference speaker, media contributor and has published two books, Business is Beautiful and Wild Thinking.

AVRA LORRIMER (C)

Managing Director
Hill + Knowlton Strategies
@AvrainLondon

Throughout her career, Avra has worked on many of the world's best-known and most beloved brands. She has experience across a diverse array of sectors including FMCG, travel and automotive. An American expat residing in north London, Avra lives with her husband and daughter. In her free time she reads, occasionally blogs and is an aspiring voice-over artist.

PETER MARTIN (C)

Group Managing Director
SMP & Melody

Peter is a senior marketing communications leader, with more than 20 years' experience running businesses and brands, delivering award-winning strategic campaigns and driving double-digit commercial growth. Before joining SMP, Peter served as managing partner at Cheil Worldwide Inc., managing director at Arc London and client director at Publicis.

CLAIRE MASON (B)

Founder & CEO
Man Bites Dog
@womanbitesdog

Claire is an entrepreneur, author and founder of Man Bites Dog – a multi-award-winning thought leadership consultancy with global reach. With 20 years of experience leading global strategic marketing and thought leadership programmes, Claire creates signature global campaigns for the world's smartest organisations. Specialising in technology, professional and financial services, Claire is also the leader of the Gender Say Gap® initiative to increase the visibility of expert women in business.

AMY MCCULLOCH (C)

Founder & Managing Director
eight&four

Amy is founder and MD of eight&four, a performance driven creative agency. eight&four's specialist skill is ownership of the end-to-end digital campaign process; from creative ideation and social media strategy to online video production and amplification. The agency's clients span FMCG, third sector and gaming including; Yeo Valley, London Pride, British Heart Foundation and King.

STEPHEN MEADE (B)

Chief Executive
McCann Enterprise

Stephen is CEO and founder of McCann Enterprise, a corporate and B2B specialist agency within McCann Worldgroup, and recently voted 'Best B2B Marketing Agency' by the RAR. Prior to setting up McCann Enterprise, Stephen was European and UK head of planning for McCann. He joined McCann from Springpoint, where he was managing director, having previously spent some 15 years at both Publicis and HHCL, Campaign's Agency of the Decade in 2000.

ROB MORRICE (B)

CEO
Stein IAS

Under Rob's guidance, Stein IAS has become a truly global B2B agency force. Named Business Marketing Association's B2B Agency of the Year five times, it has collected numerous global B2B awards since its inception in 2013. With locations across North America, EMEA and APAC, Stein IAS works with brands including Oracle, HSBC, Merck, Ingredion, Trelleborg, Marshalls, Tetra Pak and Weight Watchers.

RICHARD MOSS (C)

Chief Executive
Good Relations

Richard is chief executive of Good Relations, part of VCCP Partnership, one of the UK's leading PR and content agencies. He started his career in FMCG marketing, managing the Andrex, Carlsberg and Mr Kipling brands. Moving into the public relations industry, his agency's proposition today is centred around developing 'challenger' communications campaigns for brands such as Lidl, B&Q and Weetabix.

ITA MURPHY (C)

CEO
SYZYGY UK

Ita is CEO of data and digital strategic agency SYZYGY UK, which is 50% owned by WPP. Prior to this, she was managing director of Mindshare, client strategy director at News UK and head of media at Lloyds Banking Group. She is also a certified coach and practitioner in applied neuroscience, and was president of WACL in 2007/08.

JAMES MURPHY (C)

Co-Founder & CEO
New Commercial Arts

New Commercial Arts offers a new agency model that brings together brand and customer experience creativity. Launched in May 2020, the agency has already picked up several major clients, despite lockdown conditions. Prior to this, James was co-founder and CEO of adam&eveDDB. During his 11 years, the agency grew to become the largest in the UK, being named Campaign's Agency of the Year six times as well as Agency of the Decade.

ANDREW O'CONNELL (C)

Managing Director, UK
Dynata

Andrew has worked in market research for more than 25 years, starting as a research assistant at Aston Business School. His client-side roles include Bibby, RBS and Capita. During his 15 years at Dynata, he has overseen numerous product innovations, including early passive metering, advertising effectiveness, and data matching projects. He now has a team of 150 sales and operations staff who look after 800 UK clients.

GILES PALMER (C)

Founder & CEO
Brandwatch

Giles is the founder and CEO of Brandwatch, a leading social intelligence firm, which he started after leaving BSkyB in late 2005. Since its launch in August 2007, Brandwatch has grown to become one of the world's leading social listening and analytics tech companies, empowering some of the world's biggest brands and agencies across the globe. Giles lead the merger with Crimson Hexagon in October 2018 to create a US $100m revenue SAAS business.

CAROLINE PARIS (C)

Creative Director
Brave
@carolineparis

Caroline creates innovative TV, outdoor and digital campaigns. From Instagram and digital firsts to award-winning TVCs and OOH campaigns, she has a flair for vibrant work, big and small. Caroline is one of Campaign's top 30 female leaders, a Campaign Female Frontier finalist and a Pitch Magazine Superwoman, 2019. She was a festival speaker at D&AD in the summer and sits on their jury as well as the Campaign BIG and Creative Circle Gold Jury.

TIM PERKINS (C)

Deputy Group Chairman
Design Bridge

Tim has over 30 years experience of international brand design and has been an integral part of the Design Bridge team for 25 years. Now one of the most successful and respected brand design agencies, Design Bridge has a reputation for delivering award winning work across a broad range of clients such as Diageo, Unilever, AkzoNobel, Mondelez and Fortnum & Mason. Tim is a champion of long-term relationships built upon bold creativity, simplicity and honesty.

JULIAN PULLAN (C)

**Vice Chairman
& President International**
Jack Morton Worldwide

Julian is vice chairman and president international of brand experience agency, Jack Morton Worldwide. Rated among the top global brand experience agencies, Jack Morton Worldwide integrates live and online experiences, digital and social media, and branded environments that engage consumers, business partners and employees for leading brands everywhere.

SANDY PUREWAL (B)

Founder
Superfied
@sandypurewal

Sandy has more than 22 years of sales, marketing and PR experience, advising B2B brands from global blue chips to disruptive startups. He founded Octopus Group (now Superfied) and has spearheaded its award-winning Brand to Sales proposition combining comms, creative and technology to accelerate demand. Sandy's experience includes working with Vodafone, Cisco, Accenture, Travelex and Adecco on both local and international programmes. Sandy has been a PRCA Council Member and has been a regular in the PR Week Powerbook.

LISA RIORDAN (C)

Creative Director
Imagination Ltd

Lisa directs and leads a multi-skilled creative team, responsible for delivering award-winning events and experiences globally for a variety of luxury brands including Rolls-Royce, Jaguar Land Rover and Robb Report. With more than 20 years' experience, her expertise and talents lie in the overall design and storytelling of engaging, highly creative communication solutions for strategically driven projects.

SUSANNA SIMPSON (B)

Co-Founder
Definition
@susannasimpson

Susanna is the co-founder of the UK's most awarded UK B2B PR agency, Definition. With offices in London, Leeds and Dubai, Definition defines, protects and projects the reputations of brands across industry sectors including tech, professional and business services, healthcare, transport as well as financial services. Susanna is also a non-executive advisor to agency founders through Cactus, the UK's leading agency growth consultants.

GRAHAM SYKES (C)

Creative Director
FITCH

Graham has led the creative charge for some of the world's leading brands including Amazon, adidas, Lynk & Co and Dell. Prior to joining FITCH, his leadership experience extended across small boutique agencies, tech start-ups and global network agencies. In his current role, Graham oversees a portfolio of international brands including Nestlé, L'Oréal and LEGO. Specialising in campaign, brand, digital and experiential design, Graham is passionate about how innovative design can lead to category-defining solutions.

JADE TOMLIN (C)

Creative Director
Tribal Worldwide London

Since graduating from Central Saint Martins in 2008, Jade has worked for advertising agencies ranging from Bartle Bogle Hegarty to Cx boutique Hugo & Cat. She has 12 years diverse creative experience across lifestyle brands such as Sony, Starbucks, Levi's, Ford Mustang and Burberry. She found her home at total experience agency Tribal Worldwide London, DDB where she has joined the leadership team as creative director.

ADRIAN WALCOTT (C)

Managing Director
Brands with Values &
Co-Founder, BAME2020

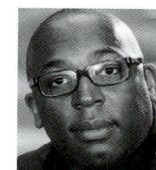

Adrian is a multi-award-winning brand marketeer and change maker, with more than 20 years' experience, currently leading Brands with Values, a culture change business. Adrian has led global projects to manage business growth and rationalisation, drive inclusion and diversity. Adrian is also a co-founder of BAME2020 (No Turning Back) a social enterprise that focuses on encouraging more people from diverse ethnic backgrounds to enter the marketing, media and communications sector. In addition, he is an emerging author and keynote speaker on brand, culture and inclusion.

GUY WIEYNK(C)

Global CEO
AnalogFolk

Guy has more than 25 years of experience in scaling future focused agencies and helping brands leverage digital channels and technology to deliver tangible business results. In his current role, he oversees independent global digital network, AnalogFolk. Prior to this, he founded Serum Consulting, a creative consultancy specialising in proposition development and digital transformation services which he sold to AnalogFolk. Before this, he was CEO of Publicis Worldwide UK and Western Europe and spent 17 years building AKQA into a global network.

DAVID WILLAN (B)

**Co-Founder &
Former Chairman**
Circle Research (now Savanta)

David has spent a lifetime in B2B research. Having co-founded BPRI and sold this business to WPP, he became chairman of Circle Research, which is now known as Savanta. David oversaw the sale of this business to Next 15 plc. He is currently a member of the Advisory Board of Green Square, M&A specialists in the marketing services sector and deputy chair of the University of Portsmouth.

DYLAN WILLIAMS (C)

CSO, Droga5 London &
Managing Director
Accenture Interactive

In his 25 years in commercial communications Dylan has worked at three of the industry's best agencies – BBH, Mother and Droga5. Amongst numerous accolades, he has won Campaign Agency of the Year and been voted the number one strategist in the industry at each agency. Dylan also sits on Facebook's EMEA Client Council, the Effies UK Council and was a founding member of the Tech City Advisory Board at 10 Downing Street.

PROF. ALAN WILSON PHD (B)

Professor of Marketing
University of Strathclyde
@ProfAlanWilson

Alan is a professor of marketing at the University of Strathclyde Business School. Before joining the University, he was a senior consultant at a London-based marketing consultancy. He is the author of several business books and has written numerous articles on corporate reputation, customer experience management and branding. He is also a Fellow of both the Chartered Institute of Marketing and the Market Research Society.

QUALIFYING BRANDS

The brands listed here have all qualified for the status of Business (B) or Consumer (C) Superbrand in 2020/21 by scoring highly with the Business or Consumer Expert Council, and the Consumer or Business Professional audiences. Where brands perform strongly with both Business and Consumer voters, it is possible for them to qualify as both a Business and a Consumer Superbrand.

3M	B
7-Up	C
A-Plant	B
AA	C
ABB	B
Abbott	B
AbbVie	B
ABP (Associated British Ports)	B
ABSOLUT VODKA	C
ABTA	B
Acas (Advisory, Conciliation & Arbitration Service)	B
ACCA	B
Accenture	B
Access Self Storage	B
Acer	B
Actimel	C
Activia	C
adam&eveDDB	B
Adecco	B
adidas	C
Admiral	C
Adobe	B
ADT	B
Aegis Group	B
Aegon	B
Aggreko	B
AIG	B
AIM	B
Air France	B
Air Liquide	B
Air Products	B
Airbnb	C
Airbus	B
AkzoNobel	B
Aldi	C
Alexander Mann Solutions	B
Alfa Laval	B
Alfa Romeo	C
Alka-Seltzer	C
Allen & Overy	B
Allianz	B
Alpen	C
Alpro	C
Alstom	B
Alton Towers	C
Always	C
Amadeus	B
Amazon	C
Ambre Solaire	C
Amcor	B
AMD	B
American Airlines	B C
American Express	B C
American Express Global Business Travel	B
Amey	B
AMV BBDO	B
Anadin	C
Anchor	C
Andrex	C
Anglo American	B
AO.com	C
Aon	B
Apple	B C
Aquafresh	C
Arcadis	B
ArcelorMittal	B
Argos	C
Ariel	C
Arm	B
Arriva	B
Arsenal FC	C
Arup	B
ASDA	C
ASOS	C
Aston Business School	B
AstraZeneca	B
Atkins	B
Atlas Copco	B
Atos	B
Audi	C
Aunt Bessie's	C
Aussie	C
Auto Trader	C
Autodesk	B
Autoglass®	B C
Avanti	B
Avast	B
Avaya	B
Avery	B
Avis	C
Aviva	B C
AXA	B C
B&Q	C
Babcock	B
BaByliss	C
Bacardi	C
BAE Systems	B
Baileys	C
Bain & Company	B
Baker McKenzie	B
Balfour Beatty	B
BAM Nuttall	B
Bank of America	B
Bank of Scotland	B
Barclaycard	B C
Barclays	B C
BASF	B
Basildon Bond	B
Baxi	B
Baxter	B
Bayer	B
Baylis & Harding	C
BBC	C
BBC Children in Need	C
BBH	B
BCG	B
BDA (British Dental Association)	B
BDO	B
Beck's	C
Beechams	C
Ben & Jerry's	C
Benylin	C
Berghaus	C
Bertolli	C
Best Western	B
BHP	B
Bibby Line	B
BIC	B
Biffa	B
Big Yellow	B
Bird & Bird	B
Birds Eye	C
Birmingham Business School	B
Bisto	C
BLACK+DECKER	B C
BlackBerry	B
Bloomberg	B
Bloomsbury Professional	B
Blue Arrow	B
Blue Circle	B
Blue Dragon	C
BMA (British Medical Association)	B
BMI	B
BMW	C
BNP Paribas Real Estate	B
BOC	B
Bodyform	C
Boehringer Ingelheim	B
Boeing	B
Bold	C
Bombardier	B
Bombay Sapphire	C
Bonjela	C
Booker	B
Booking.com	C
Boots	C
Bosch	B C
Bose	C
Bovril	C
bp	B C
BPP	B
Braemar	B
Brakes	B
Branston	C
Braun	C
Brewers	B
Bridgestone	C
Bristol-Myers Squibb	B
Bristow	B
British Airways	B C
British Chambers of Commerce	B
British Council	B
British Gas	C
British Gas Business Energy	B
British Gypsum	B
British Heart Foundation	C
British Land	B
British Red Cross	C
Britvic	C
Brook Street	B
Brother	B
Brunswick	B
BSI	B
BT	B C
BT Sport	C
Budweiser	C
Buildbase	B
Bulmers	C
Bunzl	B
Bupa	B C
Bureau Veritas	B
Burger King	C
Business In The Community	B
Buxton	C
Bywaters	B
Cadbury	C
Caffè Nero	C
Calor	B
CALPOL	C
Cambridge Judge Business School	B
Campbell's	C
Canary Wharf Group	B
Cancer Research UK	C
Canon	B C
Capgemini	B
Capita	B
Capital FM	C
Capri-Sun	C
Captain Morgan	C
Carat	B
Carex	C
Cargill	B
Carlsberg	C
Carphone Warehouse	C
Carte D'Or	C
Carte Noire	C
Carter Jonas	B
Casio	B
Cass Business School	B
Castrol	B
Cat	B
Cathay Pacific	B C
Cathedral City	C
CBI	B
CBRE	B
CEMEX	B
Center Parcs	C
Centrum	C
Cesar	C
Channel 4	C
Channel 5	C
Chelsea FC	C
Chevron	B
Chubb - Insurance category	B
Chubb - Security category	B
Churchill	C
Cif	C
Cigna	B
CIMA (Chartered Institute of Management Accountants)	B
CIPD	B
CIPS (Chartered Institute of Procurement and Supply)	B
Cisco	B
Citi	B
City & Guilds	B
Clancy Docwra	B
Clarion Events	B
Clarks	C
Classic FM	C
Clear Channel	B
Clearasil	C
Clifford Chance	B
Cluttons	B
Clyde & Co	B
CMI (Chartered Management Institute)	B
Co-operatives UK	B
Coats	B
Coca-Cola	C
Coca-Cola London Eye	C
Colgate	C
CollectPlus	B
Colliers International	B
Colman's	C
Colt	B
Comfort	C
Comic Relief	C
comparethemarket.com	C
Compass Group	B
Computacenter	B
comScore	B
Confused.com	C
ConocoPhillips	B
Continental	C
Converse	C
Cornetto	C
Corona	C
Corps Security	B
Corsodyl	C
Costa	C
Costain	B
Costco	B
Cosworth	B
Courvoisier	C
Cow & Gate	C
Cranfield School of Management	B
Cravendale	C
Crayola	C
Credit Suisse	B
Crowdcube	B
Crown	B
Crown Paints	C
Crown Trade	B
Crowne Plaza	B C
Cummins	B
Cunard	C
Cuprinol	C
Currys	C
Cushelle	C
Cushman & Wakefield	B
DAF	B
Daikin	B
Daily Mail	C
Dairylea	C
Daisy	B
Dale Carnegie	B
Danone	C
Dassault Systemes	B
David Lloyd Clubs	C
DB Schenker	B
De La Rue	B
De Vere	B
Deep Heat	C
Deliveroo	C
Dell	B C
Deloitte	B
Deloitte Real Estate	B
Delta	B
Dettol	C
Deutsche Bank	B
DeWALT	B
DHL	B
Digital Cinema Media (DCM)	B
Digitas	B
Direct Line	C
Direct Line for business	B
Disney	C
Disney Channel	C
Domestos	C
Domino's Pizza	C
Doritos	C
Dove	C
Dow	B
DP World	B
DPD	B
Dr Pepper	C
Dr. Martens	C
Dr. Oetker	C
Drax	B
Dropbox	B
DS Smith	B
DueDil	B
Dulux	C
Dulux Trade	B
Dun & Bradstreet	B
Dunlop	C
dunnhumby	B
DuPont	B
Duracell	C
Durex	C
Durham University Business School	B
Dyson	C
E.ON	B C
E45	C
Early Learning Centre	C
easyJet	B C
eBay	C
Ebiquity	B
Eddie Stobart	B
Edelman	B
Eden Project	C
EDF Energy	B C
Edwardian Hotels London	B
EE	C
Elastoplast	C
Elementis	B
Elopak	B
Elsevier	B
Embraer	B
Emirates	B C
Epson	B
Equifax	B
Equiniti	B
Equinix	B
Ericsson	B
Etihad	B C
Euromillions	C
Euromoney Institutional Investors	B
Euronext	B
Europcar	C
Eurostar	B C
Eurotunnel	B C
Eutelsat	B
Eversheds Sutherland	B
evian	C
ExCeL London	B
Expedia	C
Experian	B
ExxonMobil	B
EY	B
Facebook	C
Fairtrade Foundation	B
Fairy	C
Fanta	C
Farnell	B
Febreze	C
FedEx	B
Felix	C
Ferrero Rocher	C
Filofax	B
Financial Times	C
Finastra	B
Finish	C
First	B
First Security	B
Fisher-Price	C
Fitbit	C
Fitch Group	B
Flash	C
Flora	C
Flymo	C
Foot Locker	C
Ford	C
Forrester	B
Foster's	C
Fox's	C
Fred Perry	C
Fred. Olsen Cruise Lines	C
Freightliner	B
Freshfields Bruckhaus Deringer	B
freuds	B
FSC (Forest Stewardship Council)	B
FTSE Russell	B
Fujitsu	B
Funding Circle	B
G4S	B
Galaxy	C
Galliford Try	B
Gallup	B
Gap	C
Garnier	C
Gartner	B
Gatwick Airport	C
Gatwick Express	B
Gaviscon	C
Gazprom Energy	B
GE	B
GfK	B
Gillette	C
GKN	B
GlaxoSmithKline (GSK)	B
Glencore	B
Glenfiddich	C
Glenmorangie	C
Global	B
Global Payments	B
GlobalData	B
Globalstar	B
GoCardless	B
GoDaddy	B
Goldman Sachs	B
Goodyear	C
Google	B C
Gordon's	C
Gourmet	C
Graham	B
Grant Thornton	B
Great Ormond Street Hospital Charity	C
Great Portland Estates	B
Green Flag	C
Greggs	C
Grey Goose	C
Grey London	B
Grosvenor	B
Groupon	C
Guinness	C
Gumtree	C
H&M	C
Häagen-Dazs	C
Habitat	C
Halfords	C
Halfords Autocentre	C
Halifax	C
Hall & Partners	B
Hamleys	C
Hannover RE	B
Hanson	B
Hapag-Lloyd	B
HARIBO	C
Harris	B
Harrogate Convention Centre	B
Harvey Nichols	C
Havas	B
Haymarket	B
Hays	B
Head & Shoulders	C
Heart	C
Heathrow	C
Heathrow Express	B
Heineken	C
Heinz	C
HELLA	B
Hellmann's	C
Hendrick's Gin	C
Henkel	B
Henley Business School	B
Herbal Essences	C
Hermes	B
Hertz	C
Hewlett-Packard; Enterprise	B
Highland Spring	C
Hill+Knowlton Strategies (H+K)	B
Hilti	B
Hilton Hotels & Resorts	B C
Hiscox	B
Hitachi	B
Hogan Lovells	B
Holiday Inn	B C
Holland & Barrett	C
Homepride	C
Honeywell	B
Hoover	C
Hornby	C
Hotels.com	C
Hotpoint	C
House of Fraser	C
Hovis	C
Howden	B
Howdens	B
HPB	C
HP Sauce	C
HRG	B
HSBC	B C
HSS Hire	B
Huawei	B C
Huggies® Wipes	C
Hula Hoops	C
Iams	C
ibis	B
IBM	B
Ibstock	B
ICC Birmingham	B
Iceland	C
ICM Unlimited	B
IET (The Institution of Engineering and Technology)	B
IKEA	C
Imperial College Business School	B
Imperial Leather	C
Indeed	B
INEOS	B
Informa	B
Infosys	B
Ingenico	B
Initial	B
Inmarsat	B
innocent	C
Instagram	C
Intel	B
Intelsat	B
Interserve	B
Intuit	B
Investec	B
Investors in People	B
IoD (Institute of Directors)	B
Ipsos MORI	B
Iridium	B
IRN-BRU	C
Iron Mountain	B
Irwin Mitchell	B
Isobar	B
ISS	B
ITV	C
ITV Media	B
IVECO	B
iZettle	B
J. Walter Thomson (JWT)	B
J.P. Morgan	B
J2O	C
Jack Daniel's	C
Jacob's	C
Jacob's Creek	C
Jacobs	B
Jaguar	C
Jameson	C
Jammie Dodgers	C
JCB	B
JCDecaux	B
JD Sports	C
Jewson	B
Jiffy	B
JLL	B
JLT	B
JobServe	B
Jobsite	B
John Deere	B
John Frieda	C
John Lewis & Partners	C
John West	C
Johnnie Walker	C
Johnson & Johnson	B
Johnson Controls	B
Johnson Service Group	B
JOHNSON'S	C
Johnstone's Trade	B
Jordans	C
Jury's Inn	B
JUST EAT	C
Kantar	B
Karmarama	B
Kaspersky	B
Keller	B
Kellogg's	C
Kelly	B
Kelly's of Cornwall	C
Keltbray	B
Kenco	C
Kenwood (Kitchen Appliances)	C
KETTLE Chips	C
Kew Gardens	C
KFC	C
Kidde	B
Kier Group	B

Please note that this list reflects the brands as presented in the Superbrands research voting process; brands may subsequently have been altered or entirely rebranded, while others may no longer be sold or operational.

Brand	Qualifier
KIMBERLY-CLARK PROFESSIONAL	B
Kindle	C
Kingsmill	C
Kingspan Group	B
Klarna	B
Kleenex	C
KLM	B
Knight Frank	B
Knorr	C
Komatsu	B
Kompass	B
KONE	B
KP	C
KPMG	B
Krispy Kreme	C
Kronenbourg 1664	C
Kuehne + Nagel	B
Kwik Fit	C
L'Oreal Elvive	C
Lacoste	C
Ladbrokes	C
Lafarge Cement	B
Laing O'Rourke	B
Lakeland	C
Lambert Smith Hampton	B
Land Rover	C
Lavazza	C
Le Creuset	C
Lea & Perrins	C
Legal & General	C
LEGO	C
LEGOLAND	C
Legrand	B
Lemsip	C
Lenor	C
Lenovo	B
Leo Burnett London	B
LexisNexis	B
Lexmark	B
Lexus	C
Leyland Trade	B
Leyland Trucks	B
LGB	C
Lidl	C
Liebherr	B
Lilly	B
Linda McCartney	C
Linde	B
Lindt	C
LinkedIn	B
Linklaters	B
Listerine	C
Liverpool FC	C
Lloyd's	B
Lloyds Bank	B C
LloydsPharmacy	C
Lockheed Martin	B
Logitech	B
London Business School	B
London Metal Exchange (LME)	B
London School of Economics and Political Science (LSE)	B
London Stock Exchange Group	B
Loomis	B
Lucozade	C
Lufthansa	B
Lurpak	C
Lynx	C
LyondellBasell	B
Lyreco	B
Mace	B
Macfarlanes	B
Maclaren	C
Macleans	C
Macmillan Cancer Support	C
Madame Tussauds	C
Maersk	B
Magnet Trade	B
Magnum	C
Makita	B
Malmaison	B
Maltesers	C
Mamas & Papas	C
MAN	B
Manchester Central	B
Manchester City FC	C
Manchester United	C
Manpower	B
Marie Curie	C
Marks & Spencer	C
Marmite	C
Marriott Hotels & Resorts	B C
Mars	C
Marsh	B
Marshall	B
Marshalls	B
Martin-Baker	B
Martini	C
Marvel	C
Massey Ferguson	B
Mastercard	B C
McAfee	B
McCain	C
McCann London	B
McCoy's	C
McDonald's	C
McKinsey	B
McLaren	B
McVitie's	C
Meccano	C
MediaCom	B
Medtronic	B
Menzies	B
Menzies Aviation	B
Menzies Distribution	B
Mercedes-Benz	C
Mercer	B
Mercure	B
Merkle	B
Michael Page	B
Michelin	C
Micron	B
Microsoft	B C
Miele	C
Mind Gym	B
Mindshare	B
MINI	C
Mini Babybel	C
Mintel	B
Miracle-Gro	C
Mitie	B
Mitsubishi Electric	B
Moleskine	B
Mondi	B
MoneyGram	B
MoneySuperMarket	C
Monster	B
Moody's	B
Moonpig	C
Morgan Sindall	B
Morgan Stanley	B
Morphy Richards	C
Morrisons	C
Mother	B
Mountain Warehouse	C
Mr Kipling	C
Mr Muscle	C
Müller	C
Munich Re	B
Murphy	B
Nando's	C
NatCen	B
National Express	B C
National Grid	B
National Trust	C
Nationwide	C
Nationwide Platforms	B
NATS	B
Nature Valley	C
NatWest	B C
NEC	B
Nescafé	C
Nespresso	C
Nestlé Cereals	C
Netflix	C
NETGEAR	B
Neutrogena	C
New Holland	B
New Look	C
Next	C
NFU	B
NFU Mutual	B
Niceday	B
Nicorette	C
Nielsen	B
Night Nurse	C
Nike	C
Nikon	C
Nintendo	C
Nissan	C
Nivea	C
Nokia	B
Northrop Grumman	B
Norton	B
Nottingham University Business School	B
Novartis	B
Novo Nordisk	B
Novotel	B
npower	B C
NSPCC	C
Nurofen	C
Nutella	C
O2	C
OCS	B
Octopus Energy	B
ODEON	C
Office Angels	B
Office Depot	B
Ogilvy	B
Olay	C
Olympia London	B
Olympus	B
OMD	B
Omega	C
Onken	C
Openreach	B
Optrex	C
Oracle	B
Oral-B	C
Ordnance Survey (OS)	B
Osborne Clarke	B
OSRAM	B
Otis	B
Oxford Black n' Red	B
OXO	C
P&O Cruises	C
P&O Ferries	C
P&O Ferrymasters	B
PA	B
Paddy Power	C
Pampers	C
Panadol	C
Panasonic	C
Pandora	C
Pantene	C
Paper Mate	B
Parcelforce Worldwide	B
Park Inn by Radisson	B
Park Plaza	B
Parker	B
PARKER	B
Patak's	C
PAXO	C
PayPal	B C
PayPoint	B
PC World	C
Pearl & Dean	B
Pedigree	C
Pepsi	C
Perrier	C
Persil	C
Pfizer	B
PG Tips	C
PHD	B
Philadelphia	C
Philips	B C
Phoenix Group	B
Photo-Me	B
PHS Group	B
Pickfords	B
Pilkington	B
PILOT	B
PIMM'S	C
Pinsent Masons	B
Pirelli	C
Pitman Training	B
Pitney Bowes	B
PizzaExpress	C
Plastipak	B
Play-Doh	C
PLAYMOBIL	C
PlayStation	C
Plenty	C
Plumbase	B
Plusnet	B
Polo	C
Polypipe	B
Portakabin	B
Post Office	C
Post-it	B
Pot Noodle	C
PowWowNow	B
PPA	B
Premier Inn	B C
Primark	C
Princess Cruises	C
Pringles	C
Prudential	B C
Publicis London	B
Pukka	C
Puma	C
Purina	C
Purplebricks	C
PwC	B
PYREX	C
Qatar Airways	B C
QEII Centre	B
QinetiQ	B
Quaker Oats	C
Qualcomm	B
Quality Street	C
Quorn	C
RAC	C
Rackspace	B
Radisson BLU	C
Radisson Hotels	B C
Radox	C
Ramada	B
Randstad	B
RAPP	B
Raytheon	B
Red Bull	C
Red Tractor	B
REDBOX	B
Reebok	C
REED	B
Reed & Mackay	B
Reed Exhibitions	B
Regus	B
RELX	B
Rennie	C
Rentokil	B
Rexel	B
RIBA (The Royal Institute of British Architects)	B
Ribena	C
Ricoh	B
Ricoh Arena	B
RICS	B
Right Guard	C
Rightmove	C
Rio Tinto	B
River Island	C
Robertson's	C
Robinsons	C
Roche	B
Rolex	C
Rolls-Royce	B
Ronseal	C
Rotary	C
Rothschild & Co	B
Rowntree's	C
Royal Albert Hall	C
Royal Bank of Scotland	B
Royal Caribbean International	C
Royal Doulton	C
Royal London	B
Royal Mail	B C
Royal Worcester	C
RS	B
RSA	B
RSPCA	C
Russell & Bromley	C
Russell Hobbs	C
RWE Generation UK	B
Ryanair	B
Ryman	B
Ryvita	C
S.Pellegrino	C
S&P Global	B
Saatchi & Saatchi	B
Sage	B
Saïd Business School	B
Sainsbury's	C
Saint-Gobain	B
Salesforce	B
Samaritans	C
Samsung	B C
San Miguel	C
Sandals Resorts	C
SanDisk	B
Sandvik	B
Sanex	C
Sanofi	B
Santander	B C
SAP	B
SAS	B
Savills	B
Savlon	C
Scalextric	C
Scania	B
Schindler	B
Schneider Electric	B
schuh	C
Schwartz	C
Schwarzkopf	C
Schweppes	C
Scott's Porage Oats	C
Scottish and Southern Electricity Networks	B
ScottishPower	B
Screwfix	B C
SEA LIFE Centres	C
Sealed Air	B
Searcys	B
SECOM	B
Securitas	B
Seiko	C
Selco Builders Warehouse	B
Selfridges	C
Sensodyne	C
Serco	B
Seven Seas	C
Sharp	B
Sharwood's	C
Sheba	C
Shell	B C
Sheraton	B
Shopify	B
Shred-it	B
Shredded Wheat	C
Siemens	B C
Siemens Healthineers	B
SIG	B
Silentnight Beds	C
Silver Cross	C
Silver Spoon	C
Simple	C
Singapore Airlines	B C
Sir Robert McAlpine	B
Skanska	B
SKF	B
Sky	C
Sky Media	B
Skype	B C
Slaughter and May	B
SMA	C
Smart Group	B
SmartWater	B
Smeg	C
Smirnoff	C
Smith & Williamson	B
Smith+Nephew	B
Smiths Group	B
Smiths News	B
SMMT (The Society Of Motor Manufacturers And Traders)	B
Smurfit Kappa	B
Smyths Toys Superstores	C
Snap-on	B
Snapchat	C
Sodexo	B
Sofitel	B
Softcat	B
Sony	C
Sony Professional	B
Sophos	B
Southern Comfort	C
Spaces	B
Specsavers	C
Speedo	C
Speedy	B
Spencer Stuart	B
Sports Direct	C
Spotify	C
Sprite	C
STABILO	B
STAEDTLER	B
Stagecoach	B
STANLEY	B
Stansted Express	B
Starbucks	C
Stella Artois	C
Stobart Energy	B
Stobart Group	B
Stora Enso	B
Strepsils	C
Strongbow	C
Subway	C
Sudafed	C
Sudocrem	C
SUEZ	B
Superdrug	C
Superdry	C
Sure	C
SurveyMonkey	B
Swarovski	C
Swiss Re	B
Swissport	B
Symantec	B
Syngenta	B
Tabasco	C
TAG	B
TAG Heuer	C
TalkTalk	C
TalkTalk Business	B
Tampax	C
Tango	C
Tarmac	B
Tata Communications	B
Tata Consultancy Services	B
Tate & Lyle	B
Tate & Lyle Cane Sugar	C
Taylors of Harrogate	C
TBWA\London	B
Ted Baker	C
Tefal	C
TEMPUR	C
Terex	B
Tesco	C
Tesla	C
Tetley	C
Tetra Pak	B
Texas Instruments	B
Thales	B
The Baltic Exchange	B
The Billington Group	B
The Body Shop	C
The Daily Telegraph	C
The Famous Grouse	C
The Guardian	C
The Institute of Financial Accountants (IFA)	B
The Institution of Civil Engineers (ICE)	B
The Law Society	B
The Myers-Briggs Company	B
The National Lottery	C
The North Face	C
The Open University Business School	B
The Royal British Legion	C
The SEC (Scottish Event Campus)	B
The Soil Association	B
The Sun	C
The Times	C
Thistle	B
Thomson Reuters	B
Thorn	B
Thorpe Park	C
Thwaites	B
thyssenkrupp	B
Ticketmaster	C
Tipp-Ex	B
Tissot	C
TK Maxx	C
Toblerone	C
tommee tippee®	C
TONI&GUY	C
Toolstation	B
Topman	C
Topshop	C
Toshiba	B C
Total	B
Totaljobs	B
Tottenham Hotspur FC	C
Toyota	C
Trainline	C
TransferWise	B
Travelodge	C
Travis Perkins	B
Trelleborg	B
TRESemmé	C
TripAdvisor	C
Triumph Group	B
trivago	C
Tropicana	C
TSB	B
TUI	C
Twinings	C
Twitter	C
Typhoo	C
Tyrrells	C
Uber	C
UBS	B
UK Power Networks	B
Uncle Ben's	C
Under Armour	C
Unipart Logistics	B
Unisys	B
United	B
University of Bath School of Management	B
University of Edinburgh Business School	B
UPS	B
Utilita	B
Vaillant	B
Vanish	C
Vaseline	C
VCCP	B
Velvet	C
Vent-Axia	B
Veolia	B
Verisign	B
Verizon Media	B
Vicks	C
Viking	B
Viking Cruises	C
Vimto	C
Virgin Atlantic	B C
Virgin Holidays	C
Virgin Media	C
Virgin Media Business	B
Virgin Mobile	C
Viridor	B
Visa	B C
Vision Express	C
VMware	B
Vodafone	C
Volkswagen	C
Voltarol	C
Volvic	C
Volvo	C
Volvo CE	B
Vue	C
Waitrose & Partners	C
Walkers	C
Wall's Ice Cream	C
Warburtons	C
WARC	B
Warwick Castle	C
Waterstones	C
Wates	B
WBS (Warwick Business School)	B
WD-40	C
Weber Shandwick	B
Wedgwood	C
Weetabix	C
Weight Watchers	C
Weir	B
Western Union Business Solutions	B
WeTransfer	B
WeWork	B
WhatsApp	C
Whiskas	C
WHSmith	C
Wickes	B C
Wikipedia	C
Wilkinson Sword	C
William Hill	C
William Reed	B
Willis Towers Watson	B
Willmott Dixon	B
Winalot	C
Wincanton	B
Wolseley	B
Woolmark	B
Workday	B
Workspace	B
Worldpay	B
Wrigley's	C
Xbox	C
Xchanging	B
Xerox	B
Yahoo!	C
Yakult	C
Yale	B
Yell	B
Yeo Valley	C
Yodel	B
Yorkshire Tea	C
YouGov	B
Young's	C
YouTube	C
Zara	C
Zenith	B
Zoom	B
Zoopla	C
ZSL London Zoo	B
Zurich	B C

Key

B - Business Superbrands Qualifier

C - Consumer Superbrands Qualifier